Praise for *Occupy*

"*Occupy Spirituality* is a careful, thoughtful,
have to choose between spiritual fulfillmen
Bucko's dialogues enable us to spy the Promised Land of social justice through
fresh eyes. This book will challenge your mind, complicate your politics, and re-
energize your spirit!"

—Marc Lamont Hill, social critic, activist, and author of
Beats, Rhymes, and Classroom Life: Hip-Hop Pedagogy and the Politics of Identity
and *The Classroom and the Cell: Conversations on Black Life in America*

"Thank you, Adam Bucko and Matthew Fox, for nurturing the radical spiritual activism and moral imagination which is growing all our souls and changing our world."

—Grace Lee Boggs, activist and author of
The Next American Revolution: Sustainable Activism for the Twenty-First Century

"The monologue of the Religious Right is over. And a new dialogue has begun. This
book is a sign of that dialogue. You may not agree with everything on these pages
(I didn't), but you can't help but be stirred to join the conversation—and to dive
into a movement that is reimagining the world. Fox and Bucko refuse to see faith
as just a ticket into heaven, and they invite you to join them—and to join God—in
bringing heaven down to earth."

—Shane Claiborne, activist, lover of Jesus, and author of
The Irresistible Revolution: Living as an Ordinary Radical and
Red Letter Revolution: What If Jesus Really Meant What He Said?

"One can hope that the next great social transformation will include not just political
freedom and social justice, but a transformation of the human soul as well. One can
hope that the activists of this era will be spiritual visionaries. One can hope that the
contemplatives of this era will speak truth to power and take it to the streets. With
this book, Matthew Fox and Adam Bucko increase the possibility that it will be so."

—Kabir Helminski, activist and Sufi, author of
Living Presence, The Knowing Heart, and *Love's Ripening*

"These fresh and buoyant original voices summon us to radical habit change and life-
giving compassion in action guided by wisdom's insightful eye. That is the mission
of bodhisattva leaders and awakeners like Adam Bucko and Matthew Fox, dedicated
'servant leaders' who are fomenting a beloved community committed to witnessing
and working towards social justice, peace and harmony, and higher consciousness."

—Lama Surya Das, author of
Awakening the Buddha Within and *Buddha Standard Time*

"The Occupy movement moves us from self-centeredness to other-centeredness. The most courageous act that any of us can do is to dare to care about others. Since our destinies are metaphysical we should start now and Occupy Spirituality. Let this book be our manual."

—Sharon Gannon, co-creator of Jivamukti Yoga, author of
Yoga and Vegetarianism: The Diet of Enlightenment

"This book gives heartfelt expression to the marriage of inner and outer activism that has the potential to transform our world."

—Charles Eisenstein, author of *Sacred Economics* and *The Ascent of Humanity*

"In *Occupy Spirituality*, Adam Bucko and Matthew Fox remind us that authentic spirituality is action. Spirituality without engagement is empty. Activism without spiritual roots is dissipative and fragmenting. Spirituality needs to empower and inspire us to action. *Sadhna* (meditation) and *seva* (service) are complementary. Spirituality and Action need to reunite. In this time of corporate rule and greed, we need to heed the message of *Occupy Spirituality*."

—Dr. Vandana Shiva, environmental activist, author of
Earth Democracy: Justice, Sustainability, and Peace, and
Soil Not Oil: Environmental Justice in an Age of Climate Crisis

"In *Occupy Spirituality*, our friends Adam Bucko and the Rev. Matthew Fox have begun a multigenerational conversation that is becoming critical to accomplishing the kind of change we want to see in spirituality today. Being deeply connected to the two ends of the spectrum of adult life, and looking together at the growing edge of spirituality and modern culture, they are helping all of us to find our way."

—Netanel Miles-Yepez and Rabbi Zalman Schachter-Shalomi, coauthors of
A Heart Afire: Stories and Teachings of the Early Hasidic Masters

"*Occupy Spirituality* brings to the forefront the need for spirituality in our lives and through us in the lives of nations around the world. Materialism and morality, Gandhi said, have an inverse relationship. When one increases the other decreases. The decay in our 'civilization' today is caused by material greed. This may just be the blueprint for the survival of humanity. Everyone must read this book."

—Arun Gandhi, author of *Legacy of Love* and *The Forgotten Woman;*
President, Gandhi Worldwide Education Institute

OCCUPY SPIRITUALITY

A RADICAL VISION FOR A NEW GENERATION

ADAM BUCKO AND MATTHEW FOX

Forewords by Mona Eltahawy and Andrew Harvey
Afterword by Lama Surya Das

North Atlantic Books
Berkeley, California

Published by
North Atlantic Books
P.O. Box 12327
Berkeley, California 94712

Adam Bucko's article "My God Lives on the Street" was first published in slightly different form in the *Huffington Post*, December 21, 2012. It is reprinted here with permission.

Cover art © iStockphoto.com/mustafahacalaki
Cover and book design by Mary Ann Casler
Printed in the United States of America

Occupy Spirituality: A Radical Vision for a New Generation is sponsored by the Society for the Study of Native Arts and Sciences, a nonprofit educational corporation whose goals are to develop an educational and cross-cultural perspective linking various scientific, social, and artistic fields; to nurture a holistic view of arts, sciences, humanities, and healing; and to publish and distribute literature on the relationship of mind, body, and nature.

North Atlantic Books' publications are available through most bookstores. For further information, visit our website at www.northatlanticbooks.com or call 800-733-3000.

Library of Congress Cataloging-in-Publication Data
Bucko, Adam, 1975–
Occupy spirituality : a radical vision for a new generation / Adam Bucko and Matthew Fox.
    pages cm
Includes bibliographical references.
Summary: "This book is a call to action for anyone interested in pursuing a radical approach to spirituality and using their talents in service of compassion and justice"—Provided by publisher.
ISBN 978-1-58394-685-5
1. Christian life. 2. Generation Y—Religious life. I. Title.
BV4501.3.B833 2013
248—dc23   2013006211

1 2 3 4 5 6 7 8 9 Sheridan 18 17 16 15 14 13
                        Printed on recycled paper

We dedicate this book in solidarity with the young everywhere who are seeking a world of values, not power games; of solidarity, not hierarchy; of fun, not dourness; of sharing, not hoarding; of sustainability, not extinction; of gratitude, not regret; of expansiveness, not tribalism; of respect, not domination. May we—elders, mentors, and youth—know we are in the struggle together.

Acknowledgments

We wish to thank the following people for their contributions and help in creating this book:

Andrew Harvey for his support and generous foreword and for including us in his Sacred Activism Series; Emily Boyd, Doug Reil, Jessica Moll, Jennifer Eastman, Louis Swaim, and everyone at North Atlantic Books for helping us birth this book; Vania Kent Harber and Rory McEntee for their help; Taz Tagore and the Reciprocity Family for their support and inspiration; Mona Eltahawy and Lama Surya Das for their thoughtful foreword and afterword; Kurt Johnson, Rev. Diane Burke, Pir Zia Inayat-Khan, Mirabai Bush for their contributions; Pancho Ramos-Stierle for "being the change"; Occupy Worldwide for showing us all that it's possible; Dena Merriam and everyone at the Contemplative Alliance for creating a forum for intergenerational dialogues that matter; Loma Huh for masterful transcribing of our conversations; all the young leaders and activists for contributing their thoughts to this book by way of filling out surveys and sitting for film interviews; Steve Torma for introducing us to Earthaven citizens; all the people who read and endorsed this book for their generosity; and, finally, our families and friends (you know who you are) for continuing to pray for us and for supporting us.

Contents

Foreword

Does God Support the Revolution?
Mona Eltahawy

Was God in Tahrir Square? Was She chanting for Bread? Was He shouting "Liberty"? Was It demanding Social Justice?

"The air in Tahrir is more sacred to me than the air in Makkah [Mecca]," said Emad Effat, who is called the Sheikh of the Revolution. If this man of God felt more of a divine urgency in the square than in the birthplace of Islam, toward which Muslims turn in prayer five times a day, he must've seen God there.

By day, the sheikh would issue fatwas—religious edicts—and by the end of office hours, he'd change out of his clerical robes and into civilian clothes and join the revolution. He was a cleric at al Azhar—the Sunni Muslim world's seat of learning—but he was also an Egyptian who cared about justice.

A long time ago, when we were children, the man who would grow up to be the Sheikh of the Revolution and I used to play together, along with his brothers. His family was my paternal grandparents' neighbors. His father used to give us rock sugar when we ran into his study.

Almost forty years later, we encountered God in different ways, very close to Tahrir Square.

On November 24, during clashes on Mohamed Mahmoud Street—just off the square—riot police beat me, broke my left arm and right hand, and sexually assaulted me. I was detained for twelve hours by the Interior Ministry and then Military Intelligence. At one point, surrounded by the riot police, I fell to the ground. Eye level with their boots, I heard a voice say, "Get up now or you will die!" To this day I don't know how, with fractures in both arms, I managed to get up. Was that God?

On December 16, Sheikh Emad was shot dead as he was standing at the Tahrir Square entrance to Qasr Al-Aini Street, as the army was attacking a sit-in protesting Egypt's then military junta. God had answered his prayer for martyrdom, his wife, Nashwa Abdel-Tawwab, told reporters.

Both my arms were in casts and I was high on painkillers when I read that the Sheikh of the Revolution had been shot dead. I read that thousands attended his funeral the next day, but I didn't connect him with my childhood friend until I was speaking with my family, and my mother said, "Did you hear about Emad Effat, may God have mercy on his soul."

For too long in Egypt and other countries in the region, clerics were less men of God and more men of the state—or, more appropriately, the yes-men of the state. If the regime wanted to launch a big family planning campaign, for example, out came a fatwa. Clerics would too often preach patience and obedience, but where were the fatwas against the torture that was systematic in so many of our countries? Where were the fatwas against slums left to drown in sewage? Where were the fatwas against hunger and willful neglect of the poor?

According to his wife, Emad Effat joined almost every sit-in and demonstration, because he couldn't "bear the thought of abandoning anyone who was suffering injustice."

A few weeks before he died, he is said to have been asked by a caller whether it was ever legitimate to fire upon protesters. His fatwa was clear: never.

That's why Tahrir Square felt so pure to the Sheikh of the Revolution. It was a sort of fatwa—an indictment, certainly—of torture, police brutality, dictatorship, hunger, and the things that too many yes-men of the state were quiet about. That's why Emad Effat's death was so painful for the revolution, and that's why many people suspect the Sheikh of the Revolution was deliberately targeted.

God is definitely on the side the Revolution: God is the minority and the Revolution is always about the minority. As one of my heroes, the late liberal Muslim scholar Nasr Hamed Abu Zeid used to say, "The majority never brings about change—it's too invested in the status quo."

The majority might pretend to own moral values, but if it closes its eyes to hunger, dictatorship, and injustice, those values are not mine. The yes-men of the state might try to stand between us and God, but my God does not rub shoulders with dictators and their enablers. I worship the God of Bread, Liberty, and Social Justice.

When you worship the God of Bread, Liberty, and Social Justice, your revolution is global and not specific to one part of the world. The book you hold in your hands is from another part of the world, with its own history and its own revolution. But we share common times as well as common values—bread and equality and justice—and today we all live in a common, global culture that is bleeding from the same wounds. The lessons I learned from the Sheikh of the Revolution and from my own protests are food for those young people who are celebrated and supported in this book. We are in this together. We will fall together or rise together. We share courage and solidarity together. We need our elders and our youth standing up together. I believe this book is a boost to that movement of justice we all seek.

Foreword

The Last and Best Hope
Andrew Harvey

The last and best hope for an endangered humanity is in a worldwide, grassroots revolution of love-in-action. Nothing less will
deconstruct the now lethal omnipotence of the corporations; nothing
less will send a signal to their lackeys, the politicians of all parties, that
business-as-usual is no longer acceptable at any level: nothing less will
galvanize the devastated heart of humanity, paralyzed as it is before
the immensity of the problems of its own making. It is to inspire such
a revolution that I wrote *The Hope: A Guide to Sacred Activism*. Time
is running out for the human race, and the stakes are desperately high.

Perhaps the greatest sign that such a revolution is possible was the
outbreak, inspired by the Arab Spring, of the Occupy movement. For
all its disorganization, lack of coherent goals, and occasional lapses into
violence, the Occupy movement sent a worldwide signal that young
people are sickened by the bankruptcy and terrible inequality of the
capitalist dream of endless growth; they do not want to live in the soul-
less, degraded world it has engendered; and they are prepared to put

their lives on the line for a more just and sustainable world. And even though the powers-that-be—in an unholy alliance between the banks and government—quickly tried to dismantle the movement, many of us who had despaired of the young realizing the disastrous situation they are in and rising to meet it with courage and vision were given fresh and lasting hope.

Occupy Spirituality is a brilliant and profound meditation on the Occupy movement, its goals and real achievements, and on what needs to happen next for humanity to have a chance of surviving the chaos exploding on all sides. It is in the form of a dialogue between a fiery, radical master theologian and prophet in his early seventies, Matthew Fox, and a young sacred activist, Adam Bucko, who has devoted his life to helping homeless teenagers and who cofounded the Reciprocity Foundation. Both share a passionate love for the Christ, humanity's most challenging revolutionary of love-in-action, while being open to all authentic forms of world spirituality: both remain soberly optimistic and fertile with creative, vibrant, and exciting challenges and suggestions. The beauty of the dialogue between these two extraordinary human beings lies in its immediacy, honesty, mutual nakedness, and radical passion for justice in all realms of our world. Adam and Matt's dialogue mirrors the open conversation and communication that urgently needs to take place between elders honed by sometimes brutal experience and the wise and impassioned young hungry for a way out of terminal disaster and for a way of life commensurate to their hunger for a new way of being and doing everything.

My deepest hope for *Occupy Spirituality*—and the hope of its authors—is that this dialogue will reach a wide and avid audience of young people. The continuing, bewildering success of inanely narcissistic new age mysticism makes it clear that the baby boom generation is unlikely to wake up any time soon, let alone commit its immense resources to doing anything real or radical enough to avert or temper catastrophe. Any real hope for our future lies in the energy, passion, wisdom, and commitment of the young, and *Occupy Spirituality* is a sustained prayer to all young people everywhere to understand finally that what is being offered to them by a collapsing world is not only emptiness, anguish, and disaster but also an extraordinary opportunity to create a radical movement for justice and balance. If the young seize this opportunity, inspired by the honed wisdom in this book and others, then a new world is still possible. If they don't, then the human race will face extinction.

Three essential suggestions for young sacred activists arise from Matt and Adam's dialogue. The first is that they really grasp the epochal significance of the Occupy movement and what a radical break in the long, stifling paralysis and anomie it represented. The second is that we all learn quickly from its improvisatory, haphazard mistakes: the next wave of radical protest will have to have a far deeper and more sustaining spiritual foundation, a far wiser organization, and far more coherent and comprehensive goals to be effective. There is no time left to fail: the next wave of protest will have to have the inner depth and outer cohesiveness of the great transformatory movements of Gandhi and Martin Luther King, but on a worldwide scale. The third suggestion is one that echoes again and again through Matt and Adam's conversations: it is the urgency of building on the inspiration of "Occupy" and starting such a movement immediately. Both Matt and Adam know that any further denial, despair, and procrastination will only permit the destruction of our world to become terminal.

Although the Occupy movement was, in its large-scale activities, effectively detoured, nevertheless, astonishing and largely unreported underground work by many inspired by it continues. Teams of former Occupiers played an extensive role in helping those afflicted by Hurricane Sandy; others have continued to set up brave alternative communities and to do battle with our absurd legal and political systems to help immigrants and homeowners broken by foreclosure debt. The passion and vision of the Occupy movement, as Matt and Adam make clear, was not destroyed: it lives on in flames of sacred activism that it is this book's intention to fan into a transformatory forest fire. Adam

Bucko's desire to create a global movement of sacred community living, which he calls HAB, will be immense nourishment and inspiration to young people seeking another way of life and a living spirituality as a base for wise, radical action. I call on all my fellow spiritual elders to do everything in their power to support it.

Occupy Spirituality is not a gloomy, haranguing tract; it is a juicy, playful, exuberant, sometimes dazzling dance between two great minds and hearts, full of both visionary inspiration and down-home practical suggestions. May we all be inspired by it to risk whatever we need to set about preserving our world.

Introduction

D r. Howard Thurman, the African American mystic and prophet who was in many ways the spiritual director behind the civil rights movement, was present at the March on Washington in 1963 that included Dr. King's "I Have a Dream" speech at the Lincoln Memorial. He leaves us with this—at first glance—surprising observation:

> The thing that made the deepest impression on me at the cer-
> emonies at the base of the Lincoln Monument . . . was not the
> vast throng, as thrilling at it was to be a part of such a tre-
> mendous movement of peoples on the march; it was not the
> inspired oratory of all the participating speakers, including the
> dazzling magic of the music and utter vitality springing from
> the throat of Martin Luther King; it was not the repeated refrain
> of Eugene Blake, saying on behalf of the church, we are late but
> we are here—no, it was none of these things. What impressed
> me most was a small group of young people representing

student nonviolent groups, fresh from the jails and violences of the South, who time and time again caught the spiritual overtones of the speakers and led the critical applause which moved like a tidal wave over the vast audience. I do not know but this observation may be an embarrassment to them, but this is how it seemed to me. These young people were tuned to the spiritual dimension of what they were about even as what they were about was the exercising of their civil rights inherent in their citizenship.[1]

This profound and holy man, Howard Thurman, who traveled to India with his wife in 1935 and met Gandhi and brought his nonviolent techniques for social change back to the black community in America, and whose book *Jesus and the Disinherited* was such a gospel to Dr. King that he took it with him each of the thirty-nine times he went to jail while protesting social segregation in America, does not remember King's great oratory or even the hundreds of thousands who marched for freedom and justice so much as he remembers the young. Those who had the courage to themselves go to jail and take on an evil system replete with numerous "violences" and who "exercised their civil rights inherent in their citizenship." And why did they make so profound an impact on Thurman's awareness? Because they were leaders in catching "the spiritual overtones" of the historic moment. And because of their courage.

It is this same spirit of admiration for today's youth that motivates the book you hold in your hands. We believe that today's younger generation, who started a global movement by camping out on Wall Street and its equivalents around the world and who are often choosing a road less traveled rather than joining the military-industrial-academic-prison complex—these people are prophets in our midst. They are putting human and ecological values ahead of rapacity and greed. They are leading often with silent witness and appeals to moral imagination rather than reptilian brain confrontation or anal-retentive political wish lists. They are angry, but they are committed to an alternative set of values that will put community ahead of survival of the few and the fittest. They are not only exercising their civil rights inherent in their citizenship, they are attuned to the spiritual overtones of our times.

We write this book both to encourage them and to hopefully assist these young adults in their spiritual path, a path that combines contemplative quieting of the reptilian brain with the moral outrage that so many people are feeling today. This marriage of contemplation and action, mysticism and prophecy, is greatly needed in our time, and they are leading far more than our often tired and dried-up political and religious systems and institutions. Proof of the depth of their protest and spirituality is their *courage*—whether in Cairo or Libya, New York City or Tunisia—they have been willing to make sacrifices for the values they believe in, those they choose to deepen and to share. We honor them for that. We believe courage is the first sign of spirit at work.

We also feel these young people have a message for the rest of us, all of us, whether we be of the age of elders or mentors, grandparents or parents. That is a second reason for this book—to give the young a voice, to let their values sound more deeply into our collective economic, political, educational, and religious consciousness. As anyone not married to denial can see, these systems are in crisis the world over. Our species needs to wake up fast, to stand up strong, and to deepen its value commitments, as time is rapidly running out on this planet. We salute and honor this Occupy generation—those involved and those not yet involved—and we hope and pray that they will be joined by other generations, and that all will work together to reinvent the way our species lives and carries on its business on this special planet of ours. We hope this book speaks both to the younger generation and to their parents and elders.

That is one reason why we—a seventy-one-year-old theologian and a thirty-seven-year-old advocate for homeless youth—have teamed up to write this book: to demonstrate how useful it can be for different generations to dialogue together. We have consciously and deliberately chosen to write this book as a dialogue. Dialogue is a wonderful methodology into which everyone can be invited. It represents the impulse toward democratic interaction and responding to each other in a way that encourages wisdom to emerge through shared participation. Our exchange represents a dialogue between two generations and between two different lives and stories. As institutions lose their credibility, as is happening in all our institutions today, we go to stories and especially autobiographies. The stories of individuals are more trustworthy than the tired stories of self-serving institutions (consider the scandals of guardians of Penn State University or hierarchy in the Roman Catholic Church, who put institutional reputation ahead of caring for children in pedophile cover-ups). Putting human stories ahead of institutional stories is one reason why, early in our book, two chapters are devoted to the autobiographies of the authors. We hope they invite others' stories into the dialogue.

Ultimately, this book is about spirituality—a Radical Spirituality for a Radical Generation already known for its courage. Since everything humans engage in and give birth to carries a shadow with it, so this movement too needs a mature and examined spirituality that can support its success and reinforce its authenticity and that can assist it to incarnate its truth with both honesty and effectiveness—in this way we hope to provide some language that allows it to dialogue with other generations and multiple spiritual traditions even while it takes seriously the call to birthing new forms and new expressions of spirituality.

Given today's crises the world over, we can no longer afford to hide our contemplatives in comfortable monasteries. We need to reunite contemplation and action, we need spiritual activists and, indeed, spiritual warriors on the streets and in all our professions and institutions, who can reinvent them with ecological values and the values of social justice that assure our sustainability as a species, as well as the health and beauty of this planet.

We feel it is important to underscore that the Occupy generation— what defines it, and what kinds of dreams it cherishes and gives birth to—does not depend on the success of Occupy Wall Street or the Arab Spring. Its vision is more long-term than that. Revolutions will come and go. Movements will change names and forms. But what is emerging in people's hearts will continue. Most likely it will continue quietly, in small communities, among friends, mostly unacknowledged by the dominant media. It will continue quietly creating a counterpoint to all the institutions and power structures, eventually moving the center of life from values that no longer serve life to relationships that nourish and celebrate life.[2]

The late Thomas Berry, an eco-prophet of immense stature and a deep student of contemporary science and cosmology, reminds us that "the dark periods of history are the creative periods; for these are the times when new ideas, arts, and institutions can be brought into being at the most basic level." He gives as examples the Middle Ages in the West and the third century in China, when the dissolution of the Han dynasty gave birth to a period when Buddhist monks and Confucian scholars and artists "gave expression to new visions and new thoughts at the deepest levels of human consciousness" and that allowed the Chinese to survive and thrive as a people and as a culture. The darkness eventually gave birth to a revival of wisdom traditions that "are not the transient thoughts or immediate insights of journalists concerned with the daily course of human affairs; they are expressions in human form of the principles guiding human life within the very structure and functioning of the universe itself."[3] If we are living through a dark age currently, it may be the door to a brighter future, and the young may be the leaders of that brighter future. But they can't do it alone, and they can't do it on the terms of the journalists of the dominant media conglomerates, who operate merely at the level of information and—so often—titillation. The questions of the young are deeper, and their actions come from a place of spirituality.

While most pundits still argue about whether another world is possible, the youth are already living it . . . they are living it in how they choose to interact with each other, in how they do spirituality, in how they say no to politics as we know it, by moving from wanting to impose a fixed rule to proposing a new way of life, one in which we put aside our egos and relate to each other in ways that can produce communities that work for everyone. Indian writer and activist Arundhati Roy used to say, "Another world is not only possible, she is on her way. On a quiet day, I can hear her breathing." Kids definitely can already hear her breathing.

We open this book with a chapter on Religion versus Spirituality, how the God of Religion is too often distinct from the God of Life, and how all religious renewal requires a return to experience of spirituality and what will characterize the emergent spirituality. Then we talk about a new emerging and world-changing spirituality for the Occupy generation. Next, after our two autobiographical chapters, we turn to an absolutely central issue with young adults: vocation or calling. We present *vocation* as a spiritual path that allows people to claim their gifts, offer them in service of compassion and justice and creating communities that can nurture one's calling. Chapter six considers spiritual practices, both personal and communal, such as ritual. Chapter seven considers the relationship between young people and mentors and elders. Chapter eight considers issues of new economics and new communities, including New Monasticism. Finally, the conclusion treats the topic of spiritual democracy and the Occupy generation, themes that draw together the other issues of this book.

In addition to our dialogues we incorporate the words of young people, derived from the twenty-some hours of filming young leaders that we have done in New York City, at an ecovillage named Earthaven in North Carolina, on a permaculture farm in Colorado, and in the San Francisco Bay Area, as well as from surveys we have distributed widely. We also include some observations from elders whom we respect.

The facts of life for many young people today speak loudly to the profound challenges they face and the profound changes that are called for. Unemployment is soaring among young people the world over—in Spain it stands at 60 percent. In America in 2011 over half of college graduates were jobless or underemployed. Over 350,000 Americans with advanced degrees were receiving food stamps or some other form of public assistance. College loan debt has tripled in the past ten years and now averages $24,000 per student; today more than one-third of college graduates have a zero net worth. The median net worth of eighteen- to thirty-five-year-olds has dropped 68 percent since 1984. It now stands at less than $4,000. Meanwhile, however, the 1 percent— the richest Americans—tripled their share of income between 1980 and 2006. Their median net worth is over $5,000,000.

As for education, while consumer prices in general have approximately doubled since 1985, tuition has risen almost 600 percent. Total state education cuts in 2012 were $12.7 billion, which is just about the exact amount that 285 of our nation's largest companies avoided in state taxes each year from 2008 to 2010. The state of Arizona doubled college tuition costs in four years. K-12 schools in California have one counselor per eight hundred students. Pennsylvania's governor proposed cutting higher education funding by half, and New Hampshire did exactly that. Corporations are sitting on trillions of dollars but are reluctant to hire. Apple employs forty-seven thousand people and makes a profit of $420,000 per employee. "Yet most Apple store workers make about $12 per hour."[4]

Paul Bucheit, who cofounded the social network company Friendfeed and worked as an engineer with Google for years, comments, "For those of us who weren't particularly good activists in the 60s, age has widened our perspective, and the lack of opportunities for our children has given us a second chance to protest, to help make it clear how the leaders of my generation have abandoned the people they no longer need." His advice to the young? "First you have to get mad."[5] Getting mad is what prophets do, Gandhi was mad and King was mad and Jesus was mad; anger has its place. But it needs direction, it needs contours. Moral outrage is and always has been a light that sets fire to social change. But it takes discipline, such as the discipline the civil rights movement instilled in its nonviolent practices. It takes a spirituality.

It is our experience, in interviewing dozens of young people and in studying the surveys we distributed widely and in working with young people, that moral imagination is on the rise. A growing number of young people are living in community—a choice that begins with an economic survival motive but usually evolves into a sharing of values, ranging from gardening to friendship; conviviality to common cooking; part-time work that mirrors one's real values, with time for meditation and spiritual practice and political protest—we find many young adults are people with their imaginations in overdrive. They are not wilting before the onslaught of the adultism that rules our institutions from Wall Street to Washington, from media powerhouses to the Vatican. They are beginning to create their own societies. As one twenty-two-year-old woman put it, having escaped from fundamentalism when she was fourteen years old, "my generation is aching for a living spirituality." One might call this the "aching generation" as well as the Occupy generation. But it is a spiritual quest they are on as much as a political quest. It is the task of mentors and elders to join forces with them.

It is good to heed the teaching of Walt Whitman, who first coined the term "spiritual democracy." He writes especially to the young. "The people, especially the young men and women of America, must begin to learn that religion, (like poetry,) is something far, far different from what they supposed. It is indeed too important to the power and perpetuity of the New World to be consign'd any longer to the churches, old or new, Catholic or Protestant—Saint this, or Saint that. It must be consign'd henceforth to democracy *en masse*, and to literature. It must enter into the poems of the nation. It must make the nation."[6]

Today we are thinking and acting beyond just "the nation" to the species and beyond our species to the Earth itself. But the issue of "spiritual democracy" remains the same. Our hearts and minds, bodies and imaginations, must be consigned to democracy *en masse* and to literature entering the poems and, therefore, the heart of all nations and all places.

Pancho Ramos-Stierle is twenty-six years old and was arrested at

Occupy Oakland while meditating. Modern poverty, he says, boasts "two kinds of slaves: the intoxicated—the prisoners to the addiction of consumption, and those who aspire to get intoxicated—the prisoners of envy. . . . We ourselves must be strengthened and changed, for we have to experience an inner independence even before the corporations, police states, and governments grant the outward one. . . . We really need to step up as citizens of the world." What does it mean to Pancho to be an Occupier? "We are the early adopters of a revolution of values, and we are the evidence that the totalitarianism of corporate capitalism—the machine that has devastated the planet and human beings—we are the demonstration that system doesn't work and that we need a new system."[7]

Pancho sees the issue as a marriage of spirituality and activism:

It is time for the spiritual people to get active and the activist people to get spiritual so that we can have total revolution of the human spirit. Because we have the idea that the self-indulgent people are just meditating—they are going to caves and meditation centers while all this madness is happening or you have people at these meditation centers that are asking how can you bring peace and calm and harmony to the world if you do not have that in your heart?

I think that we need both now, and that we need to combine this inner revolution with the outer revolution to have the total revolution of the spirit. Then you can build the alternatives to a collapsing system built on structural violence.[8]

Are we up to the task? This we know: it cannot be accomplished without the generosity and imagination and hard work and courage of the young. Howard Thurman offered this observation about young people, "Youth is a time of soaring hopes, when dreams are given first wings and, as reconnoitering birds, explore unknown landscapes. Again and again a man full of years is merely the corroboration of the dreams of his youth. The sense of fancy growing out of the sense of fact—which makes all healthy personalities and gives a touch of romance and glory to all of life—first appears as the unrestrained imaginings of youth."[9] This truth underscores the stakes of young and old working together on this great adventure that calls us all today. We call that adventure *spiritual democracy*. It is bigger than any one of us; bigger than any generation. It is about our ancestors and our descendants; it is about the now and the future. It is about despair and promise. We invite you to deep listening and deep acting.

1

Is It Time to Replace the God of Religion with the God of Life?

To me G*d is the unfathomable mystery that connects everything in existence, everything that ever was and ever will be, the oneness and power that moves through us all.

K.R., Female, 27

I don't like the word "God." It's too loaded and I'm too small of a being to try to assign language to something so large.

A.B., Female, 29

God is my vertical connection which asks me to connect horizontally.

N.B., Male, 33

How narrowly people define God always cracks me up! Often the Atheists I talk to don't believe in the "Old White Dude up in the Clouds," yet have a reverence for the miracles of nature, and the power of our own consciousness . . . to me that is a part of God.

K.R., Female, 29

I used to go to Friday Muslim prayer regularly, but I got tired of hearing views that don't match my own. I really like a mosque in another city and go there when I can.

K.C., Female, 28

Spirituality burns hot while religion is lukewarm if not cold.

S.W., Male, 28

I don't practice the Buddhism of my parents or the old ladies of the temple. I think spirituality is more of a personal experience. Buddha taught that we need to experience it for ourselves and not just believe him. We need to question him and see it for ourselves. It is only when we experience the truth for ourselves that we can know for sure.

A.N., Male, 35

Spirituality enlivens religious practices so they don't become meaningless.

K.C., Female, 28

God is within me at all times and around me even when I am too busy to notice.

J.H., Male, 17

I think youth today are less encumbered with (or you could say more ignorant of) traditional religions, so they can emphasize simple practices that help increase spirituality and spread harmony in the world instead of getting caught up in different doctrines.

K.C., Female, 28

Spirituality plays a very important role in my life. I think though for a long time I was ashamed about being a spiritual person. Like, it wasn't "cool" to be spiritual (beyond your religion) and to recognize that . . . Well . . . spirituality is far more powerful than "religion."

We are all connected, regardless of religion, skin color, gender, sexual orientation. . . .

Also, spirituality is important when it comes to my menstrual cycle. Honoring my menstrual cycle through rituals, letting myself rest and reflect, means a lot to me.

L.Y., Female, 22

God is the way that I integrate all of my experience into a coherent whole so as to feel more connected to what is at the center of my being and the mysterious void from which all things emerge. Spirituality, for me, also involves the process of becoming more sensitive to the subtleties of life.

S.W., Male, 28

I am sure that a nature-centered spirituality contains within it solutions to all of life's problems. If the soil is healthy, the plants and animals will be healthy. If the plants and animals are healthy, the people will be healthy. It is as simple as that.

Many of our industrial, social, and economic systems that have been established over the last century are beginning to show fracture lines. It seems as if many of these structures and systems are going to crumble in the lifetime of the current youth population. The challenging task of maintaining these systems will indeed fall onto our shoulders but if they are not built upon a solid foundation they will inevitably collapse. Ultimately it is going to be the task of the current youth to redesign systems that are based on a more stable foundation.

P.P., Male, 27

ADAM BUCKO: Imagine a group of protestors gathering together at one of the Occupy sites. Suddenly, one of them does what they call a "human microphone" check. The mic is on. The ritual of call and response is about to begin. The liturgy of hope is about to start.

Most of the people there are young, in their twenties. Looking around, one can see people from all walks of life. There are college students, young professionals, mothers with babies, artists, even former Wall Street employees who decided to join in. Many are eager to participate in this regenerating ritual. Some feel broken, worried about what kind of future their kids will have.

Many are holding signs. There is one kid holding a sign that says, "That we're young only means we have the most to lose by standing idle." There is someone there with a sign that reads, "Obama is not a brown-skinned antiwar socialist who gives away free healthcare . . . you're thinking of Jesus." There is an elderly woman who looks like she could be the grandmother of any of these kids. Her sign says, "I'm 87 and mad as hell."

MATTHEW FOX: There is much to be angry about in today's world, whether you are young or old, but certainly if you are young. Adultism reigns. The debts the young are inheriting, which include not only unheard-of educational debts but the debts of foolish wars and the debts of a depleted Earth system and the loss of so much beauty and richness and variety of species, the deteriorating health of the planet, climate change, ineffective political systems and religious systems—they all cry out for grieving. And anger is the first level of grief, after all. The question is not "Who is angry and why?" but "What are we doing with our anger? What is the most effective use of it?" What Howard Thurman and Mahatma Gandhi and Martin Luther King Jr. teach us is that it is possible and necessary to steer anger into useful protest and authentic change.

ADAM BUCKO: There are also signs that say, "I won't believe corporations are people until the state of Texas executes one" and "If only the war on poverty was a real war, then we would be actually putting money into it." There is even a dog there protesting, holding a stick in his mouth with attached little flags that read, "Democracy gone . . . to dogs." Finally, there is a sign that reads, "Sorry for the inconvenience. We are trying to change the world."

A passerby, upset that his favorite coffee truck had to move because of this spectacle, shouts at one of the kids, "Why don't you get a job!" He answers, "I would, but there are no jobs."

The kid is right. There are no jobs. He is part of a "lost generation" that has been marked by "debt, joblessness, insecurity, and hopelessness" and abandoned by "its market-obsessed, turn-a-quick-profit elders."[1] Today this kid is gathering with many others to reclaim the promise of a word so often used in the Bible: he is here to reclaim hope.

MATTHEW FOX: For many young people on the economic margins, joining the military seems like the only available option. We spend a trillion dollars on war in Iraq and Afghanistan, and there is nothing left for schools and construction jobs and infrastructure at home. The abandonment that young people feel from churches, schools, and government is a sign of how we are in a moment of great change, and our institutions have not caught up yet by any means. But time is running out. And if despair takes over, grave danger awaits us all. The great medieval philosopher Thomas Aquinas said that while injustice is the worst of sins, despair is the most dangerous, because when you are in despair, you care neither about yourself nor about others.

ADAM BUCKO: I recall meeting a homeless girl at a shelter some years ago. Like all of the other kids there, she too had dreams. She dreamed of a future in which she could make something of her life. She had all the odds working against her: poverty, lack of funds for college, no mentors who could help her find her way, yet she still had the courage to dream.

She desperately wanted to start her life anew. She wanted her American Dream—nothing too extreme, just a good and meaningful job that could give her a sense of self-worth, a modest apartment, perhaps a future family.

So there she was, looking for her promise and looking for her dream. But there were no jobs except for one, the US Army. This job accepted her with a smile. I don't know what happened to that girl, but my guess is that she signed up and was shipped to Iraq on her eighteenth birthday. What a way into hope, what a way into her dream and her future. Is this all our society has to offer?

Then just last week, while walking around my neighborhood, it dawned on me that there aren't any youth centers in my neighborhood. No youth centers, yet two US Army recruiting centers. Why worry about our kids when we can ship them off to Iraq? Perhaps there they can learn what life is all about: death, destruction, mayhem, the "enemy." Then they return to our country with PTSD and haunted memories for a lifetime.

A cover story of *Time* magazine in July 2012 reported that the suicide rate among US soldiers had reached one per day. This is unprecedented. Suicide deaths are higher than combat deaths.

Was the girl I met at the homeless shelter one of the soldiers who died today, I wonder? Or have we only done our best to set her up for a tortured life?

MATTHEW FOX: I like the teaching from the eco-philosopher David Orr that "hope is a verb with the sleeves rolled up." We need to get to work to provide what is real for the next generation across the board: real education, real jobs, real values, real politics, real religion.

The great Howard Thurman makes an important distinction between the "God of Religion" and the "God of Life." They are not always, unfortunately, the same thing, and when they are not, we have to return to the God of Life to rebegin not only religion but culture itself. I think we are living in such a time. Just like the God at Penn State was a God who cared not about innocent children but about the preservation of that institution, and the same can be said of the God of the Roman Catholic Church, so we have to begin anew with the God that Thurman says "is the life within life" and the "heart of the universe" that puts love first and justice first.

So easily can the God of Religion saddle up to the Gods of Empire, of Commerce, of Greed, of Power, of Militarism. That is why we always have to criticize the idols around us and within us. Idolatry is alive and well; we have to pay attention.

ADAM BUCKO: Speaking of hope being a "verb with the sleeves rolled up," while protesting outside the White House against the militarization of our country, Chris Hedges gave a beautiful speech called "Real Hope Is about Doing Something."[2] I want to bring some selected passages from that speech into our conversation.

> Hope does not mean that our protests will suddenly awaken the dead consciences, the atrophied souls, of the plutocrats running Halliburton, Goldman Sachs, ExxonMobil or the government. . . .
>
> Hope does not mean we will reform Wall Street swindlers and speculators. . . .
>
> Hope does not mean that the nation's ministers and rabbis, who know the words of the great Hebrew prophets, will leave their houses of worship to practice the religious beliefs they preach. Most clerics like fine, abstract words about justice and full collection plates, but know little of real hope. . . .
>
> Hope knows that unless we physically defy government control we are complicit in the violence of the state. All who resist keep hope alive. All who succumb to fear, despair and apathy become enemies of hope.
>
> Hope has a cost. Hope is not comfortable or easy. Hope requires personal risk. Hope does not come with the right attitude. Hope is not about peace of mind. Hope is an action. Hope is doing something. . . . Hope, which is always nonviolent, exposes in its powerlessness the lies, fraud and coercion employed by the state. Hope does not believe in force. Hope knows that an injustice visited on our neighbor is an injustice visited on us all. . . . Hope sees in our enemy our own face.

Hope is not for the practical and the sophisticated, the cynics and the complacent, the defeated and the fearful. Hope is what the corporate state, which saturates our airwaves with lies, seeks to obliterate. Hope is what our corporate overlords are determined to crush. Be afraid, they tell us. Surrender your liberties to us so we can make the world safe from terror. Don't resist. Embrace the alienation of our cheerful conformity. Buy our products. Without them you are worthless. Become our brands. Do not look up from your electronic hallucinations to think. No. Above all do not think. . . .

The powerful do not understand hope. Hope is not part of their vocabulary. They speak in the cold, dead words of national security, global markets, electoral strategy, staying on message, image and money. . . . Those addicted to power, blinded by self-exaltation, cannot decipher the words of hope any more than most of us can decipher hieroglyphics. Hope to Wall Street bankers and politicians, to the masters of war and commerce, is not practical. It is gibberish. It means nothing.

I cannot promise you fine weather or an easy time. . . . I cannot pretend that being handcuffed is pleasant. . . . If we resist and carry out acts, no matter how small, of open defiance, hope will not be extinguished. . . .

Any act of rebellion, any physical defiance of those who make war, of those who perpetuate corporate greed and are responsible for state crimes, anything that seeks to draw the good to the good, nourishes our souls and holds out the possibility that we can touch and transform the souls of others. Hope affirms that which we must affirm. And every act that imparts hope is a victory in itself.

MATTHEW FOX: A powerful message indeed, combined with his witness as well. I too have found hope and moral imagination, a renewal of energy therefore, in visiting Occupy sites in Boston, New York, North Carolina, Colorado, San Francisco, and Oakland.

ADAM BUCKO: I love it when Chris Hedges says that "any act of rebellion, any physical defiance of those who make war, of those who perpetuate corporate greed and are responsible for state crimes, anything that seeks to draw the good to the good, nourishes our souls and holds out the possibility that we can touch and transform the souls of others." Somehow I feel that this captures what happens when kids from the Occupy movement come together.

MATTHEW FOX: One often gets the impression from people of the Occupy generation that they are listening especially deeply to their vocations, their callings, rather than just listening to the noise of the media and of incessant advertising, whose goal is to feed Wall Street with addicted consumers. In this regard, I like what Howard Thurman says about listening deeply to that call inside us, "There is something in every one of you that waits and listens for the sound of the genuine in yourself. It is the only true guide you will ever have. And if you cannot hear it, you will all of your life spend your days on the ends of strings that somebody else pulls."[3]

ADAM BUCKO: I remember being at Occupy with some young people from our community during the protest. I felt there a certain kind of energy, a kind of spiritual and moral power. It felt like we were able to come together in a way that created an opening for this energy to enter the world. It literally felt like the world cracked open and let this moral, soulful force come in and do its healing work. I remember marching the streets and looking around at the bankers and corporate executives standing there in their suits, watching us. I saw that they too were feeling this energy. They could see that this was not just another dress-up game of angry and frustrated college students. It was a manifestation of moral authority that was here to change things. I swear I saw a recognition in them that things would change.

MATTHEW FOX: I think one reason for this is that they found something positive to do with their grief and their anger. On the right, the Tea Party is also fueled by anger and outrage, but I fear that most of their solutions are hardly thought out at all. Yet they have been amazingly successful in getting their people elected and in changing political discourse (not always for the better, I fear) in America. Hopefully the Occupy movement will also spawn dedicated political leaders and alternatives with well-thought-out principles and policies that defend Main Street and the 99 percent. Already their protests have assisted to redefine the debate around economics and to reintroduce values of justice and fairness into the political discourse.

ADAM BUCKO: This reminded me of an experience that I had in Europe. When the Occupy movement began I was given an opportunity to go to my home country, Poland, and speak at the Warsaw Stock Exchange. While there, I spoke on a panel with some leading Polish politicians who remembered Poland's struggle for democracy and were very sympathetic to the Occupy movement in New York City. After our panel, a Wall Street banker came up to me and asked, "Do you think things will really fall apart?"

I looked at him and I could see the fear in his eyes, but I could also see hope. There was a fear of losing everything. The hope, however, was that if things did change, it would relieve him from participating in a corrupt system. He no longer would have to justify supporting his own children in a way that prevents others' children from being fed and given opportunities—opportunities that all children deserve.

It is this fear and this hope that I see in the 1 percent. They fear losing their way of life, but deep down they also hope for it. They hope, like we all do, for a world that can nourish everyone, not just the 1 percent or not only the 99 percent, but one that can work for 100 percent.

MATTHEW FOX: One thing I have learned from seventy-two years of living is that the primary signs of spirit are courage and generosity. They go together nicely because to stand up for justice is always demanding in terms of generosity. It requires giving to those you may not even know personally. Giving to future generations. It also requires courage, of course, because one is always taking on powerful forces when one stands for justice and speaks truth to power. Without courage and generosity we do not have spirituality. With it, we do.

Consider the many sacrifices of those in the Middle East who have been standing up to dictatorships and often paying the ultimate price for it. Consider the civil rights movement in this country fifty years ago, which brought alive the courage and generosity of the tens of thousands of persons who participated, often at great risk to themselves. Consider those in South America who did the same a generation ago, when they stood up to the dictators (often supported by our government, I'm sorry to say) and transnational corporations who then and still today are raping the Amazon rainforest and its indigenous peoples for their gods of mammon. It is a pity that so many so-called religious leaders do not stand up with courage and generosity toward the young and the future but are busy playing games that insure the security of their institutions.

Recently I spoke to a gathering of world youth leaders sponsored by UNESCO, and I told the following story, which I think reinforces the principles of courage and generosity and caring. A few years ago a whale was trapped off the coast of San Francisco in ropes laid by fishermen. As she thrashed around in the ropes she made them even tighter and it was clear that she was so enmeshed that she was going to die. Five men went out in rubber dinghies and in wetsuits with machetes to try to free her. It was a dangerous mission—one swing of her tail, and they could be killed. They spread out around her and starting chopping at the ropes that imprisoned her. The operation took about forty-five minutes, and she was freed. First she swam a big circle out of sheer delight; then she swam over to each of these men and individually touched each one, thanking them. The men said afterward that it was the "most transcendent experience" of their lives.

Some of the lessons I draw from this is what an organic relationship we have with the other creatures, who need not be afraid of us, and with whom we share this interdependent planet. But also that it took genuine caring and, with it, both courage and generosity on the part of these men to accomplish their task. It took a deep spirituality. One of them, who was cutting the ropes in the whale's mouth, was eye-to-eye with the whale for the entire forty-five minutes. He said he would never forget that encounter.

ADAM BUCKO: This, indeed, is a beautiful example of spirit, courage, and generosity. Speaking of which, when young people in Egypt began to take to the streets, I remember wondering about our spiritual leaders. Where were they? In the midst of the uprising, I decided to peek on Twitter to see what kind of messages our spiritual leaders were sending to the world. Were they standing up in solidarity with the youth as the Egyptian secret police brutalized them in Tahrir Square? Or were they too busy organizing their speaking tours and television appearances?

What I found disgusted me. They were pushing books on "spiritual weight loss," "miracles of manifesting wealth," and many other absurd things. It was capitalism at its worse. No wonder the Occupy generation is not impressed with them! No wonder they are turning away from that kind of leadership and witness! No wonder young people are convinced that this kind of spirituality has nothing to do with the "kingdom of God," and everything with the "kingdom of the empire," be it religious or corporate.

While young people in Tahrir Square and many other places around the world were standing up for Truth and risking their lives, these so-called spiritual leaders were continuing to push their latest books and "magical solutions" to life. One has to ask, how are these leaders any different from Wall Street executives? And the answer, sadly, is that they may be even worse. At least with Wall Street there is some degree of honesty about their purpose, which is to make money at all costs.

I am not saying that any spiritual leader who has had some success is insincere or that none of the leaders of our time have stepped up to the plate. There are genuine spiritual teachers and elders who do feel called to play a role in what is happening. The fact is that what is trying to emerge through these movements desperately needs them. The challenge for these leaders, though, lies in abandoning their usual role of the teacher who shows up and tells everyone how things should go. When leaders show up with ideas and without paying attention to what is trying to be born there, they simply miss the mark, they miss the evolutionary possibility. Their ideas and life experience are needed, but they need to share these in a dialogue with the energy that is arising in kids' hearts and lives. It's a spiritual energy, a moral unfolding and fire. It cannot be ignored. Ignoring it is like doing what the Muslim Brotherhood is doing in Egypt when they tell Arab women, "thank you for your participation in the revolution but now you can go home. We know how to take it from here."

This is not the time for top-down management. This is not the time for monologue. It is the time for dialogue. Trying to tell people what to do is missing the spirit of the times that we live in. Now is the time for these spiritual elders to engage in heartfelt conversation and spiritual democracy, allowing new things to be born as a result of these meetings of the hearts.

MATTHEW FOX: This is part of the meaning of *spiritual democracy* that we will want to develop later in our conversations. Moving from hierarchical and top-down dynamics to circle dynamics. A more horizontal than vertical model is needed. Spirit works through circles, after all, and not just from top down. Main Street is about circles—people look each other in the eye there on a daily basis; Wall Street is about ladders; it is very top-down. Dorothee Sölle, the feminist and liberation theologian from Germany, said that the opposite of hierarchy is *solidarity*. I think the Occupy movement is teaching us a lot about solidarity. So did the crew that saved that whale.

ADAM BUCKO: The spirituality of the Occupy generation does not come from the top down, nor does it come from New Age experts who show up and try to play the role of gurus, convinced that they know where things need to go. This moral power that is felt in the movement is those kids' spiritual teacher. They are getting a direct transmission from the entity of justice that is emerging in their midst. As they stand up for what's possible, and as they relate to each other in the spirit of mutual aid and direct democracy, this power seizes their hearts and initiates them into a new kind of spirituality. It is a spirituality of Life, not a spirituality of morally bankrupt institutions. This new spirituality is about doing something to help the world in way that requires sacrifice rather than being spoon-fed easy answers. It is about discovering your true calling, your unique gifts, and offering them as an active prayer in service of compassion and justice. I believe movements like Occupy are initiating many people into what this kind of life is really like.

When I look at history, I realize that this is not the first time that spiritual revolutions have happened in this way. This was the spirituality of Jesus, Kabir, Ramakrishna, Gandhi, and many others. George Fox, the founder of Quakers, at the age of nineteen realized the corruption of the religious institutions surrounding him, and not being able to find a "priest" who could speak to his condition, he turned inward and found his "teacher within." This "inner light" then guided him into a life of courage, transformative compassion, prophetic witness, and spiritual democracy.

In our own day, eco-warrior Julia Butterfly Hill embodies this type of courage. In 1997, at the age of twenty-three Julia felt called to protest the destruction of ancient redwood forests by a market-driven corporation. She climbed high into a thousand-year-old redwood tree and didn't come down for 738 days. Her aim was to prevent the destruction of the forests by making it impossible to destroy the tree without killing her. In the process, through heartbreak and love, she was guided into surrender and also began to sense this inner guidance that we are speaking of. From nature and from life, she found the courage to stay in that tree, to hope and to survive. That guidance transformed her into a sacred leader who now inspires millions of young people all around the world.

And, so here we are today. Will we choose the God of Religion or of Wall Street, or do we have the courage to choose the God of Life? The future depends on our choice.

Some time ago I saw a wonderful piece of art published in *Adbusters* magazine that captured what this new movement of spirit is about. It portrayed a group of Occupy protestors with the following prophetic message:

> Hey you up there! The rumbling has started. The pressure is rising. Can't you see capitalism is heaving under its own swollen brain? The fractures are splintering into every corner. The golden goose is dead. The magic beanstalk dried out. The pot of gold got fenced. No policy can fix it. We all know what's ahead: a quickening beat of ecological, financial, political, spiritual, and personal crisis. Everything about this insanity is the same. It's time to wake from this dead dream. There are millions of us out here so listen good.
>
> We're not gonna have a future unless we rise up and start fighting for a different kind of future.[4]

MATTHEW FOX: The role of the prophet has always been to wake people up from their slumber or their denial (which tend to be the same thing). I certainly hear the Occupy movement trying to do just that. It is so needed. There is so much denial in our culture, our media, our religions, our politics. How badly we need to be awakened. After all, the very name *Buddha* means, "the awakened one." And Paul and Jesus both talked about "waking up." And the ancient Indian mystic Kabir says, "You have been sleeping for millions and millions of years. Why not wake up this morning?" And the great Western mystic Meister Eckhart says, "God is the denial of denial." So to wake up, to cut through denial, is to let the Divine flow again—just as we are promised by the prophet that "justice will flow like water."

2
Radical Spirituality for a Radical Generation

We want to heal the world by acknowledging and embracing its inherent divinity and imperfect perfection.

R.P., Male, 32

The spirituality that my generation is interested in is less compartmentalized than that of our parents' generation. For my parents they had their work life, their family life, their religious/spiritual life, and all of these things existed separate from each other. This resulted in a lot of fragmentation of self, and I think a lot of people my age recognize that in their parents. We want a version of life that doesn't ask us to compartmentalize these things. We want our work and our families and our spiritual practice to be one and the same, to find a way to live a full life of devotion that reflects our truest self in everything that we do.

V.H.K., Female, 30

I was raised Protestant Christian. I have more respect and understanding for Christianity now as a Muslim than I did when I was a Christian and I felt I had to conform to certain ways of thinking that rubbed me the wrong way. Now I feel free to believe what I want. I feel very close to Jesus, and I sometimes say I'm a Muslim whose Sheikh is Jesus.

K.C., Female, 28

I was raised within several traditions . . . Christian, Sufi, and Indigenous Spirituality. I was told that life was magic, and secrets are woven throughout nature. I was deeply confused by Sunday school but loved the Indian stories I was taught.

S.W., Male, 28

I wear jewelry with Jewish stars that I received from my Bat Mitzvah, I throw around some Yiddish jargon every now and again, I am grateful for my Jewish ancestors and their traditions . . . but honestly, I am in my own world, with my own spiritual traditions, and would be glad to just let the Judaism go. My parents want me to marry someone Jewish (if I marry)—not that they wouldn't love me or the guy if he was not Jewish—but my parents are biased.

L.Y., Female, 22

Many in my generation are wary of the terms religion and spirituality. However, I think we are hungry for something that encourages questioning, curiosity, depth, and meaning. Our generation has the opportunity to redefine spirituality as something that is truly healthy and inclusive of things like art, science, and having fun!

E.B., Male, 30

The spirituality that my generation is interested in is personal, non-structured and all-encompassing. We tend to use numerous methods to deepen spiritual experience, including nature, yoga, meditation, conscious-community, art, and activism. We take and blend what we believe serves our spiritual path from numerous sources, including religion, ritual, psychology, and movement. Because it is sourced from our personal experience, we don't feel pressured or compelled to conform to a specific teaching or institution.

C.C., Female, 35

I don't think of my generation as spiritual. I think of my generation as materialistic and concerned with their own desires and needs above all else.

C.M., Female, 35

We are an 'intra-spiritual' generation. I, for example, consider myself to be part of Christianity, Universalism, Earth-Based Traditions, Yoga, and Sufism. I, like many of my generation, like to mix and match my spirituality.

K.R., Female, 27

The spirituality of today is very different from the spirituality of the past. There are many things today, like media/internet/cellphones, that didn't exist in the past. Those things make it more difficult to be centered and spiritual. At the same time, because of them information about spirituality is much more accessible to us. We can read about it, explore it, and connect with people practicing it all around the world. In the past, we would have been stuck with our family/village/town's religion and could have been killed or disowned by our family for wanting to explore something different. Now we can go to church on a Sunday and do Buddhist meditation during the week.

A.N., Male, 35

Essentially living a deeply spiritual life does not allow for segmentation of our spirituality and the other parts of our lives. I try to make sure that I bring my spiritual values into all aspects of my life. I try to learn how to dance this dance with balance and grace. At times it is tempting to just want to get away from it all and live in the mountains.

My grandmother always told me, "Much is expected from those to whom much is given," I don't feel it would be spiritually responsible of me to try to remove myself from the world. . . . G*d is everywhere and we awakened light bearers need to be everywhere as well.

K.R., Female, 27

To me, the spirituality of my generation is about following an instinct, an impulse, which arises from deep inside. It requires a constant fidelity to the relationship aspect of the universe, or the friendship aspect of God. I feel that this brings the whole of one's life into the process of spiritual development, hence integration is natural, free flowing, and unique. There is an openness to the movement of the Spirit which leaves all of Life exposed to Its breath.

R.M., Male, 35

ADAM BUCKO: All social movements, across generations, need a solid spirituality. A solid spirituality is one that enables people to energize their moral imagination, to make their motives conscious, and to use and deepen their talents to give birth to a new tomorrow.

As we mentioned in the previous dialogue, the Occupy generation is being initiated into a new kind of spirituality, one that is ready to replace the God of Religion (or a God of any other morally bankrupt institution) with a God of Life. This spirituality is democratic, transformative, and dedicated to the healing of ourselves and our world. It is an active and all-encompassing spirituality that leaves nothing untouched, but rather it completely transfigures people and society.

This spirituality is already emerging. It is present in small circles of friends, Occupy-inspired groups, and certain spiritual communities. It is also emerging in the dialogues of young and old coming together in the spirit of reciprocity. It is present anywhere there is a direct meeting of hearts, which makes a meeting with God not only possible but inevitable.

Here is a collage of themes, some named for us by the youth of the Occupy generation and some named by us as we engage with the new generation with deep respect, appreciation, and hope. We will touch upon these themes throughout the book, sometimes through stories, sometimes through practices, and sometimes through sharing our own personal experiences.

We call it *Occupy Spirituality*. Its promise is no different from what Martin Luther King Jr. called the "beloved community." We deeply believe that this spirituality has the potential to change both individual lives and the world as a whole.

The first characteristic of this new spirituality is that it is deeply ecumenical, interspiritual and post-traditional. In an article in *Los Angeles Times*, Philip Clayton, a dean of faculty at Claremont School of Theology, talked about the fastest-growing religious group in the United States, sometimes called "the nones," "nonaffiliated," or "spiritual but not religious."[1] As he pointed out, 75 percent of Americans between the ages of eighteen and twenty-nine now consider themselves "spiritual but not religious." Young people are not necessarily rejecting God, they just simply feel that "religious organizations are too concerned with money and power, too focused on rules and too involved in politics."[2] It is for this reason that Philip Clayton feels that the rise of "spiritual but not religious" is not a sign of spiritual decline but rather "a new kind of spiritual awakening."[3]

Looking at this from a perspective of young people that I work with, I think that young people are very much interested in spirituality, but they find it outside of organized religion. They tend to adopt spiritual practices from various traditions, have interspiritual mentors, and thus create a post-religious and interspiritual framework for their spiritual lives. Even young people who are still connected to a specific tradition usually have a different relationship with that tradition than their parents did. They may feel rooted in the tradition but not stuck in it. So while many of our religious leaders and media pundits still argue whether Muslims and Christians worship the same God, our young people have already moved beyond that. Not only do they believe that there is one underlying reality at the foundation of all major world religious, but they are also convinced that different traditions and their unique approaches to God complement each other.

MATTHEW FOX: Can I just respond to that? Just to give an example, I have a friend who's Buddhist, from Thailand, and two summers ago he did the pilgrimage to Santiago de Compostela on foot. I think it's about a four-hundred-kilometer walk; he got halfway, and his feet were bleeding so badly he had to quit. But then the following summer he went back and started where he had ended and finished the pilgrimage. And as far as he knew, he was the only Buddhist he met on the entire journey. He's in his young thirties. I think it's very interesting that this Buddhist was happy and willing to make this sacrificial pilgrimage.

And I asked him what he learned, and he said, "Well, I learned that God is in everyone and everything—but, of course, I knew that already." But again, to me, this just underscores what you just said, that this generation is not the least bit hesitant to mix practices and traditions. And that's a pretty new phenomenon.

ADAM BUCKO: I think that is because they are sensing that the God they want to experience is a God of Life and not a God of Religion. It's about deepening their experience of life.

A second point is that this new spirituality is contemplative and experience based. It starts from life rather than concepts. Nonetheless, concepts are celebrated as tools to connect the dots and deepen the experience. So this new spirituality is lived in a constant dialogue between experience and concepts, where one informs the other, thus leading to subtler and subtler understandings. And, of course—you mention it often—Thomas Aquinas said that to teach spirituality, experience is not enough, you also need the concepts. I think this new generation really understands that.

Some of the older spiritualities and more traditional paths started from concepts. An idea of enlightenment or grace, or whatever, was introduced, and then one was given a path that one had to follow for five, ten, fifteen, twenty years to get to that experience. The problem with that approach, as I experienced in my own life, is that it convinced me that God and the experience of God needs to happen outside of my life. This then created a certain kind of detachment from my life and the world around me. In contrast, this new approach goes back to that God of Life. Rather than thinking that God will happen outside of our lives, it's about starting from what we are already experiencing, acknowledging the sacredness of it, and then using practices and other things to deepen that experience and to sustain that experience.

MATTHEW FOX: Here I'm thinking, when it comes to concepts, that the Four Paths of Creation Spirituality could be really helpful.[4] The Four Paths are conceptual, but they're thoroughly grounded in experience, and they return to experience. The backbone of the Creation Spirituality tradition is its naming of the spiritual journey in the Four Paths. The Four Paths address the question, where will God—where will the experience of the divine—be found in our life? Creation Spirituality responds: the divine will be found in these places:

> In the Via Positiva: in the awe, wonder, and mystery of nature and of all beings, each of whom is a "word of God."

In the Via Negativa: in darkness and nothingness, in the silence and emptying, in the letting go and letting be, and in the pain and suffering that constitute an equally real part of our spiritual journey.

In the Via Creativa: in our generativity, we cocreate with God; in our imaginative output, we trust our images enough to birth them and ride them into existence.

In the Via Transformativa: in the relief of suffering, in the combatting of injustice, in the struggle for homeostasis, for balance in society and history, and in the celebration that happens when persons struggling for justice and trying to live in mutuality come together to praise and give thanks for the gift of being and being together.

Since I've been teaching them for forty years, I've had a lot of feedback from so many different kinds of people, and I find that they validate not only individuals' experiences but the lineage. They validate the naming of archetypal religious icons that are still useful to us, whether we're talking in Christian language about the cross or about the resurrection, or about the mystical experience that creation is, or about compassion. But I find that they work across the board, and they help to explain when our spiritual practices are just one experience of the spiritual journey—such as, for example, the process of emptying, the process of silence, and so forth—as valid and important as that is, it's only one part of the journey. So, these Four Paths give us an integrated conceptual framework that can help us create a well-integrated spiritual life.

ADAM BUCKO: I agree, the Four Paths are extremely useful here. They really deal with all of life and all of what we are and are capable of as human beings. If you don't have the whole picture, it's easy to just take one of those paths and practice it, thinking that it's the whole path. And it's not. I think that the beauty of the Four Paths is that they really reconcile different schools of spirituality that perhaps traditionally have not always agreed with each other. They reconcile things like action and contemplation, and contemplation and creativity, creativity and social justice.

MATTHEW FOX: Each of the paths is valuable in itself. But also, any one of the paths done on its own could be seductive. For example, the fourth path, being an activist: I remember one of my students said to me, when I first met her, "I am a cause junkie." One can become a cause junkie—one can make one's whole life social activism and leave no room for the soul, no room for the mystical juice that, first of all, is the very goal of social justice. The goal of social justice is that the whole community can live life fully. It's about celebration of life. If you've left that out of your path because you're so married to being this warrior twenty-four hours a day, seven days a week, then first of all you're going to run out of steam and juice, but also you're not going to taste what it is you're really trying to bring about, which is the flow of justice that allows the flow of life to move on.

So there is a danger that any one of these paths can be an end in itself. That's one of the great values of the Four Paths: to remind us that we move in and out, in and out. That's how they feed one another, and that's literally how one stays young, because one is staying spiritually alive.

ADAM BUCKO: I feel that experience without concepts could be almost dangerous. You can have many experiences, yet not be changed by them, because you don't have a framework that can connect the dots, connect those experiences. I have observed people who have had many experiences, but each time, because they don't have useful concepts, they have to go back and start from scratch.

MATTHEW FOX: That's a very important point. Also, you can become addicted to these experiences. It's experience for experience's sake exclusively, and you're not growing from it, and you're not serving others through these experiences.

Of course, the opposite is also dangerous and, in fact, is probably far more of a disease than the first, and that is to live just in a conceptual world with no experience. And that, I think, is at the essence of defunct religion.

ADAM BUCKO: Because it leads to fundamentalism.

MATTHEW FOX: That's right, and then it leads to ideology. Then all the juice of your faith is put to defending your ideology. Anyone who's not in it is out and lost. So then faith becomes a fortress, it becomes a system that beats up on others, but it's also beating up on those inside it, because their souls are shrinking; they're not growing.

ADAM BUCKO: A third point in this new spirituality is that practice goes beyond traditional contemplative exercises. People still practice meditation and contemplative prayer, but this new spirituality understands that the journey needs to include good psychology and shadow work, as well as integration of the body through things like yoga, sacred sexuality, and deep human relationships. This includes conscious romantic relationships as a path into life and into spirituality. Basically this new spirituality expands the focus of transformation from just one dimension of our being—the soul—to all aspects of our being.

MATTHEW FOX: Yes, and included too, I think, would be the role of creativity as a path, as a spiritual discipline, as a yoga—what I've called and practiced, through thirty-some years of teaching spirituality, "art as meditation." So that focusing through clay, through dance, through painting, through music, and so forth—that too is meditation, and that too incorporates the body. All art is bodily. And that can be missed. Of course, for many people, it also includes athletics, sport—running or climbing or walking or hiking. These should not be denigrated as inferior, so long as you bring your heart and your focus to it. Or even exercising, working out—if it is just about beefing your body up, well, that's one thing. But if it's also about centering and about focusing, there's definitely a spiritual practice to it.

I know people who run on a treadmill while listening to discourses on spirituality and mysticism and so forth. So again, I think the world has opened up so much, and part of it is the availability of electronic teaching devices—and music, of course—that there are so many more ways to practice spirituality. Massage too. And they're all saying what you're saying, that including the body is including the soul. It's not leaving it at the door. And in a way, I think, we may be just beginning as a species to integrate in this regard.

ADAM BUCKO: I think it's a completely new development as a species.

MATTHEW FOX: And yet, of course, if you look back to olden times, the work, for example, that the monks did, and the struggle to survive that our species has gone through at so many times in so many cultures, that very much included the body. The monastic vision was that work is prayer, too—working in the fields or carving the stones for the buildings in which you're living, and so forth—that all of work can be prayer, as part of carrying your meditative consciousness with you. You can take that consciousness wherever you go.

As a Dominican, I was taught that study is also prayer, so study can be a spiritual practice—and needs to be. When we secularize study, which we've done in our culture, you get bad results. You get very unhappy professors, you really do. You get people set up for addiction, and you have a joyless educational project. The joy is missing, because facts in themselves, knowledge in itself, does not satisfy the soul. There's something deeper that we yearn for and ache for, and that needs to be integrated in all of our life efforts.

ADAM BUCKO: Speaking about exercising and listening to discourses, there is a very good biography of Henri Nouwen called *Wounded Prophet,* and in it there's a description of him exercising and listening to a tape of *Creation Spirituality*.

MATTHEW FOX: Really? Wow, that's funny! So Henri Nouwen listened to my book while exercising. Well, I'm edified! My respect for Henri Nouwen has taken a leap forward—one, that he exercised, and two, that he had me along!

ADAM BUCKO: Point number four is related to what you were saying—that this new spirituality says that spirituality that does not include action is no spirituality at all. But it's not just about any action—it's about action that comes from one's deepest calling. This spirituality does not accept the reality of living a divided life, such as complete withdrawal or a separate career divided from one's soul and its deepest aspirations. Those dualities of the past no longer apply here. For young people today, the sense of vocation and the sense of a calling become the very doorways into spirit. So this new spirituality also realizes that the new world can be created only if people incarnate their unique gifts and callings in the world and employ them in the service of compassion and justice.

MATTHEW FOX: As I reflect on the topic of vocation, I remember the distinction I make in my book *The Reinvention of Work*, in which I point out the difference between a *job* and *work*. A job is something we do to pay our bills. Work is the reason we are here on Earth. It is a call; it is our purpose; it is how we give back. Today I find lots of young people who are willing to sacrifice an overcommitment to job in order to devote themselves more to their work. This entails living a simpler lifestyle, of course, and often living in community. Vocation raises to importance in such a value system.

ADAM BUCKO: This point is especially important for me, because I feel that this is definitely my path, which is service—sacred activism and karma yoga. This idea of a calling or vocation is, in my opinion, uniquely inspired by Western traditions. If you look at the Eastern traditions, there is less focus on an individual calling. The *Bhagavad Gita*, for example, talks about the importance of service, but it's more about fulfilling your role or duty. It says that as long as you're not attached to the results of your actions, your service will lead you to union with God. In Western traditions, there is more of a concept of individuation. You're literally called by name to a specific kind of task. In this way, sensing your calling becomes a very deep connecting point with life and God, because you really discover your unique expression in life and the unique contribution that you can make.

I sense that in people today. They sense some kind of gift emerging in them, and they want to say yes to it, because it's so personal and so connected to the soul and because it's a doorway into spirit. That's why the divisions of the past, the dualities of the past, no longer make sense. Making a sacrifice and saying no to this gift is like saying no to life.

MATTHEW FOX: Very well said. And the kind of action we're talking about is action that comes from nonaction, comes from being—it comes from where the deep call is. Again, to introduce some concepts here, which is always useful, because concepts can help you to go deeper, and they provide a certain objectivity, the ability to step back and analyze our deep experiences. One of the concepts that I have always found useful is the dialectic between mysticism and prophecy. Or, if you will, contemplation and action, or that which constitutes a spiritual warrior—that a warrior, as distinct from a soldier, has an interior life and undergoes practices that feed one's deepest level of being, not just the compulsion to act.

I also observe in younger people that they're not content to just live at the level of action and recovering from action, but rather, as you said, action as an expression of their being and of their calling. And in a way, this is also talking about everyone living their lives artfully, because that's what art is. As the psychologist Otto Rank said, for the artist, his or her work is their life. Their work and life come together in vocation, because there's a calling and because there's a love affair going on. So when we can learn to love our work, because it is our calling and because it is in service for others, then there's a loop—there's a return. You don't burn out nearly as quickly, and you don't need that much to live on. You can live a simpler life, because, for one thing, you don't have to be dashing away to expensive resorts to heal.

ADAM BUCKO: And you don't have to act out to get a break from things, because you're being fed by your work.

MATTHEW FOX: Exactly. You're being fed by your work. And that's a wonderful loop to be in. And, again, a sign of that is joy. The joy is embedded in the loop, because you're receiving joy as well as putting it out.

ADAM BUCKO: This takes us to point number five, which is that this new spirituality includes joy, sensuality, celebration, and heartful aliveness.

MATTHEW FOX: Fun!

ADAM BUCKO: Fun, absolutely. This new spirituality celebrates life through meaningful connections, works of art, music, and all things that essentially help to grow the soul.

MATTHEW FOX: Exactly. And again, to invoke a concept, you are speaking of the Via Positiva—that there is a joy of life, a celebration of life that permeates and that really holds all the crises and all the breakdowns and all the chaos and all the vicissitudes that life also offers. But that fun is itself a value is something that many, many spiritualities have not taught over the centuries. We've skipped over the Via Positiva; we've kind of let it go, turned it over to secular powers, such as advertisers, to give us their pseudo definitions of pleasure and what supposedly provides profound joy. I think we have to take that back. It's kind of like the word *eros*. We gave that away to the pornography industry, whereas, in fact, an erotic life is a juicy life, an alive life, and we all have a right to it. And as Audre Lorde, the New York poet, said, "I'm erotic when I write a poem, when I make a table, when I bake bread, or when I make love"—eros is the passion for living that we bring to everything we do.

Again, I think a big part of honoring the celebrative dimension to life and spirituality is this feminist thinking. I think it's one reason that we've underplayed the Via Positiva. Marija Gimbutas, the feminist archeologist, says that for the goddess civilization, the essence of it all was a celebration of life. I think when patriarchy established its norms and its definitions of religion and so forth, it very much short-changed the celebration of life. I think that a new spirituality that's truly profound and grounded will again bring back the divine feminine to balance the sacred masculine. But part of that gift in the divine feminine is that the celebration of life is primary. And as I said earlier, even the struggle for justice as service is precisely so that people can celebrate life. It's not to be right; it's not to win in court. The point is to create a culture, a civilization, a community in which all can enjoy, for as many years as they're on this Earth, the gifts that life has to give.

ADAM BUCKO: The sixth point is that this new spirituality is more democratic. As a result, the role of the teacher changes from a traditional tell-you-what-to-do teacher to a spiritual friend. The role of the teacher is to point students back to their own experience and to name their experience for them so that they can start paying attention to the movement of the spirit within. Discernment becomes a big part of this new democratic and dialogical way of being. Elders are not so much recognized for their titles, résumés, or fame, but rather their ability to relate to the younger generation from their lived experience.

Our friend Jamie Manson, who writes for the *National Catholic Reporter* and in whose prophetic column, "Grace on the Margins," I always find deep nourishment and encouragement, related to me a profound story of this change in the youth. In teaching theology, she often assigns her students the task of designing their own religion. In the many times she has done so, no one has designed a priesthood or a hierarchical leadership structure. The students' religions are always built around small communities working with a collaborative methodology. The bulk of what the communities do centers around meditation, which I find very, very interesting. Everyone, even students who have never meditated before, seem to know that something in their spirit longs for it. It is so telling that if left to themselves, the youth would design religious frameworks that are completely at odds with traditional religious structures.

This new spirituality is much more about taking off the masks of pretense and cultivating genuine heart connections that inspire growth in both elders and youth, rather than in keeping with tradition or respecting authority. It is all about true aliveness and entering into life in a more full and deep way.

MATTHEW FOX: Yes, and I think it's taking seriously the advancement of the Enlightenment consciousness that fought so hard for democracy—so the American Revolution and its great thinkers, the French Revolution, and so forth. The whole idea that we're not eternally bound to hierarchy, to monarchy in any of its forms, to dictatorships—even benign ones—that we're not just in vertical relationships. We're in horizontal relationships also, and we are individuals. That is, I think, one of the major accomplishments of the modern-era enlightenment consciousness: the dignity of the individual. That spirit works through democratic and horizontal directions and through circles, not just down from ladders.

So a spiritual democracy incorporates the wisdom of the Thomas Jeffersons of the world, if you will, that this is not just about a secular, political shift of power. It is a spiritual insight, and it's not unrelated to the teachings of Jesus and the Cosmic Christ and Buddha and the Buddha Nature, and so forth. The Iroquois were already practicing democracy centuries before the Europeans landed here.

The notion is that the spiritual works through democracy, through a shared distribution of power, through debate and disagreement and compromise, and through every citizen having an insight about what life is about. So again, it's about moving from the vertical idea to horizontal.

Now this does not mean that you're without leadership. But it means that, first of all, leadership can evolve, and no one is meant to be a king for life, and we have to elicit leadership from one another. And it's not an ego trip; therefore, it's not a power trip. Leadership is, again, a mode of service, as Jesus tried to teach. So it's not as if we're without a leader, but that ultimately the leader is responsible to the group itself, and the group is responsible for itself. You're not surrendering power to some kind of individual.

ADAM BUCKO: There's an element of trust at play, too. Trust in human nature and human insight, and trust that we can relate to each other in such a way that allows wisdom to come through everyone participating in it. It doesn't mean that people don't have different gifts or different callings. It just means that there's a fundamental respect for what our gifts are and a trust that those gifts are there.

Well, you know, Matt, we're calling it a "new spirituality" incarnating itself in the younger generation, but it's very obvious to me that you have been talking about all of these points for the past forty years. Essentially, all of these points can be traced back to what you envisioned to be Creation Spirituality.

MATTHEW FOX: Well, I would not deny that. And I carry a few battle scars from promoting these sometimes unpopular (and sometimes labeled *heretical*) ideas over the years, but I have always sensed a deep affirmation of these principles in many students and listeners. Now, I think, with this new generation that we are talking about, the time has come for these ideas to become more mainstream.

I think that point number seven is that this spirituality is meant to be lived in communities. And, I think that you and I would agree that hints and echoes of what we're talking about have already emerged in Base Communities in Latin America—which, interestingly, were so badly treated by the Vatican, by hierarchical powers, almost to the point of wiping them out. And yet their resilience is such that today they are simply divorcing themselves from organized religion, from the church as such, from the institutional church, and continuing their practice of democratic spirituality and democratic leadership—in other words, the church of the people.

ADAM BUCKO: And serving not the church, but humanity, which is also life.

MATTHEW FOX: Exactly—serving life and humanity, and letting the church go in its own direction as it travels down the path of death.

So there have been movements that had this kind of spirituality. Certainly the civil rights movement is a North American example, led as it was by prophets like Howard Thurman and Dr. King—we can see that the spirituality we're talking about is not just beginning at this moment. It's been stirring, and it's already drawn many heroes and saints, even martyrs—martyrs in South America and North America, who include Óscar Romero, Dr. King, Malcolm X, Dorothy Stang, and others.

But I think now a whole generation is primed for this, and it's a global thing. It's not just about the Americas, but there's a stirring and an aching among young Buddhists in Southeast Asia and among Muslims in the Middle East and in many people around the world. Hopefully, anyway.

ADAM BUCKO: That is why later on we will be talking about the Occupy generation and a vision for a community-based approach or a New Monastic approach, so to speak, one that could take these points and put them into practice in small communities. This is very much what the Base communities were doing, what the civil rights communities were doing, what Catholic Workers have been doing, and what some of the Sufi orders have been doing. Because we're talking about the whole generation, this could really be a new way of relating to life and relating to each other. In the process, it can be a way of changing ourselves, our communities, and the world.

3
Adam's Story

ADAM BUCKO: I recently was reading something by the German Benedictine Anselm Grün, who used a very beautiful metaphor that went like this: Before you are born, God pronounces a word or a sentence over you. Then, once you get here, your goal is to live your life in such a way that other people—the people around you—can hear it. I thought it was very beautiful, because it's saying that if you're in your purpose, people can hear it and smell it, you know?

MATTHEW FOX: It's very close to the Aboriginal teaching in Australia. Of course, the Aboriginals may be the oldest tribe in the world at this time, certainly one of the oldest. They say that God sings every being into existence, and your job is to find your song and then find how it matches up with other people's songs, so that you make music together. So it's very analogous, isn't it?

ADAM BUCKO: That's beautiful, because that's like ... not only service, but community ... and gift giving, and also receiving the gift of the other.

MATTHEW FOX: Absolutely. Think of an orchestra. Each instrument has its own notes to play and its own tone and feeling. It's an acknowledgement of the beauty of diversity. We're not just here to hear one song, but many songs.

ADAM BUCKO: And to sing our song!

MATTHEW FOX: So how did you find your song?

ADAM BUCKO: I was born in 1975 and grew up in Poland during the seventies and eighties, in a time of a Communist totalitarian regime. When I was six years old, I believe, Poland went into what is called a "state of emergency" or a "state of war," which meant that, all of a sudden, we woke up in the morning, and there was an announcement made on the radio that, basically, we're entering a state of war and that we should all stay home. After that there was no radio, no TV to get news from; we went outside, there were tanks on the street, soldiers. It was crazy. Everyone was panicking, asking, "Who knows what is going to happen?" "Is the Russian army going to invade us?"

When I look at my childhood, I had a very happy childhood. I had a wonderful, loving family, but at the same time, when I look at the society in which I grew up, it was very violent. Lots of oppression. Lots of instability. Then, later on in my life, Chernobyl happened.[1] We only found out a few days after it happened, because our government didn't tell us. We found out through Radio Free Europe that this huge catastrophe was happening. Our bodies were exposed to radiation, and then we had to deal with the consequences of that. So there was all this insecurity and systemic violence that was crushing people's spirits.

MATTHEW FOX: Elaborate on your insecurity.

ADAM BUCKO: The insecurity that I felt when I was growing up led me to this big question, which was: Who (or what) can I rely on? What that did for me is that as a child, I realized that I had to look for something deeper than what I saw around me. So I decided to go inward. I remember, as a child, when other children were playing outside, I decided to build an altar at home and to say mass. At that time, my idea of a spiritual person or a person who is in communion with God was this archetype of a priest. I remember building an altar and just standing there for hours experiencing this presence, which now I call God. That presence filled my heart with security—with some kind of reassurance that while there was all this craziness and suffering around me, nevertheless, life is worth living.

MATTHEW FOX: What happened as you grew up?

ADAM BUCKO: And so as I got older, I became fascinated with people who were fighting against the totalitarian system and trying to change the world. Looking at it from a perspective of time, I realize that there were some priest-activists in Poland who left a very deep imprint on my soul. The two priests whose stories were especially important to me were Fr. Jerzy Popieluszko and Fr. Stanislaw Suchowolec. Both of them were chaplains for the Solidarity Movement. Both came from the same region of Poland as me and one was my parish priest. They were both really transformative figures. John Dear called Fr. Jerzy "a towering prophet . . . mighty nonviolent resister" and "the Martin Luther King of Poland."

It just so happened that both of them were brutally tortured and killed by "the system." In case of Fr. Jerzy, a lot of it later was shown on TV to scare everyone. Having those two examples of activist-priests was very instructive, because I realized early on that to be faithful to that presence that I was experiencing during my home ritual of mass and to truly say yes to God requires me to say no to injustice and anything that violates God's love and justice.

Seeing those two guys brutalized and killed also showed me what happens to people who decide to make a choice like that. There's a cost! And that was very frightening to my young psyche.

Eventually all of this led me to both spirituality and activism, a journey that I continue to this day.

MATTHEW FOX: It sounds like you had great role models to help you develop your courage.

ADAM BUCKO: I did have great role models. My first role models were my parents. They guided me with love. Since I was a child, they always encouraged me to trust my inner unfolding and truth. That was such an invaluable lesson and support.

Then the movement became my teacher. As a child I was observing people who, within a couple of decades, were able to transform Poland's political system. That was proof for me that social change is not just theoretical aspiration; it can actually happen. Participating in that change with my friends and family was an empowering experience. That gave me so much courage.

Finally, my more "formal" activism began at the age of fourteen, when I became part of the anarchist youth movement. The logic of the movement at that time was to embrace the principles of spirituality, compassion, democracy, eco-justice, and mutual empowerment. The principles of that movement planted many seeds in my life. By the time I came to the United States, it was very clear to me that my life's work would be helping to create positive change in my community and the world.

MATTHEW FOX: When did you come to the United States and begin your work with homeless youth?

ADAM BUCKO: When I came to the United States, it was a big opportunity for my family. I was seventeen and didn't know any English, and I did not want to come here. At first it was a very difficult experience for me. I felt really alienated, disconnected. It took me some time to learn English and to be able to communicate with people. Also, we were "illegal immigrants" for the first five years, so work was difficult to find. The two choices that I had as a teenager for making a little bit on the side—while I was also in school—was to either play music on the subway (which I did) or work construction (which I also did).

MATTHEW FOX: What about playing music on the subway?

ADAM BUCKO: When I came to the States, I sang poetry in Polish on the New York City subway for maybe two or three years. That was my first job really. I started on my second day in the United States. I brought a guitar and went to the subway. In many ways, that was my way of coping with being in a new place; it was my way of grieving; and it was my way of connecting with people without being able to speak to them.

MATTHEW FOX: That's wonderful. I never heard that story before. How much money did you make?

ADAM BUCKO: You could make fifteen, eighteen bucks an hour. So it wasn't that bad. I could only do it for three to four hours a day, because the voice wouldn't take it for longer. But I also ran into trouble with the New York City police department, because it wasn't necessarily legal to do that without having a specific license. I couldn't speak English, so every time they came up to me, I just packed my stuff and left the station.

MATTHEW FOX: Did you have a microphone or just do it—

ADAM BUCKO: No, I liked to play in small stations, because for me it wasn't so much about reaching a lot of people. It was more of a therapeutic and spiritual practice for me, so I liked intimate stations, where I would get people in between trains, stations with good acoustics. Usually I could sing three to four songs in between trains. People really connected with it, and it felt like a kind of unitive experience for me. It was my way of connecting to my new life. And of course, that's where I was exposed to some of the homeless people, and I even played with one homeless person. He was a master flute musician, who made his own flutes, lived in the New York City subway. We became friends, and he would join me.

MATTHEW FOX: That's beautiful.

ADAM BUCKO: After two years in the United States, I experienced a huge depression. When I think of it now, I realize I was experiencing both symptoms of depression and also a post-traumatic stress disorder. And I remember lying in my bed for a week freaking out. My body, everything felt sick; I was completely falling apart. My whole body felt sick. I felt like I was dying. Then this fear would just take over, and I would want to die, and I would get to a point where I would say, "Take me," because it was too painful to stay in my body. And yet—nothing would happen. I just had to deal with the pain. I kept on surrendering to it, but it wouldn't go away. It was a very intense experience.

At that time, my mother found a counselor from an ad in a Polish newspaper in New York—and I went to see that counselor. It turned out that that particular person was also a spiritual practitioner, and her room looked like a Hindu temple. Like an ashram.

She started counseling me, using holistic healing techniques and teaching me meditation. In one week, things got so much better. I went to see her a few times a week, and one day I said, "Wow. This is good." After working with her for a couple of months, I was saying, "This is great." I started meditating, and I started having dreams of an Indian saint whose picture my counselor had on her walls. I was like, "What the hell is going on? I mean this is very interesting, but what am I supposed to do with it?" She said, "Well, here is a name of a bookstore, why don't you go there, pick up some books, and then you'll see." I remember walking into a bookstore, seeing a book, opening it, and there was a picture of an Indian monk, or *sadhu,* with long dreadlocks, and I said, "This is good, this is my guy." I already had dreadlocks, so I thought I was on my way to becoming like him.

I started reading the book, and started really getting into meditation, and again, I went back to the counselor and asked, "How can I live my life? You know, my perspective has changed completely." She said, "Well, there are lots of monasteries here, why don't you just call one of them, and get on the bus and go there?"

So I found one ashram in Virginia, got on the bus, and that changed my life. I really embraced a contemplative life. At first I stayed there for a month, then went back to New York, started studying theology, and went back to the ashram the following summer for a few more months. My goal was to be a contemplative. At first I wanted to spend as much time in the monastery as possible. But, eventually, years later, I realized that my calling is really to be a contemplative in the world, someone who can be engaged with life from a deep place of a contemplative heart. Today I call that being a "New Monastic."

MATTHEW FOX: What about your India experience?

ADAM BUCKO: Some years later, before I discovered my true calling of being a contemplative in the world, I went to India to spend time at a Himalayan hermitage. It was a Hindu-Christian hermitage in the tradition of Father Bede Griffiths and Swami Abhishiktananda. My heart's longing was to spend time living as a monk in India and drink from India's spiritual depth.

Shortly after arriving in India, I met a homeless child who came up to me, took my hand, and walked with me for five, ten minutes—it seemed like forever. She was just skin and bones—very damaged body. Cigarette burns on her face. Crazy stuff. She was just asking for food. "Take me to a restaurant." Before going to India, I heard so many stories. People said "never give any money to beggars because they will never leave you alone," and "it's all bullshit—don't do it."

But this—there was something different about that particular situation. All of a sudden, it wasn't just some beggar—it was a child. And that child was holding my hand. And there's something about touch. I just couldn't let go of that.

The next day I called an old friend of mine who was a very interesting character, he used to be a drug dealer in the seventies and had been addicted to heroin for about seventeen years.[2] He had lived in Amsterdam and was a kind of wild person. He himself, when he talks about his life, says, "I've never met anyone who had a more extreme life than me." So—crazy stuff.

But at some point, when he was trying to get clean, after seventeen years of addiction, he had an experience of Jesus. Jesus appeared to him, and that changed his life. And as a result, he went to India, where he was trying to figure out what to do with his life. One day he saw a dying heroin addict on the street, and he brought him into the room that he was renting. Eventually, his enterprise grew into a village of broken people, about two hundred people living together. It was an ashram, a very holy place of Grace.

In many ways it was an ashram that combined what Father Bede Griffiths was doing and what Mother Teresa was doing. It was about prayer, about contemplation, and at the same time, probably 97 percent of all the people living in that ashram were people rescued from the streets. About 70 percent of them had tuberculosis, very often multidrug-resistant tuberculosis. About half of those people were also HIV positive. A lot of them were kids, street kids.

MATTHEW FOX: What followed for you?

ADAM BUCKO: After meeting the homeless child, I called the founder of the ashram, who came to pick me up. As he was driving me to his place, all of a sudden, he stopped the car. He said, "Come with me, I need to take care of something." We went under a bridge, and there was a guy lying there in the gutter, just skin and bones, surrounded by people shooting heroin. I mean, it's like, one big syringe circling around. It was crazy stuff. Some people were fighting, and I didn't know how to deal with that. He just picked up the guy, brought him into his car. The guy started bleeding—his feet started bleeding; it had the smell of rotting flesh. Finally, we got into this small temple that had been converted into an emergency rescue center. They took him in, took off his bandage, and part of his foot just fell off. Someone said, "Even the maggots are already dead."

I was just so broken by that. It was the craziest experience that I'd ever had. Then we went to my friend's community, the ashram. It was beautiful—all these happy kids jumping around—but at the same time, I'm like, "Why are they jumping?" Most of them had only one leg. You know, they were on the street—bone tuberculosis happened or gangrene—and it was too late to save their bodies intact, so parts of their bodies were missing.

During the first night of my stay there, my friend asked me this question: "Where do you want to sleep?" He said, "you can sleep on the roof or with that guy in that room." That guy was basically dying; he had AIDS, tuberculosis, and cancer. Skin and bones, vomiting blood. It was a pretty small room, and so I answered, "The roof." In my mind, I said, "Shit, this India business is not working out—screw this. I want to go home, I want to go home." Really, but I was too embarrassed, because it felt like such a failure to just go back.

I went to the roof, but then it started raining—it rained for three days, so I had to stay in that room with the guy. And the first night, I was freaking out, I couldn't sleep at all. The guy was trying to get to the bathroom at night, and he was vomiting, and I was like, "I'm not touching you." It was fear, fear, fear. I was terrified, I was broken. And I just wanted to run.

Then something happened, and I remembered words of a theology professor who once said, "It's easy to just run. Stay with it, and something will open up, if you stay with it long enough." I felt that by staying with it, something did open up. I felt like the part in me that wanted to objectify other people's suffering and detach from it some-how collapsed a little bit. All of a sudden, the suffering that I was seeing in that person was also my suffering. The only thing to do after that was to decide to move into that community and to work there with those people. That was really the beginning of my vocation.

MATTHEW FOX: Your story is very powerful. You learned compassion the hard way, by being broken open. You went to India to do what the book said to you, to become a spiritual aesthete, a monk, so to speak. And yet you ended up working on the streets.

ADAM BUCKO: Yes, I went there to follow my Himalayan dreams, to find God in the silence of meditation . . . and yet it seems to me that I found God and my calling in the noise of the streets—in the broken bodies and souls of homeless children. India brought me back to Earth. And when that happened, I realized that in order to have a fully embodied life with service, my spirituality, my practice, and everything in my life needed to change. The ideals that I previously embraced belonged to another era. They belonged to an era of detachment. I felt that I was being called to a different kind of spirituality, a spirituality of integration.

Prior to that, in my training I was taught detachment. And what I understood by that was disengagement. So I was disengaging from parts of myself, from my body, from my sexuality, from my feelings, from . . . you name it. And the promise of that was that if you do that, you're going to arrive at this peace that the saints are searching for. And you know, I did feel pretty peaceful, but also very numb.

MATTHEW FOX: Very numb?

ADAM BUCKO: Numb, because I felt like I kept detaching, detaching, detaching. And then I was almost cornered, and parts of me died. Yes, there was peace, but it was almost like being in some kind of a spiritual coma. I couldn't relate to people. I was like in an in-between state. I remember hearing a Carmelite hermit quoting St. Teresa of Ávila, who said the first step on a mystical journey is to fall in love with life. And I thought, shit, I must be doing something wrong, because I'm definitely not in love with life. In fact, I don't feel alive at all.

MATTHEW FOX: So it had sucked your passion out.

ADAM BUCKO: Yes.

MATTHEW FOX: I take it that you got those lessons of detachment both from your Catholic background and from some of the Eastern practices, too, is that right? They were both kind of giving you the same message in that regard?

ADAM BUCKO: I think it was a combination. I think that a lot of the teachings came more from the Eastern background. But some of them came from my experience in Poland. As a child, I was fairly ill, weak, and also—as I mentioned before—I was exposed to all the violence and political turmoil that was happening around me. All of that created in me some sort of mistrust of life. In addition to that, I grew up around big statues of Stalin, Lenin. So in a sense, those statues gave me the feeling that the particulars in life didn't matter. Big ideas did. Because all of those guys, you know, they were not real people.

MATTHEW FOX: They were idols.

ADAM BUCKO: They were these huge idols. It almost didn't matter what they did in life. They represented ideas. And that's what we were supposed to turn our lives into—into those ideals. So, I feel that when I discovered Eastern spirituality, in a sense it was a perfect theology for me, because it justified mistrust in life.

MATTHEW FOX: That's interesting. So, going back to your journey. You didn't stay in India?

ADAM BUCKO: I couldn't stay in India for very long. My body couldn't handle it. I was sick all the time. After few months I had to come back. I was broken. I crashed, and I was very disappointed in myself. Up to that point, my life story was supposed to be one of following in the footsteps of contemplatives I admired. Looking at it now, with the perspective that time gives, I think I always had an inner sense that India was more of a training ground for me rather than a permanent destination. Yet it was difficult to accept. At that time, I didn't see many models for this New Monastic way. I later discovered it through great souls like Brother Wayne Teasdale and Raimundo Panikkar, who named it for me as a way of living a contemplative life in the world while, at the same time, fully engaging with life. They laid open the possibility of being in a loving relationship and dedicating my life to both prayer and service.

I came back to the States feeling like a failure. It took me a while to realize that this was really part of the unfolding of my spiritual life. My own vision for my spiritual life fell apart so that God and Grace could enter. I crashed so that God could take over. So in reality, leaving India and the ashram and monastic-like setting deepened my vocation and gave me a new spirituality. I moved from a spirituality of detachment to a spirituality of integration. Later, it also led to me to cofound the Reciprocity Foundation, an organization that works with homeless youth in New York City.

MATTHEW FOX: After India, you went to Florida and worked with street youth there. Tell me what you learned from that experience?

ADAM BUCKO: First of all, I realized that we have people in this country who live in conditions very similar to those in India—it just doesn't happen on a main street of our cities. So, when I got back to the States, I started working with street kids in Florida. I was working for one of the largest organizations in the country that deals with youth homelessness. Most of the kids I was working with were involved in sex work and a lot of other horrible things. My job was to become part of their street fabric, to be there, so that when they were ready to leave that environment, I could literally take them out of that space.

One night I was outside this very sketchy hotel where all these kids doing sex work would stay. This one girl came up to me and said, "Help me." She was prostituting at night, two of her small kids were sleeping at the hotel, and during the day she was looking for a job. She said, "Help me, help me get out, I need a job . . . I need something." But I couldn't help her, because if I took her to the shelter, her kids would be taken away from her. On top of that, she would be asked to get a minimum-wage job that wouldn't be sustainable. At that point I realized that the system I was representing, the system that I was part of, was not set up to be able to address her problems. And there were many other things that I witnessed on the streets that convinced me that the traditional approach to youth homelessness was not working. So I just begun to have this intuition that a new approach and a new way was needed.

MATTHEW FOX: Now tell me about the origins and the start-up of the Reciprocity Foundation in New York City. How did that come about, and what do you see as your most valuable accomplishments?

ADAM BUCKO: The vision for Reciprocity Foundation arose out of a shared longing that my cofounder, Taz Tagore, and I had. Just like I had my experiences that initiated me into this work with homeless youth, so did Taz. Her journey begun as a teenager where "by accident" she wandered into a homeless youth shelter in downtown Toronto. Reflecting on that experience, she recently wrote:

> I was sixteen the first time I walked into a homeless shelter, and I was sure it was an accident. I was looking for a student

art show, not broken youth. But a voice within told me to stick around. There was something here for me. I spent the afternoon talking with the youth, and found that we had much in common. I was the adolescent child of parents who fled their home country overnight and found shelter in Canada. I too felt lost, disconnected and unsure of how to express myself in the world.

When my suffering met the youth's suffering, I experienced pure grace. Instead of my heart closing—as it often had in the face of poverty—my heart opened. I spent the next decade raising awareness and funds for homeless youth. The work was helping others, but it was also changing me. I was learning to lead others and to express myself. I was also developing insight into my real purpose in the world.[3]

Our desires to live a life of meaning and purpose brought us together and helped us form a deep friendship. Eventually it lead to the founding of the Reciprocity Foundation.

But our life experiences were very different. Taz had learned to approach social injustice by developing a vision, a team, and by leveraging the resources of public and private organizations to help those in need. I had come at it from a person-to-person approach—working on the streets to find forgotten, homeless youth and working directly with homeless children in India. Taz and I spent many formative years building a bridge between our two frameworks. I had to learn how to be part of an organization with a clear vision, goals, and partners, and Taz had to learn when to let go of the managerial tasks and goals and to trust the process of loving and supporting each youth that walked through our doors. We both had to learn to trust that our combined care and energy would offer homeless youth more than either of us working alone or in isolation from our many partners and community. This way of working also reinforced our belief that our service was a central part of our spiritual journey and practice. The more we worked from a place of deep intuition and heart, the more every working day felt like a day of spiritual practice.

What held us and our organization together during the early years was the belief that homeless youth deserved to live a rich, fulfilling, and engaged life. So many youth development and antipoverty agencies focus on employment or short-term housing—believing that if youth found work or stable housing that the rest of their issues would fade into the background. But Taz and I held firm in the belief that deeper healing occurs when you help an individual move beyond work to discover their true calling—a vocation that enables them to express their gifts and be connected to others in a positive and healthy way. When we are deeply committed to and engaged in meaningful work—irrespective of how we define meaning as individuals—we feel alive in a profound way. We can touch our purpose. We trust life again. And we trust that we are alive for a clear and powerful reason. For a homeless youth to feel that way after a life of abuse and abandonment is what Taz and I strive for every day at Reciprocity. It is a joy to bear witness to youth shifting from a defensive posture toward life to opening completely to the world around them. This process also helped Taz and me trust another of our original impulses—the belief that homeless youth are capable of becoming leaders and visionaries in our society. We believe that any human being who undergoes a profound personal transformation as a result of illness, poverty, or brokenness can cultivate the vision and compassion necessary for leadership.

As the organization has matured over the years, we have honed our process for serving homeless youth. What we've learned is that to fully awaken a person who has been deeply traumatized, you need to work at the level of the body, of the mind, and of the spirit. You have to tightly integrate all three in order to have a deep and sustainable impact on another human being. We call this the "Whole Person approach" to personal transformation. The Whole Person approach involves looking deeply into a young person's mind, heart, and spirit and offering them tools to awaken each aspect of himself or herself.

The other critical factor is showing youth how to tap into mind, body, and spirit all the time—that these parts of themselves can be awakened at work, in relationships, on vacation—it can be present in everything they touch in life.

The Reciprocity Foundation is now in its seventh year—we have built a stand-alone holistic center in New York City to house our work, and we are proud of have worked with over nearly a thousand youth since 2004. What is most astounding is not the size or scope of our work but the radical transformations that the youth have undergone with the support of the Reciprocity community. Not only are they realizing their career goals of becoming designers and activists and educators, but they are truly stepping into leadership roles in our world. Seven of our youth were nominated for an Emmy award for a film they created about youth homelessness—others are advocating or making media that is changing legislation and the way Americans think. Many of them also return to Reciprocity as mentors or are inspired to start their own projects for social change.

MATTHEW FOX: What kind of gift did Reciprocity give you?

ADAM BUCKO: I have received so many gifts from Reciprocity, too many to name. Perhaps the biggest is that Reciprocity took me into my vocation; it did for me what it does for our kids. It took me into that sacred space where I felt the impulse of God in my life. When I said "yes" to that impulse, a "method" of spiritual direction emerged that I now use with young people. The method helps me to be present in young people's lives in a very specific and encouraging way, so that they too can touch the essence of their calling and live from there.

A couple of years ago, I was on a silent retreat, and just before bed, I went to the chapel. I had a deep, prayerful experience there. I engaged God in a conversation, and I began to feel the presence of Jesus in a very special way. I felt like a child, exposing and opening every corner of my life to God. It felt like I was relating to God in a new way, in a way that I never experienced before. I felt completely known and affirmed.

That night, I woke from my sleep with a sentence vibrating in my heart. It said, "Reciprocity was for you to learn the method of working with people, now you can use that with everyone."

Since then my work has begun to expand. I will always work with homeless kids; they are my children, and I never want to leave them behind. However, I have also now begun working with young people from all walks of life, offering them spiritual direction and helping them to build contemplative lives that revolve around their unique callings.

MATTHEW FOX: When you spoke of leaving India and the monastic setting, you mentioned that that gave you a "new spirituality." Can you say more about that?

ADAM BUCKO: At some point I started doing psychotherapy with a contemplative therapist who was also a Zen priest. That led me to a real break of my usual identity. I remember it happening during one of the first sessions. He was asking me questions and kind of deconstructing my identity. All of a sudden something cracked—I literally heard a sound of it cracking. After that I just laughed, maybe for three hours. I felt so free and alive.

I think what happened was that I was so attached to this spiritual identity that I had. I needed many practices to fix that identity. All of my spirituality was based on my need to fix my identity so it could be "pure" and so it could reflect "holiness." Every other identity was bad, so I was constantly fighting with my shadow, because if the shadow is real, then this is not real. It was like a war, in a sense, with my body, my sexuality—you name it. After that initial break of my identity, I realized, "Wow! There are many identities, and I can go to the pre-identity stage, where it's just aliveness."

I think that is when the deepest dimension of my true calling or vocation really dawned on me; I discovered that my calling is more about being in touch with that aliveness and invoking that aliveness in others.

MATTHEW FOX: This is a powerful experience you are sharing with us— your being "cracked open"—and it is so interesting that it happened in a therapy session with one who was both a therapist and a spiritual practitioner. I can see why you honor the gift that therapy gives: a true "breakthrough" that liberates your self-doubts and preoccupations about your worthiness.

That phrase you used about pre-identity reminds me of Eckhart's phrase. He talks about "returning to our unborn self and becoming as free as you were before you were born and as free of knowledge as you were before you were born." He calls that a "breakthrough," and that's in his great sermon on the Sermon on the Mount, which is a commentary on Jesus's speaking of being poor of spirit. That's how Eckhart interprets poor of spirit, that it's the ability to return to your unborn self and, as you say, your self without masks, and your true self. Your self that comes from inside you, not from someone else's version of what holiness is or what religion is or who you are.

To me, coming from a Christian tradition, the radicalness of Jesus is that the spirit works through us all, and all of us can sense her calling. But it does require that we get into our real self, our true self, our unborn self, or our pre-identity self, to use your phrase. It entails moving beyond the "false self" or the illusory self that society (and religion) can often instill in us. And that often takes being "cracked open" or being broken through and through. It is special that this opening for you ended with laughter and joy.

ADAM BUCKO: This experience really transformed my whole spirituality.

MATTHEW FOX: Did Creation Spirituality also offer you some language for your new spirituality?

ADAM BUCKO: Absolutely! I first discovered your work when I was a student of theology. I was looking for my theological guides and found that your work on Cosmic Christ could help me reconcile my experiences from a Hindu ashram with the Christian contemplative tradition. Once my experience of breakthrough happened, I truly dived into your theology, which helped move me from a life-denying framework of traditional patriarchal religion into a more life-affirming and creation-centered spirituality of wholeness. Creation Spirituality really gave me permission to trust my experience and to say yes to what was emerging in me. In addition, it helped me connect with allies within our tradition who could guide me on this new journey.

MATTHEW FOX: I remember receiving a letter from you some time ago about a new spiritual community that you started. It was a community for young people, a community focused on helping young people experience their true calling and build their lives around it. It also included giving them the tools to create communities of friends who share, pray, and develop their spiritual lives together, lives dedicated to truth, authenticity, deep transformative spirituality, and sacred activism.

ADAM BUCKO: Yes, the community is called HAB, and it is a part of this larger unfolding of New Monasticism. It is an attempt to begin to bring some of the fruits of this movement to a broader audience, especially to youth. I have been working for quite some time on this unfolding of New Monasticism, working closely with another young New Monastic, Rory McEntee, with whom I cowrote the manifesto, "New Monasticism: An Interspiritual Manifesto for Contemplative Life in the Twenty-first Century."[4] Rory was a close mentee of Br. Wayne Teasdale and is now very involved in the interspiritual movement. He and I have spoken many times on the need for an intergenerational alliance that bridges the gap between many of the elders in our traditions and younger people, many who do not feel called to be in a particular tradition, but who are hungry for a nonsectarian brand of spirituality that embodies the same type of contemplative depth. We have been working closely with elders such as Kurt Johnson[5] and Fr. Thomas Keating to begin to envision what this looks like and slowly to begin to build the structures and the relationships to bring this about.

HAB is one of these manifestations that we believe can help create a truly authentic and genuine contemplative option for young people.

MATTHEW FOX: Perhaps it would be appropriate to conclude this conversation on your journey with some quotes from that letter about HAB, because that letter really summarized this unfolding of your life into this new phase. In the letter you said the following:

> I felt a sense of calling to start this community of friends so we could share our journey towards true aliveness in God and help each other become a healing presence in the world.
>
> Among the many things that inspired this idea were: Spiritual guides like Father Bede Griffiths, who combined the contemplative wisdom of East and West. . . . My time at Sewa Ashram in India, where prayer and activism met beautifully in sacred service offered to victims of AIDS, abuse, and social estrangement. . . . Prayerful searchings at a small hermitage in the foothills of the Himalayas, where the sound of the Ganges permeated my heart and began opening it to what really matters. . . . My heartbreak at vigil-like meetings with homeless youth, in whom God was present in secret and anonymous ways waiting to be recognized by all of us. . . . Childhood memories of activist priests of Poland, killed by the totalitarian regime for knowing that saying yes to God requires saying no to injustice. . . . And, finally my "post-ascetic" experiments with "shadow-work" which helped me move from

life-denying framework of traditional patriarchal religion, into a revolutionary, creation-centered and inclusive spirituality of wholeness. . . .

All of these influences have been woven together into my spiritual vow—through the inspiration and guidance of mentors and elders, who helped me listen, affirm and understand what it means to be faithful to God's loving impulse and action within me.

This new community will be called HAB and its charism will reflect the meaning of this Aramaic word. HAB represents the active dimension of love. Love, that moves from inside out and uses the "dry parts of our lives" to kindle a fire that transfigures deadness into life. This community will be rooted in the tradition of contemplative living and radical spirit-based activism. The examples of Fr. Bede Griffiths, Swami Abhishiktananda, Dorothy Day, Mahatma Gandhi, Lanza del Vasto, and Mother Teresa will offer us guidance. Our goal will be no less than a transformation of the whole-person so that our lives can become life-giving signs of hope in a world so broken by war, rivalry, greed, lack of concern for the other, and the impoverishment of spirit. Our journey will begin in a very simple way. We will meet weekly and share in contemplative prayer, sacred reading, heartfelt reflection, friendship and celebration. In the process, we will begin to discover God's loving presence and action in our lives. Our task will be to offer each other support and spiritual friendship so we can have the courage to say yes to what is emerging in us, so that our lives can become an expression of HAB in the world.

MATTHEW FOX: This sounds like a powerful and fresh version of a new but old kind of Base Community. Small communities are where Spirit is working in particular today.

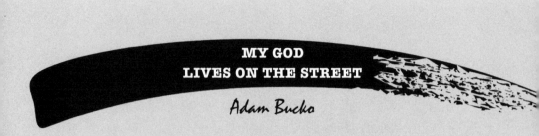

MY GOD
LIVES ON THE STREET

Adam Bucko

It's nighttime. I am walking outside the Port Authority Bus Terminal, that depressing brick behemoth on 42nd Street and Eight
Avenue that is the main hub for buses arriving to and depart-
ing from New York City. I am looking for homeless kids, trying
to spot new arrivals that might still be hanging out, unsure of
where to go. I keep my gaze active, scanning the outside and the
various crevices of the building.

Tonight, like every night, there are about four thousand kids
in New York City who will spend the night on the street. While
most of us will be comfortably resting in our beds, many of these
four thousand will sleep on the subway, in an abandoned building,
or with a person with whom they will have to compromise their
dignity in exchange for a place to sleep. I want to reach them
to offer help before they disappear into the Manhattan sinkhole.
But I am not the only one looking for them. As soon as they step
off the bus, there is a chain of pimps waiting for them, ready to
promise them the future that they dream of. Ready to mesmerize
their minds, stab their souls and imprison their consciences.

In 2004, Taz Tagore and I co-founded the Reciprocity Foundation, an organization that offers street youth support and
helps them build healthy and successful lives. Our job is to catch
the kids before they become victims of this never-ending cycle of
horror, abuse and prostitution. It is just a question of who gets
to them first.

A long time ago, I learned that if I want to be effective in
my work, I have to walk the streets with certainty. I have to act
and feel as if these streets are an extension of my living room.

This aura of ease confuses all the pimps and the other sketchy characters here that are used to seeing fear in everyone around them. They are not sure what to make of me. They don't know who I know or who I run with, and so they leave me alone.

I walk into the station to see if I can find any newcomers. Kids come here from all around the country for various reasons. Some come because they were asked to leave by their parents. Some because their families were too poor to take care of them. Some because they aged out of the foster care system. Upon turning seventeen or eighteen, they were simply dropped off at the Greyhound bus station and told to follow their dreams. Some come here because they have suffered abuse by a family member, and the only way to escape that—other than suicide—is to run away. Some kids come to New York City because they are gay, and they have been kicked out by religious parents who believe that the harsh reality of the street will convince them to "change their ways."

Over the years, I have met thousands of homeless kids. Some I was able to help, and some I lost. So, here I am today walking these streets, prayerfully knowing that each time I see a kid, it might be the last time. Knowing this changes everything. Knowing this lends urgency to my work.

As I continue to walk, faces of kids I have known appear in my mind's eye. There is Tanisha who got shot by a pimp. There is Nicky who was kidnapped by two fellow shelter residents and turned into a prostitute. There is Larry, calling me on the phone crying, telling me he was just diagnosed with HIV. There is Tony, telling me how he is haunted by the memory of his father killing his mother, as he looked on, a frightened child. These stories are so horrifying and yet so typical. They are the shared daily experiences of thousands of street kids. I take a few more steps into a dark alley only to notice a kid I know getting into a stranger's car. God only knows what will happen once she gets into that car.

Seeing this, it is so easy to just give up. But I cannot do that. The kids we have helped through the Reciprocity Foundation tell me that we are their only family. They say our center is the only place they have ever felt loved. I stop for a moment and recall all the happy faces I have seen over the years. Kids who went through our program and whose lives were changed. Kids who discovered their talents and now work with other struggling teens. Kids who graduated from college and are now beacons of hope in this hopeless world of the streets. Kids who recently made a film called "Invisible: Diaries of New York's Homeless Youth." It aired on a major network, was nominated for an Emmy Award and showed everyone that homeless youth, once given proper attention and care, are capable of doing great things. All of them came to us in a state of despair, and through the foundation, got what they needed to lead purposeful and meaningful lives. Thinking of them, I know that I cannot, I will not, give up on those in need of help.

It is 3 a.m. and time to go home. As I walk toward the subway I try to hold all of those faces in my heart and offer them to God. Along the way I hear a mad street preacher desperately screaming, "Where is God? Where is God? Where is God?!" I look at him and the words of Mother Theresa come to mind:

"Jesus is the Hungry—to be fed. Jesus is the Thirsty—to be satiated. Jesus is the Naked—to be clothed. Jesus is the Homeless—to be taken in. Jesus is the Lonely—to be loved. Jesus is the Unwanted—to be wanted."

Where is God? He is here on this street, lying naked in the gutter. He is here on this street, homeless. He is here on this street, in all the lonely and unwanted, waiting for our love.

As I continue my walk toward the subway I wonder, what will it take for us to notice Him?

4
Matthew's Story

ADAM BUCKO: Why do you do what you do?

MATTHEW FOX: I enjoy it. I find it meaningful for myself and presumably for others. I feel passionate about the changes I call for, both personal and societal transformations, and I see them as deeply related. If you don't work on yourself, then much of your politics is merely projections. We have to walk our talk and do the inner work that allows the outer work to be authentic and also effective. I get enough positive feedback (and negative too, such as the Vatican saying a major work by me was "dangerous and deviant") to let me know I'm on the right track, more or less.

ADAM BUCKO: How did you discover your vocation? Was there someone who helped you name it? Is priesthood a big part of your vocation? How does that relate to what you tell young people when you say, "Priest is the posse"?

MATTHEW FOX: The "posse is the priest" phrase means to me that priesthood is not restricted to those who slogged through seminary training by any means. The posse is the group for example that puts on a Cosmic Mass (it usually takes about thirty people including DJs, VJs, rappers, carpenters, PR people, etc., etc.) I define the priest archetype as being "a midwife of grace" so that means that all of us, when we are doing work that is healthy for others, are priests because we are midwives of grace.

My vocation obviously evolved over the years and grew, but as a teenager I was struck by my soul blowing open when I read Tolstoy's *War and Peace,* and I wanted to explore what happened to me. It was a mystical experience (as were other experiences I had had) although I did not have the language for it. I always knew others had such experiences and that they also lacked the understanding and language to understand its importance and deeper meaning. I felt that by joining the Dominican Order, I would learn both how to grasp the importance of spiritual experiences and how to share such experiences and assist others to name them as important in their lives. That is why I ended up studying spirituality in Paris.

I had polio when I was twelve years old, and doctors could not tell me if I would ever walk again. My father had been a football coach at the University of Wisconsin, and I had imagined that I would, like my older brothers, be a football hero, but now I could not walk. While I was in the hospital, a Dominican lay brother would visit me. He was a very contemplative kind of person, and I was drawn to his contemplative way of being. When, after many months, my legs did return, I remember saying a thank you to the universe and a promise that I would not take my legs for granted again. I think that is a mystical approach—not to take things for granted (for example, one's breath—which one learns by meditating on breath). I did play sports but with more abandon, one might say—that is, more for play than serious ego gratification.

ADAM BUCKO: You mentioned that one of the reasons why you were not afraid to be kicked out of the Catholic Church is because you gave up priesthood even before you were ordained into priesthood. Can you speak about that?

MATTHEW FOX: During my years of study and "formation" as a Dominican student, I often had some deep contemplative experiences, and my confessor told me I should consider becoming a hermit. At first I thought this advice very odd, but then it kind of grew on me. I did some research and found a colony of hermits living on Vancouver Island under the direction of a Belgian abbot (or former abbot). I told my provincial of my need to try out that lifestyle, and he said I was crazy to do so and that "if I went there for the summer, he could not guarantee that I would ever be ordained a priest." I said I needed to go, and I did go (with his reluctant permission). It gave me lots of energy that I ran on for over twenty years. But also it meant I left the priesthood, gave it up, before I was ordained. Thus, when I actually was ordained, I was freer than many priests find themselves to be.

Also, this experience may have helped me when I wrote to Thomas Merton, because I did tell him about it in general. It turns out he knew the abbot and the hermitage, and, moreover, he had to struggle with his abbot for six years to get permission to live as a hermit on the grounds of the monastery where he lived. That was right about the time I was doing my hermit-thing. So I guess we had that in common. It was Merton who recommended that I do my doctoral studies in Paris, and I am grateful to him for that, since I met my mentor there and I learned from him about the Creation Spirituality tradition. Also, I guess I can say that I owe Merton for all the trouble I've gotten in since.

ADAM BUCKO: You once said that your vocation exploded you out of the church.

MATTHEW FOX: My vocation has been to take seriously the spirituality side (which is the experiential side) of religion and to help others to do the same. That is why I write about mysticism and prophecy (also called contemplation and action) and define prayer as a "radical response to life." Being involved in both has been exhilarating and, at times, has put me in some trouble with institutions and those who want to defend them at all costs. I would not back down on issues of women's rights, gay and lesbian rights, eco-justice, social justice. My provincial, who ultimately expelled me (under pressure from Ratzinger, then chief inquisitor and later pope Benedict XVI), told the *New York Times*, "The church has moved to the right but Matt Fox has not." So I got exploded out of a right-wing church that, I think I have proven in my recent book, *The Pope's War*, is in fact a schismatic church today, because it has abandoned all the principles of Vatican II—from lay rights to national bishop conferences, freedom of conscience, and, above all, social justice issues. It has wandered very, very far from the spirit and teachings of Jesus and the Gospels, with all of its preoccupation with pelvic morality, for example, and its support of fascist movements like Opus Dei and Communion and Liberation. Vatican II had attempted to bring Catholicism back to the values of the Gospel, but it was abandoned by the papacies of John-Paul II and Benedict XVI.

I have written a public letter to the new pope that expresses my hope and prayers that he live up to his namesake, Francis, and truly rebuild the church; end the current inquisition; clean out the curial stables; close the Vatican bank; fire all prelates who covered up pedophile priest crimes; speak out on injustice, including eco-injustice; honor the divine feminine to balance with the sacred masculine (something Francis had in spades); invite women into church leadership; and listen to the young. We shall see soon enough what stuff he is made of.

ADAM BUCKO: You are a true spiritual radical, who challenged some of the basic tenants of Western theology, spirituality, and the church. What are some of the things you challenge in your life and why?

MATTHEW FOX: I challenge the dualisms of body versus soul, matter versus spirit, things that so dominate the fundamentalist wings of Christianity. This means I am challenging patriarchy, since patriarchy is built on dualisms, and also I challenge homophobia, since that too is built on a sexual majority lording over a sexual minority. I challenge sexism and the one-sided presentation of God as "he," which ignores the wisdom traditions of God as female. I challenge boring worship (that is, prayers from a book) that is so oppressive that even the angels aren't worshiping much in church any more (they are more likely to be found in bookstores, I am learning). I challenge denominationalism, which is at least as dark and foreboding as sexism or racism—as if God is restricted to a particular religious box. ("Deep ecumenism," as I call it, is about finding Spirit in all cultures and all religions and finding what the best of spirituality in all have in common and how they compliment one another.) I challenge anthropocentrism and all those preoccupations that prevent humans from relating in economics, politics, religion, education, and justice with the rich varieties of species other than our own. The Earth is burning up, and Rome (and religion in general) is playing the fiddle.

I challenge fascism, whether coming from the Vatican or from the Supreme Court. The Citizens United decision is pure fascism—Mussolini himself defined fascism as "the marriage of government and corporations." I fear gravely for the future of our country under that absurd decision, which wants us to believe that corporations are persons and which unleashes billionaire barons to define our politics for us. It is of great significance that five Catholics on the Supreme Court voted for that sick notion. By the way, Susan Sontag defines fascism as "institutional violence," and there is a lot of that in the Catholic Church today, including but not limited to the horrible pedophilia cover-ups. I challenge denial and cover-up and the ignorance of our Western mystical tradition.

I wrote a book called *Original Blessing*, which challenges the great investment the Western church holds in "original sin"—even though Jesus *never heard of original sin* (no Jew has—it is a term invented by

St. Augustine in the fourth century AD). I challenge popes and wannabe popes who think they and their bureaucracies hold all the truth—when, in fact, the people themselves and those working closely to them are also recipients of Spirit and of truth (*sensus fidelium* is the traditional term for this).

I also challenge educational systems that do not incorporate the body and all of the chakras, for we don't learn just with our heads. I have created models of education that have proven very successful and that include all of our brain—left and right hemispheres—as well as our heart chakras and our lower chakras, where we feel the kick of injustice. I challenge education that does not lead to creativity, since creativity is what most distinguishes us as a species. There is no excuse for education (or worship) that bores people. We live in an amazing universe and that is what university should mean—a place to find one's place in the universe. I seek wisdom schools to displace our knowledge factories, and I've established a few myself over the years.

ADAM BUCKO: Was being kicked out of the church difficult? You must have felt betrayed by your friends and brothers, and by the institution that claimed to be "the mother"? You don't seem bitter about it. How did you deal with what happened?

MATTHEW FOX: Aquinas says bitterness comes from holding anger in a long time. I recognized my anger at being treated unjustly, and I tried to deal with it with humor. (When they silenced me for a year, my opening remark after fourteen months was, "as I was saying fourteen months ago, when I was so rudely interrupted . . ."—the audience got it, but the Vatican, poor fellows, aren't real adept at humor). I also tried to deal with it by continuing to tell the truth as I saw it. I put it into creativity by continuing to teach and invent forms of education that were inclusive and not exclusive of right and left brain, and so on. I kept writing and lecturing and therefore thinking, even though that is the last thing the Vatican wanted to encourage, unfortunately. Of course, I saw then, as I see now, that my expulsion from the order in which I had lived for thirty-four years was a political act—they expelled Leonardo Boff and Eugen Drewermann, theologians from Brazil and Germany, respectively, the very same year they expelled me. It was obviously a political act, our three expulsions, meant to intimidate other theologians who were less visible than the three of us. So I tried not to take it all too personally.

Yes, there were lots of betrayals, but I learned important lessons about how some people (I am blessed not to be one of them) prefer institutional protection and safety and pseudo security to the truth. I have been amazed at how in denial many clergy still are about the inquisition that has been going on in the Church for the last forty years. I wonder if the latest attacks on Catholic sisters will bring some courage to the fore in such people. To live in denial means that one lives only partially. (Meister Eckhart says, "God is the denial of denial.") My understanding of spirituality is that it means living life fully . . . and courageously. I opt for that. Whatever the price. The French have a saying, living "sur la marge," living on the margin. That is where I have chosen to live; it is a good way to stay alive and alert and dancing and even youthful. But there's not lots of insurance there. I think more and more young people are being pushed to the margins in our time, and that can be a wonderfully creative way to live: on the margins.

ADAM BUCKO: What are the lessons you learned from taking on institutions?

MATTHEW FOX: You seldom "win." They control the information, the press, the power, even the definition of "winning" if you allow them. Lots of lies get told. For example, stories were told about what a bad Dominican I had been, but actually, until Ratzinger put more and more pressure on my province, I was well respected there. In fact, I was elected to be a *diffinitor,* one of four persons handling all provincial affairs at a gathering that elected a new provincial (though I had to bow out of that appointment, because of an operation on my back that interfered). So I was not always a "problem member." Some of my brothers were proud of my work (and I of theirs).

Often it is better to start new "institutions" than to waste one's limited time and energy trying to convince dead ones. Jesus said, "Let the dead bury the dead." You need to be able to smell death. And to smell where new life is also.

At the same time that you take on institutions, you do need to find allies who are on your wavelength, who also do not want to sell their souls for untruths or for partial living, and who are willing to struggle creatively and laugh a lot. Institutions—no matter what the Supreme Court says in its silliness and subservience to fascism—are not people. People have inner lives. We need to cultivate that and encourage it in one another. We also need to infiltrate our institutions in order to bring life and Spirit there. And find leaders or become leaders that create circles of wisdom and give birth to new forms and new movements that may eventually become institutions.

ADAM BUCKO: Your Creation Spirituality really redefined the Western spiritual tradition. How did you discover it? What is the basic premise of Creation Spirituality, and why is it so important?

MATTHEW FOX: While doing my doctoral studies on spirituality in Paris, I had a wonderful teacher who became my mentor—Père M. D. Chenu, a great French Dominican. He was the father (or grandfather) of liberation theology and had had a very great impact at the Second Vatican Council (having been silenced for twelve years by Pope Pius XII because he worked with the worker priest movement after World War II). He is the one who named the Creation Spirituality tradition for me. It answered the basic question that I brought with me to my studies: what is the relationship between mystical experience and social justice? The key is art and creativity, as Chenu demonstrated. Creation Spirituality is the oldest tradition in the Bible; it is about original blessing more than original sin; it is feminist, since *wisdom* is feminine in the scriptures (*spirit* is also in the Hebrew language); it is cosmological and not antiscience at all; it is playful and creative; it is justice oriented; and it is the tradition that Jesus came from, since all scholars agree he came from the wisdom tradition of Israel. And clearly, from the name itself, it is about preserving and saving the Earth.

The recovery of Creation Spirituality is so important because religion in the West has been on a grand detour from the teachings of Jesus, especially with the detour that took flight in the fourth century, when the church married the Roman Empire, and with the detour took place in the second century, when men took over exclusive decision making in the community, contrary to the practices of the first century of the Christian movement. One of the most radical things about Jesus was his respect for women, and the early church had women leaders. Today scholars (not popes) make these facts abundantly clear (see my book *The Pope's War* and the section on women leaders there). The fall/redemption tradition of Christianity, which begins with original sin and endorses dualism, anthropocentrism, and patriarchy, is not as ancient as Creation Spirituality, nor is it relevant to the real moral issues of our time, including ecological, gender, gender-preference issues. It reinforces a fear of the feminine and ignores healthy mystical experience, while discouraging prophetic movements for justice and liberation. It becomes a front for those who want to live the status quo.

ADAM BUCKO: You often say, "courage is the first sign of spirit." You have made some very courageous decisions in your life. What initiated you into this spirituality of courage?

MATTHEW FOX: I think I saw some courage in both of my parents when I was growing up. And, of course, people like Martin Luther King Jr. were exemplars for me, as they were for many of my generation. I had the privilege several years ago to dialogue about racism and ecology with Rev. Fred Shuttlesworth (who has since died) in the civil rights museum in Birmingham. He was a street minister in Birmingham; he convinced King to fill the jail with teenagers, since the adults had to go back to work after thirty days, and they needed the jails full. King was reluctant, but he gave in to Shuttlesworth. And with that the movement succeeded. But Rev. Shuttlesworth was beaten three times by the Ku Klux Klan with chains; his two children, eight and ten years old, were arrested by Sheriff Bull Connor; and his house was blown up while he was in it (he walked out okay). Having lunch alone with him just before our dialogue, I asked him, "Fred, where did you learn your courage?" He replied, "You can call it courage, but I call it trust. When I walked out of my house, blown to bits by their bombs, I knew they could not kill me or the movement. Oh, they might kill my body some day, but the movement would go on."

That taught me a lot. Courage comes from trust. And *faith* is the Biblical word for *trust*. King too talked about courage when he was asked, "How can you march through Skokie knowing that people want to kill you?" He answered, "You have to love something more than your fear of death if you are going to live." I loved something more than the priesthood when I became a priest; and we all have to be willing to lose our jobs and/or our status and/or our reputations over something we truly believe in.

ADAM BUCKO: What role did Native American spirituality play in your life? I think I have heard you say that you experience God in sweat lodges and not in churches? Can you tell us about some of the most life-changing experiences you had with Native Americans?

MATTHEW FOX: I don't think I would have survived spiritually or politically without the great gifts of Native American spiritual practices and spirit teachers in my life. There is an Earth-based dimension to a sweat lodge or a sun dance or a vision quest or a powwow that literally grounds one's being. There is an adventure dimension to it also; it is a challenge;

it takes you to the edge. My first twenty minutes in a sweat lodge I was looking for a fire extinguisher or a fire exit. There was neither. I thought I was going to die. Then I yielded to the experience, and great things happened from then on. In contrast, there is so little challenge in most Western worship (except staying awake). Adventure is important especially in prayer. Indigenous people have that. Plus, the ancient songs are so moving you actually feel the ancestors entering the lodge. Good souls, real people, struggling people, sacred drum touching the heartbeat of the universe and one's own, uniting all. What is there not to like? What is there not to learn from? Dancing to pray—how ancient that is, and how real a way to get back in touch with our lower chakras and with Mother Earth.

One teaching I received from Buck Ghosthorse, my Lakota teacher, was this: "In our tradition," he said, "fear is the door in the heart that lets evil spirits in. So all real prayer is developing a big heart [i.e., courage] so that fear does not enter and take over." I also had a powerful and trippy vision quest (which I relate in detail in my autobiography), which, according to Buck, meant that the spirits of the ancient animals of the land were emerging to assist my work, because "two leggeds will not always support you, but they will." This vision quest has often kept me going through rough times.

ADAM BUCKO: You practice a lot of deep ecumenism. Can you elaborate on the origin of that term?

MATTHEW FOX: I first used the term "deep ecumenism" in my book *The Coming of the Cosmic Christ;* I sort of borrowed the term from Joanna Macy and the movement of "deep ecology." That movement's goal was to bring the spiritual dimension to the ecological movement, which was more secular, driven by political opposition to ecological destruction, but did not include the dimension of the sacred. So deep ecology did include the dimension of the sacred. I felt that was also needed in discussion of ecumenism, since too much "dialogue" among religions,

I felt, was just exchanging position papers: "we believe this," and "oh, you believe that." I wanted ecumenism to go deeper into actual experience, both personal and social (including action for social justice, but also involving worship). To be spiritual is to want to travel deep, and I felt it was time that our various wisdom traditions went deep together. Thus, "deep ecumenism."

ADAM BUCKO: What role did art and science play in your spiritual formation?

MATTHEW FOX: I wrote poetry when I was a kid, but all that sort of ended when I attended high school, collage, and graduate studies with the Dominicans. But it came alive again during my sojourn in Paris, while doing my doctoral studies—the French have a wonderful appreciation of the role of art in all of our lives. It was Père Chenu, whom I referred to earlier, who said to me, the last time we visited (when he was about ninety years old), "Never forget—the worst tragedy in theology of the past three hundred years has been the separation of the theologian from the artist, the poet, the painter, the musician, the sculptor, the filmmaker." He understood the deep connection between prophecy and art—there never was a prophet who was not a social artist; "moral imagination" is what is at stake, after all, in waking people up out of their slumber into alternative possibilities for living.

More and more musicians and poets grew on me and helped to develop my soul over the years. Rilke and Rumi and Hafiz and, most recently, Mary Oliver are examples. This is why "art as meditation" is so important a pedagogical method in my educational programs beginning in ICCS in Chicago and going through the University of Creation Spirituality and now YELLAWE for inner city youth. Creativity awakens the soul. We have found, working with inner city youth, that they get genuinely excited about making their own movie, for example, and this joy of learning inspires them to stay in school instead of drop out. As Hildegard of Bingen puts it, "there is wisdom in all creative works."

Or as Meister Eckhart puts it, when you give birth, you are giving birth to the Christ.

ADAM BUCKO: How do you trust in life?

MATTHEW FOX: By being willing to enter both the Via Positiva and the Via Negativa, the brightness and the shadow. By testing your response and growing your soul and heart through spiritual practices of silence and more. By standing up to fear and not running from it. When you think about it, everyone has already trusted life, insofar as you are still around. Maybe it hasn't been easy, but we are still here to talk about it.

What is the opposite of trusting life? Cowering in a corner? What fun is that?

It also helps to study the lives of others—the mystic prophets of the world—who have shown courage and trust of life. They—our ancestors—are our teachers still.

ADAM BUCKO: You often say to young people that if they are not happy with the institutions they are part of, they should create their own. This is exactly what you did in your life. You not only challenged and questioned religion, worship, education, activism, but also created many initiatives that propose alternatives to the old systems. Can you speak about that?

MATTHEW FOX: It's about trusting our powers to give birth. We are a creative species, after all. There is great hope and promise in that. But it won't happen if we succumb to couchpotatoitis or become passive citizens or put others on a pedestal. It's about taking responsibility, standing up and being counted, being willing to make a mistake and even "fail" (whatever that means). I have always said I would rather "fail" at something exciting than succeed at something pedestrian. Adventure matters. It brings out the best in us. Takes us to the edge. Keeps us alive and alert.

Let me give a concrete example. A year ago I had to declare bankruptcy, because the LLC I formed to operate, Historic Sweets Ballroom in downtown Oakland, was not able to continue to pay the rent on the place. I purchased it by taking loans on my house and planned it to be a place to reinvent ritual and do our "Cosmic Masses." I had signed the credit cards and everything else, so the responsibility was mine. Do I regret the bankruptcy? Of course. But all sorts of "Main Street" projects went belly up when Wall Street got ordinary citizens to bail them out of the economic crisis. They got all the loans, and none of us on Main Street got any.

Do I regret saving the ballroom from destruction and putting a big (for me) amount of money into it for the sake of ritual reinvention? Not at all. It was worth it. It was an investment in the future. Reinventing forms of ritual and incorporating today's new art forms like DJ and VJ and rap is a very important work we need to do today. We did over ninety Masses either there or in other parts of the country, so we have demonstrated that (1) reinvention of worship with rave is possible, and (2) it is powerful and useful. So the bankruptcy was worth it. Furthermore, now I understand better and can identify more easily with those millions of others who were raked over by Wall Street practices, and I know concretely how badly we need a new economic system—one that works for everyone. The present one favors the rich over the poor, Wall Street over Main Street, the 1 percent over us 99 percent. (I went to over forty-four banks and lenders to get a loan, which we never got). Sadly, little has changed in the current system since that hard lesson was learned by many of us a few years ago.

ADAM BUCKO: What are your experiences like when it comes to creating intergenerational projects?

MATTHEW FOX: I always learn from young people, so it is always fun and invigorating. I also find young people today basically respectful of elders—until they prove to be bad listeners. What I most learned from inner city teenagers in the YELLAWE program was how much beauty they carry inside and how rarely our so-called educational systems even bother to bring it out of them. There is generosity and a love of life and a sense of fun and the Via Positiva in most youth, and that is catching. Like a healthy virus or something.

ADAM BUCKO: Many young activists tend to resist spirituality, thinking that religion has nothing to do with social change and is, in fact, part of the problem. What do you think about that? What are some of your personal experiences with that? Should spirituality play a bigger role in the Occupy movement?

MATTHEW FOX: Religion has wounded many people, and when we are young, we are often very vulnerable and can take in some toxic messages about life, about God, about hell and damnation, about obedience, about sexuality, about homophobia, about fear, and all the rest. Gandhi said a religion of fear is no religion at all. There is such a thing as religious abuse, and it is just as menacing as sexual abuse when you are young and vulnerable. So many people grow up wounded by religion and do not want anything to do with it, and they tend to throw spirituality in the pot with religion. But they are not the same thing. As we mentioned before, the great African American mystic Howard Thurman, whose book *Jesus and the Disinherited* Dr. King took with him every time he went to jail, talks of the distinction between the God of Life and the God of Religion. True spirituality is about the God of Life.

We also cannot erase the fact that among our greatest heroes and sheroes, there was often a deep and abiding commitment to spirituality (sometimes as part of religion and sometimes not) that sustained them in their acts of courage. I speak of people like Dr. King, Mahatma Gandhi, Dorothy Day, Óscar Romero, Cesar Chavez, Julia Butterfly Hill, and more. So yes, Occupy, like any other human enterprise, runs the risk of being in denial of its own shadow. Occupy needs spirituality to sustain its vision and values, including courage (proof of this may be that the forces it is standing up to, such as banking institutions, have long ago abandoned any spirituality). No spiritual teacher, north, south, east, or west, has ever countenanced greed and rapaciousness as values worthy of our species.

ADAM BUCKO: Why do you care so much about young people? Didn't you accept the "religious asylum" from the Episcopal Church under the condition that they will let you focus all of your time on reinventing religion and worship for and with young people?

MATTHEW FOX: I care for young people because they are searching and they can be very blunt and honest and because nothing is going to happen in reinventing new forms of worship or education if the young don't get on board and begin to lead. This is the elder's job: to assist the young in their vocations to lead. Besides, I learn from them. Spirit works through the young quite readily.

When I became Episcopalian, it was for one reason only: to assist young people to give birth to new forms of celebration and worship. I had long sensed how outdated our forms of worship are, but I agree with the African ritual teacher, Melidoma Some, that "there is no community without ritual." Ritual is very important if we are to build community again, and the young people today have all new languages at their fingertips. These ought to be honored and invited into worship to make it live again.

ADAM BUCKO: You have been a wonderful mentor to many young people, including to me. You tend to relate to young people in a different and more open manner than most other elders. What is it that other elders need to know about how to relate to the young?

MATTHEW FOX: Elders have to learn three lessons: (1) to listen, (2) to listen, (3) to listen. This means that generational smugness is not in order. The older ones do not carry all the wisdom that we need today. The present generation of young people holds a new perspective, a postmodern perspective, on life and society. They see the world differently—Thank God! They need to be listened to, first of all. They are carrying a huge burden, with the ecosystem collapsing all around us (and adults and even entire political parties in denial, and the media often selling denial to preserve the privileges of their corporate lords and masters), with the job market not delivering (I believe youth unemployment is at 60 percent in Spain today), with education costs out of control and debt over the one trillion mark, with religion being silly a great deal of the time, and so on, and so on. Elders are only useful if they first listen. Then truly dialogue as equals. Spirit works through the young, not just through the old. As Thomas Aquinas put it in the thirteenth century, "the experience of God must not be restricted to the few or to the old." Amen!

ADAM BUCKO: Speaking of young people, what do you think about the tremendous popularity of vampire novels?

MATTHEW FOX: Recently I was sent a very thoughtful sermon on . . . vampires![1] It surprised me, being the first and only sermon on vampires I had ever heard. In it, the woman preacher, who has read over 250 vampire novels, helped explain why vampires are such a powerful archetype to young people today (and how Hollywood has made over $7 billion the past two years on vampire films). "Vampire Diaries" is a big hit for young people in Europe as well. The Vampire archetype is *not* about sex, she explains; it is about power and money and the abuse of power. The question posed is this, "If you had power over others, how would you use it?"

Teens often feel powerless, and they watch as the older generation abuses power. The power of Wall Street is often vampire-like. The power of sexual predators, whether priests or college coaches in the news lately, is vampire-like. The stories are about a struggle to lead a moral life in spite of one's addiction to blood-lust—are fossil fuel and oil our blood lust? Is it the wild pursuit of money without end? Is the pursuit of power within an ecclesial structure that elevates people in the hierarchy who don't sound the alarm about predators? If we are sucking lifeblood from the planet, our prey is the planet itself. The vampire is a mirror reflecting our secret and shadow self.

ADAM BUCKO: Can you tell me about some of your mentors and spiritual friends who were or are very important to you?

MATTHEW FOX: I have mentioned Père Chenu already several times. In addition to his intellectual brilliance, he was a joyful man, without bitterness (even though he was forbidden to write for twelve years), with a richly developed sense of humor and with a great love of young people. I never once heard him put down a student in the classroom, but always built us up. There was nothing of the sadomasochistic professor/pupil relationship that one so often witnesses in academia. He walked his talk. He challenged us to "join the revolution" in 1968 that was bringing down the government and was student-led.

Fr. Jerry O'Leary was an American Dominican of my province who supported my work early by hiring me to teach in his Institute of Pastoral Studies in Loyola in Chicago; he always encouraged thinking and creativity. My fellow faculty members were so often my mentors as well, especially Sr. Jose Hobday, who was a Seneca woman and a Franciscan sister; M. C. Richards, poet, potter, philosopher, friend; Dr. Clarissa Pinkola Estés, writer and Jungian sage and more; Fr. Thomas Berry, who, with Brian Swimme, put the new cosmology into layman's language and a spiritual context; Dr. Rupert Sheldrake, with whom I have written two books (one more on the way) on science and spirituality—he has great courage to take on the dogmas of contemporary science, and I admire him greatly both for his courage and for his intellectual brilliance; Buck Ghosthorse, whom I have mentioned above; Starhawk, who has remained true to her prophetic and justice-oriented life while practicing Wicca spirituality; Jeremy Taylor on dreams, and many more. One of the gifts of running my own school for thirty years was I could surround myself with wonderful beings and teachers, and they helped me to grow and stay alive in so many ways.

Of course, the ancestors, so-called dead mystics of the past, from Jesus to Eckhart, from Hildegard to Black Elk, Howard Thurman, and Rabbi Abraham Joshua Heschel, are speaking to us still, and they too are part of my pantheon of mentors. As are so many writers, poets, musicians, and scientists.

ADAM BUCKO: What are some of the biggest life lessons that you have learned that you would like to offer to young people today?

MATTHEW FOX: Recently I heard poet Mary Oliver, now in her eighties, give a poetry reading, and in it she offered the following "lessons for living." (1) Pay attention. (2) Be astonished. (3) Share your astonishment. I agree wholeheartedly. It is mostly about the Via Positiva, to pay attention and expect to be astonished. Sharing the astonishment is about the Via Creativa and the Via Transformativa. So I say: live life deeply, which means to travel deeply through those four paths of Creation Spirituality, not getting stuck in any one. Keep moving, like the planets all do. Don't look back over your shoulder overly much. Remember that solidarity is the opposite of blind obedience (Dorothee Sölle). And the God of Life is sometimes different from the God of Religion. Keep your conscience alive. Live from that. And consider FUN a virtue (which it is).

ADAM BUCKO: How did you discover that you were a writer?

MATTHEW FOX: By writing. It was while writing my doctoral thesis on a Basque farm in southern France that one day, sitting at the typewriter, I said out loud to myself, "I am a writer because I enjoy writing so much." I enjoy writing because I find it a great way to collect my ideas and put them together and give birth to more ideas. I think it was Anaïs

Nin who said, "we write to taste life twice." Writing is a marvelous way to learn. It's a thrill, a joy, an ecstasy. When I write, I often feel myself riding the waves of the ocean of ideas. You are not in charge. The Spirit of creativity carries you along. That is exhilarating. And then, to think that others might read what you write and also get turned on—what could be more fun than that? I think all good work is like that: it begins in joy and ends in joy, though with plenty of sweat, backaches, headaches, doubts and detours and disappointments and challenges in between.

TWELVE PRINCIPLES OF CREATION SPIRITUALITY

1. The Universe (and all things in it, ourselves included) is fundamentally a blessing, and our relationship to the universe intoxicates us.

   We experience the universe as good.

2. We experience that the Divine is in all things and all things are in the Divine.

   The traditional term for this experience is *panentheism*, which is not theism (God out there) and not atheism (no God anywhere).

3. God is as much Mother as Father, as much Child as Parent, as much Godhead (mystery) as God (history), as much beyond all words and images as in all forms and beings.

   Beware of any literal name for God or clinging to our gods in only one form.

4. In our lives, it is through the work of spiritual practice that we find our deep and true self.

Through this work of meditation and silence we calm the reptilian brain and move beyond fear and into compassion and community.

5. Our inner work can be understood as a fourfold journey involving:

   awe, delight, amazement (known as the Via Positiva)
   silence, darkness, suffering, letting go, letting be (Via Negativa)
   birthing, creativity, passion (Via Creativa)
   justice, healing, celebration (Via Transformativa)

   This journey is not linear but spirals through our lives.

6. Every one of us is a mystic.

   We are born full of wonder and can recover it at any age (Via Positive).

7. Every one of us is an artist.

   Whatever the expression of our creativity, it can be a form of prayer and praise (Via Creativa)

8. Every one of us is a prophet.

   Our prophetic work is to interfere in what interrupts authentic life, that is, all forms of injustice, whether it be ecological, economic, social, gender, or gender-preference injustice (Via Transformativa).

9. The Universe is obviously biased in favor of diversity.

   So too our struggles are to honor and rejoice at the rich diversity found among individuals and among multiple cultures, religions, and ancestral traditions.

10. The basic work of God is Compassion, and we, who are all original blessings and sons and daughters of the Divine, are called to compassion.

This means we acknowledge our shared interdependence and we rejoice at one another's joys and grieve at one another's sorrows and struggle for justice and healing of the causes of those sorrows.

11. At this time in human history, Deep Ecumenism has never been more important.

Thus we honor and respect the wisdom that arises from the various wells of all the religious and wisdom traditions of the world, for while the wells vary, there is only one "underground river" of wisdom.

12. Ecological Justice is essential for human and planetary survival, constituting the very meaning of "salvation" (to preserve things in the good).

Ecology is the local expression of Cosmology, and all people with a conscience are called today to challenge their own lifestyles and values in light of this ultimate value: passing on the beauty and health of creation to future generations. The Sacredness of creation is underscored in such traditions as the "Buddha Nature" of all things or the "Cosmic Christ" as the light in all things or "Father Sky" and "Mother Earth."

5
What's Your Calling?

Are You Living in Service of Compassion and Justice?

If we understand God to be love, then each time a human denies another love, God is afflicted. If we understand God to be justice, then each time a human struggle for justice is thwarted, God becomes poor. If we understand God as peace, then each time peace is broken, God is shattered and distressed. If we understand God to be healing, joy, and wholeness, then whenever and however we disregard God's presence by committing acts such as degradation, abuse, and oppression, God is broken, God is violated, God is alienated.

Jamie Manson, Female, 35[1]

There is a thread which has been woven throughout my work thus far; following it and staying true to it leads me to my calling: to work with underrepresented young people to heal from the suffering brought onto them by forces like trauma, oppression, discrimination, and living in poverty. To me, to heal is to be able to express oneself fully: creatively, spiritually, and in relationships. In my view, all human beings deserve a chance to be their true selves, so I will continue to follow this thread.

P.L., Female, 26

My calling is to use whatever talents I have to make the world a better place. I do this through the dedication, struggle, and celebration to become more mature, more discerning, more courageous to follow the guidance given by the Spirit, the only one who truly knows what is best for the Whole . . . and finally by letting go. Whatever I do that is helpful emerges out of this space; it is unique and could only flow through this incarnation.

R.M., Male, 35

My calling is to heal and aid in the process of people who have been marginalized to empower themselves. I am called to seek and see God in every act of social justice. I am called to always come from a space of Love.

M.C., Female, 26

My calling is to support those who are on the front lines as Change Makers, transforming the world around them. Through the practices of mindful yoga and meditation, I've found tools to support my own sustainability, and it is an honor to share it with others and to bear witness to their transformation.

L.B., Female, 38

My calling is to help people to find the courage to be vulnerable, through fostering nurturing and compassionate relationships with their own bodies and minds. This radical acceptance of Self, which empowers us to accept and connect with others, has been a huge part of my continuing journey to wholeness and connection with the Divine. I think and hope that my learning and experiences can help others to do the same.

V.H.K., Female, 30

My vocation is to cultivate my inner wisdom of compassion, creativity, and play, and shine it upon the world around me.

C.C., Female, 33

My "calling" . . . has been a discovery of the connections between my own healing and the healing needed in the world around me, a discovery of how my greatest joys can meet the world's greatest needs.

K.R., Female, 27

A lot of times, people—especially in the work world—are like, "Oh, I've got to work, you know. And in twenty or thirty years I'm going to retire, and then I can worry about saving the world." I think that the bodhisattva vows speak to that, "No, you need to start now, because your world is waiting for you."

K.K., Male, 32

There's very much a relationship to spirit that feels like before I do anything, before I take any kind of action in my work, I have to feel a certain resonance that comes from another source entirely. And then once I feel that resonance, then I'm happy to do whatever it takes to follow the vision that is resonating.

C.K., Female, 32

I do not have a calling. . . . I am always listening for it though.

A.B., Female, 29

So you've been given these gifts. What are you going to do about them? And what are you going to do in this lifetime?

K.K., Male, 32

My calling is . . . to serve God as a writer, public speaker, wife, and maybe even as a priest. I want to show and tell everyone with my actions and words that they are valued, included, loved, and accepted

*by God no matter who they are and what their station is in life. I believe
everyone is worthy of respect, even if we disagree. And I believe if we
all start to respect each other despite our differences we can become a
doorway to God's love and create heaven in our midst.*

V.D., Female, 35

*I changed my work to pursue happiness above money. I'm a happier
person now and I have more time for yoga!*

M.E., Female, 28

My calling is writing. I realized I get sick and depressed if I don't write.

K.C., Female, 28

*Yes, I am living my life's purpose. And to me, at the end of the day,
even if I feel like the experiment [living in an eco-village at Earthaven]
is not going so well, I'm certain that I'm living my life's purpose by
being here and participating in this experiment. So that makes it so I
can sleep well at night and get up the next day and put a smile on my
face and do it all over again.*

A.N., Female, 35

*My passions—everything is connected to social justice. And that
involves my many interests, which are art, activism, my intellectual
work and my spiritual work. I try to unite them all with the vision of
working toward social justice. I am following my path, and that's what
I have come to this world to do. Whether it's to raise consciousness
through multiple forms, whether it's to contribute to the betterment of
the world, that's my path. And I think, as I walk it, then that's how I
am connected to the divine, because I'm listening to my path.*

S.B., Male, 31

*Self-expression . . . is that a calling? Much of my younger years I spent
in all different types of talk therapy (i.e. psychoanalysis, cognitive*

behavioral, etc.)—and I guess I developed a knack for speaking my own truths. . . . (I was anorexic). . . . Hey, the therapist doesn't deserve ALL *of my wisdom! I'd like to share that wisdom with the world! Maybe make a career out of it.*

L.Y., Female, 22

My activism is part of my path, which I feel is part of the connection with the divine as well. They're all linked together. . . . I think that's my call in this world.

S.B., Male, 31

I have always felt my calling in life is to be a vehicle of reconciliation to a broken and divided world. A world which is broken by the illusion that peoples, classes, geographies, and faiths can not understand each other. My Faith as a Christian and my calling as a priest allows my life to be but one simple bridge to help unite people to each other and to the Divine.

M.R., Male, 37

Permaculture is my calling. The pure logic of healthy soil makes a lot of sense. If you get somebody into the soil, and starting to look at some plants and watching something grow—I mean, if you can tell me something more divine than watching a plant grow or watching a seed grow into a healthy plant, and then eating that plant and using that energy . . . the spiritual path is already set. Once you get somebody's hands in the dirt, and once you get somebody's hands caring for soil or caring for compost or caring for a plant, caring about nutrition—these types of things the youth are open to.

P.P., Male, 27

Finding a vocation that you really feel passionate about and that gives you energy and you look forward to every day, that's the best—where you can just feel like you're motivated and your life's passion is in that kind of work, and where other people feel inspired and it's creative and it feeds you. Unfortunately, a lot of people don't have that kind of work. A lot of people dread their work. And so that's just a big drain on who you are, and if you're not really living who you're meant to be or doing the kind of work that you should be, then you're not being true to yourself.

S.O., Male, 33

It is hard to live a spiritual life while paying the bills, but I trust that if I am following the Holy Spirit that things will end up the way they need to end up

G.W., Male, 17

As I've grown more interested in environmental and poverty issues, I definitely see my concern for these issues stemming from my faith. Jesus's example, his life—you know, he spent the majority of his time reaching out to the poor and the generally disenfranchised. And I see the work that I'm pursuing as serving my faith, as serving Jesus.

B.M., Male, 20

I am confused about how to create a just and sustainable world; confused about what I have to abandon and take on; confused about whether it is going to work to bring the kind of change necessary to save humanity and many other species nearing extinction.

S.W., Male, 28

ADAM BUCKO: Many young people today say that spirituality without action is no spirituality at all. Yet they don't just speak of any action. They specifically refer to action that reflects the deepest sense of their calling or vocation. Bill Everson, in his book, *Birth of a Poet,* said that for the Western mind and soul, vocation is a primary pathway into spirit.

MATTHEW FOX: Yes, especially for young adults. That book by Bill Everson is in fact a collection of his teachings from a very popular course he taught for years at the University of California, Santa Cruz—in fact, it was the most popular course on campus. Which shows how natural and organic it is for the young to be excited to learn about their "vocation" or "calling."

ADAM BUCKO: I can see why young adults were especially drawn to that class. The problem with a purely meditative path is that you are left without tools for engaging with the world. I think the beauty of vocation as a primary spiritual path is that it includes contemplation, but also connects us to the world.

MATTHEW FOX: Right, and to history as well, and the linear world. You're bringing the two together, the cyclical and the linear, the mythical and the practical. Everson talks of linear time as "the world of cause-and-effect," whereas cyclical time is the world "of myth, a world not of cause-and-effect but of concurrence. The eternal return." He sees our culture as having displaced cyclical time in favor of "the power of causation." Intuition happens more in cyclical time, where "there is another world to be known, another world to be realized and to be lived. Simple and pure, it is waiting to be entered."[1] He recognizes that the mystic dwells in cyclical time, and contemplation renders us intuitively sensitive but also very vulnerable. Speaking of the cyclical, he said, "To enter the cyclical world we have to relearn the ancient art of surrender. . . . You surrender to God and you surrender to love, or there is no profound realization. It is the ancient paradox: you have to lose your life in order to gain it."

ADAM BUCKO: The beauty of it is the two interact as a result. This solves the whole problem that many of our spiritual traditions have struggled with for centuries, namely, the relationship between contemplation and action.

MATTHEW FOX: Yes, and this has always been a strong point of the Dominican tradition. Both Bill Everson and I come from the Dominican tradition. Aquinas (who was also Dominican, as was Meister Eckhart) talks about how "sharing the fruits of your contemplation" is more noble than just contemplating. That position was a big deal in his day. The new orders were fighting a constant rearguard battle with respect to the old monastic establishment, which saw action as a lesser path. The idea that you could mix action and contemplation was revolutionary, and was embraced by St. Francis and St. Dominic in the early thirteenth century.

ADAM BUCKO: Before we go any further, could you talk about Bill Everson? I think we both feel that he is a real guide for young people, a real archetype, on this journey into the spirituality of vocation.

MATTHEW FOX: I think Bill was a towering figure in many respects. A Californian and poet from the valley area, he was a conscientious objector during the Second World War and was placed in a camp for the duration of the war. That experience killed his marriage. In the late forties he fell in love with a Roman Catholic woman, who introduced him to Dorothy Day's radical worker-house movement, and he became a Dorothy Day–kind of Catholic. Later he joined the Dominican Order and took up his poetry again, devising an unusual art form of preaching by reading his poetry in many universities around the country wearing his medieval Dominican robes. His poetry is very nature based, and his deepest mentor was Robinson Jeffers, whose sense of passion and wildness in nature and the cosmos (his brother was an astronomer) influenced Everson very deeply. In the late sixties, Everson left the Dominicans to marry, and that is when he moved to the Santa Cruz area and taught his unusual course, which he declared was *lectio divina*, not academic lectures. The experience of his class transfigured many of the thousands of young people who participated in it. He was very keen on the role of shamanism and the wisdom of the ancient ancestors of indigenous cultures. He also declared that Jesus was a great shaman.

I first met him when I was a Dominican student, and he visited us in Dubuque, Iowa. I remember his speaking about the Mississippi river in the deepest way—Dubuque being on the Mississippi—and I said to myself, "This is the first truly contemplative Dominican I have ever met." Later, in his Santa Cruz days, I visited him on several occasions, and he was pleased with my work on Meister Eckhart and on the Cosmic Christ, which gave him language he was looking for. Shortly before he died, he wrote me a beautiful letter about my book *Sheer Joy*, on Thomas Aquinas, and commended me for "seizing Aquinas by scapula and capuche," hauling him "point by point through the fundamental issues of our day," and lifting "him bodily through the paradigm shift into the new millennium." How could I not love a guy like that? He also commended me, since I had just been expelled from the order by Cardinal Ratzinger, for this "highpoint of my vocation"—which also gives you a feel for his understanding of vocation as a verb. We celebrated the hundredth anniversary of his birth in 2012 with events at the University of California at Santa Cruz and at the University of California at Berkeley.

Bill was himself a fine example of one who followed his vocation through various reincarnations in his lifetime—he wore the garb of buckskin and bear-claw necklace when he taught at Santa Cruz representing his vocation as a poet-shaman (à la Whitman), in contrast to his previous garb as a Dominican friar. A fine book by one of his students appeared a couple of years ago called *The Shaman's Call,* which consists of interviews with Bill before he died and his emphasis on the shaman archetype.[2] Interestingly, he was buried in the Dominican cemetery, which was a sweet touch.

ADAM BUCKO: Archbishop Desmond Tutu, a real hero of our times, said in his book *God Has a Dream,* "Just as we are all meant to be contemplatives and to hear the voice of God in our lives, we are all meant to answer God's call to be His partners in transfiguring the world. This calling, this encounter with God, is always to send us into the midst of human suffering."[3] Bernard McGinn, in his commentary on Eckhart, said that in Christianity it's not until Eckhart that action becomes equally important or even more important than contemplation.

MATTHEW FOX: Eckhart is standing on Aquinas's shoulders, and that's the Dominican spirit. In Eckhart's sermon on Mary and Martha, you see a complete turnaround. For centuries before and since, they'd been saying that Jesus teaches that it is better to be the Mary (who sits at his feet to listen) than to be the Martha (who is busy working in the kitchen). The former represents contemplation; the latter, action. But Eckhart says that Martha was more mature, because she can do two things at once, both listen to Jesus and be active. Mary, he teaches, was immature—she could only do one thing at once: contemplate. But to be mature spiritually, you have to be both contemplative and active. And that was just a complete 180-degree turn, that one sermon of his.

ADAM BUCKO: It's a real revolution.

MATTHEW FOX: It's a revolution, absolutely. And, like most revolutions, it wasn't followed through. Today, our traditions still struggle with this.

There is a funny story about Cardinal Newman, who was recently canonized as a saint and who at one point in the nineteenth century considered joining the Dominican order. He was especially attracted to this ideal that combined contemplation and action. So he found a Dominican community in Italy and went to visit them. What were they doing? They were making perfume. After his visit he wrote, "The Dominican ideal—the noblest and now defunct."

ADAM BUCKO: Transforming the world with perfumes!

MATTHEW FOX: Yes, the olfactory meditations.

ADAM BUCKO: When Bill taught his famous class on vocation at the University of California, Santa Cruz, what was his basic methodology for helping people to find their calling?

MATTHEW FOX: Bill Everson's basic methodology was dreams. He taught his students to listen to their dreams, to pay attention to their dreams. Like a vocation, a dream is a call. It's coming from someplace deeper than just our ordinary egos.

ADAM BUCKO: Reaching our vocation always requires us to follow the signs. These signs take us to the center of our being, where the calling can be sensed, the nature of it felt, and the uniqueness of it heard. It is all about leading a guided life, and dreams can be a great help to us in recognizing divine hints. They can help us to see things that aren't directly perceived so easily. I'm thinking of a Sufi teacher, Llewellyn Vaughan-Lee, who often does dreamwork with his students, teaching them to be guided by their dreams. He has a beautiful way of describing the process:

> Our dreams take us into a world of images. Many of these dreams are just "mind dreams" in which our mind reworks and digests the images and impressions of the day. . . . But sometimes our dreams take us into a deeper realm within us, into the sacred dimension of our soul.

They have a quality, a music, a depth of feeling that belong to the sacred part of our self. Such dreams open "a little hidden door in the innermost and most secret recesses of our soul." Listening to these dreams, we can hear the voice of our deeper self. Speaking to us in its own language, a language of images, symbols, and feelings, a dream can guide us through the tortuous maze of our psyche. . . . Through sharing our dreams and listening to those of others we also learn to value the uniqueness of our own path, of our own way of journeying Home.[4]

MATTHEW FOX: Listening to dreams and sharing them is a regular practice in many Native American traditions, and, of course, the Bible is filled with moments of transfiguration that occurred because of dreams, whether Jacob's dream of the ladder stairway or Joseph's dream in the Christian Bible that instructed him to flee to Egypt with his young family. Jeremy Taylor is a marvelous teacher of dreams who taught on my faculty for many years; his special emphasis was on the healing power that all dreams bring us, including healing of societal strife and differences.

My own life has often been affected by dreams—for example, when I was worrying about traveling to Germany to lecture at Pentecost time in 2005, when Cardinal Ratzinger had just become pope. I was considering canceling my lecture tour, because I could not reconcile the "celebration" of Pentecost with the dark days I knew were ahead for the church. I asked for a dream and got one: that Ratzinger was the first German pope in many centuries, and another German theologian, Martin Luther, responded to church corruption in his day by pounding ninety-five theses on the church door in Wittenberg. I got up, wrote out ninety-five of my own theses, and then went to Wittenberg after my Pentecost lectures to pound them there.

It was also in a dream that I received my opening lines after I came out of the fourteen-month silence that was laid on me by Cardinal Ratzinger. I said, "as I was saying fourteen months ago, when I was so rudely interrupted." The audience got the humor; Ratzinger never did.

History has often been affected by dreams. When Francis of Assisi went to visit the pope to ask permission for his new order, he was turned away. But that night the pope had a dream that told him to pay attention to this pauper from Assisi; he called him back the next day and gave him permission. Francis himself had a dream that was pivotal to his vocation. The dream said, "Repair my church." At first, Francis took it literally and set himself to rebuild a dilapidated chapel in his neighborhood, but obviously it was a bigger dream than that, one that spoke eventually to his birthing the Franciscan order to repair the church at large.

Helping homeless young people to find their vocation and then helping them with tools to build their lives around it is a big part of your work at Reciprocity. What is the method that you use to help them find their calling?

ADAM BUCKO: It is a very subtle and gentle process. Speaking about it almost feels sacrilegious in a sense, like I am making it too defined, too noticeable, and too concrete. There's an element of betraying it by naming it, and I want to be respectful of that. The method is very intuitive. It is more of a "spiritual direction" in the Christian sense, with Spirit doing the work and me trying to "get out of the way."

The work usually happens in our meditation room in our Manhattan office. There we have a little ecumenical chapel. When I meet with students, I sit silently and then use questions to bring them into the present moment. Sometimes we start with a brief period of meditation and a silent prayer for guidance. For our first few meetings, we focus on two questions: "What breaks your heart?" and "What makes you truly alive?" We spend about one week on each question.

MATTHEW FOX: Your two questions sound like you are pursuing the role of the Via Negativa and the Via Positiva respectfully in each of their lives. I think they are both profound and practical, and I am not surprised that they achieve deep results.

ADAM BUCKO: The goal is not to answer these questions. The goal is to be present to them with all that we are. In a way we are following the poet Rilke's advice when he counseled the young artist, "be patient toward all that is unsolved in your heart and try to love the questions themselves. Perhaps you will then gradually, without noticing it, live along into the answer."

These questions take us into the reality of heartbreak and aliveness, and there we hold them simultaneously. We make sure that we are holding them with all that we are, with every part of our being. There we just wait faithfully, trusting that if we stay with these questions and what they evoke long enough, something will emerge. We wait for that impulse of truth to come, a movement of insight to arise in the heart, and a direction for our lives to come to the surface.

It is really a contemplative process that directs itself. It feels like a gentle wind blowing across our faces and opening us to awe. These days most of my work with people is based on this. In the past, my work was focused on addressing issues and problems. It was focused on using different therapeutic modalities to help young people go beyond the horrifying realities of their lives. But in the last few years, something new has been emerging. My work has become about prayer.

MATTHEW FOX: I think that is a very important evolution for you and your work and for the kids you work with. I commend you for putting the heart work—your heart work—first. I think that helps to explain the rich fruit your work is bearing with the kids. The reason I define prayer as "a radical response to life" is precisely to include our work as our prayer.

ADAM BUCKO: So that's what happens in this process. I simply sit with people and wait for God's impulse in my heart. When I feel the movement in my heart, I follow it. When I feel it, I say yes to it, and my words and presence become an expression of that. The more I trust it, the more it comes. My therapeutic skills, my ideas, all of them are used in this process. Somehow they are assembled and utilized in a way that I would never think of. When this happens, when I am able to open to it, I feel like it always works, and people always get what they need. It feels like I am also helped through this process, and to be honest, it is not really clear who is helping whom. In many ways, instead of helping them to figure out answers, it feels much more like I become an instrument of a transmission that is taking place. I benefit from that transmission just as much if not more than them. It feels very reciprocal. It feels like prayer.

MATTHEW FOX: It is the Via Creativa in practice—the Spirit takes over the artist at work. Remember what Aquinas said, "The same Spirit that hovered over the waters at the beginning of creation hovers over the mind of the artist at work." You are developing a new art form by combining psychological awareness with deep listening! That is very important, a great gift to be shared.

ADAM BUCKO: We sit together holding heartbreak and aliveness with all that we are. Eventually, one's usual identity, thought patterns, and feelings, and the ways in which one relates to the world begins to crack. The moment it cracks a certain kind of aliveness comes through, a certain kind of creative impulse is felt.

MATTHEW FOX: Meister Eckhart says, "if you want the kernel you must break the shell." Cracking and breakdown often yield breakthrough (the Via Negativa first, the Via Creativa next).

ADAM BUCKO: This aliveness and creative impulse is very powerful, and I can sense it when it arrives. It usually carries a message, a direction. It is important to name it for the person who is experiencing it—simply saying, "This is it. Go into it. Open to it. Say yes to it!" That gives them permission to embrace what life is giving them and where life is leading them.

When this happens, a person simply knows what is required of them. When this happens, everything changes and new life begins. It is a true spiritual birth, and that is what discovering one's calling is. It is like being born again, "being born into color," to use Rumi.

MATTHEW FOX: Bill Everson says vocation is like falling in love—you don't know what it is until you experience it.

ADAM BUCKO: So this is the process . . . and once it happens, the work of embodying those insights in the world begins.

MATTHEW FOX: One time you told me a story about a girl who was holding a flower that bloomed during one of these sessions of spiritual direction. Can you tell that story?

ADAM BUCKO: We were on a retreat with our youth. All of our retreats are lead by my cofounder, Taz. She does really beautiful work with them. I usually assist her and sometimes meet with students on a one-on-one basis between their daily retreat activities of meditation, reflective conversations, nature walks, bodywork, and healing treatments.

This day I was meeting with kids outside a temple surrounded by a pond, flowers, and trees. I sat there praying the Jesus Prayer, and once in a while a youth would come to see me for an hour-long conversation. We started each meeting with a silent meditation and then moved into a conversation. A young girl named Ebony was there. Things had begun to arise for her during the retreat, and she had difficulties expressing them. During our meeting I felt inspired to send her for a walk around the temple and asked her to find three objects that represent what is really in her heart.

She came back after about twenty minutes and brought three objects. I asked her to talk about each of them and why she picked them. One of the objects was a flower that had yet to bud. She told me that she felt like this flower. She felt there was a gift inside of her trying to emerge, but no one knew. Even she forgot it. She said, "I am like this flower. From the outside no one knows that this flower has a potential to be beautiful, to offer fragrance, and bloom unless they look inside. One day I know I will bloom, but I don't seem to be able to get there."

I was struck by how much her life was just like that. There was all of this beauty, potential, and heartfulness, but it was all hidden and guarded by the rigid pain of her past. After talking about it for a while, I told her to take her three objects and go into the temple and meditate for about ten minutes. She went in and meditated while holding her objects in her hands. Afterward, she came running up to me—I wasn't sure what happened, but I noticed that she was radiant with aliveness. "What happened?" I asked. "Look at this flower," she said. "I meditated holding it. During my meditation I felt like something happened within me, and I stopped struggling. When I opened my eyes, I was shocked. The flower had opened and bloomed in my hands."

Witnessing her words and radiant face, I smiled and said that maybe this is a sign that she is ready to release her pain and allow the gift of her life to bloom and be offered to the world. Later on she said that this little flower meditation changed her life.

I am not sure what to make of this flower blooming during her meditation, but I do know that this is exactly what she needed during the retreat. It meant the world to her. It gave her permission to emerge out of hiding and say yes to her deepest sense of aliveness. It gave her permission to trust in God and to share her heart with the world.

MATTHEW FOX: That is a powerful story and a powerful support to the art form of deep listening you are developing. What about your calling?

ADAM BUCKO: As I mentioned before, this work does for me what it does for the young people I work with. It has taken me into my vocation. When I think of my experience of discovering my calling, I realize that vocation is not a fixed thing. I often use the phrase "being in vocation," because following my calling feels more like being in the field, where I'm an expression of something that is arising in me. It has this feeling of being an expression of something that is birthing. So even saying, "hey, I discovered my calling" is not an accurate description. It's more like "I either am in this field or I'm not." And being in this field and being in my vocation requires a constant practice of receptivity, so the call, the inner arising, can be sensed and consented to.

MATTHEW FOX: That's a wonderful way of putting it, being "in vocation" and working "from" that place. I think Bill would say your vocation discovers you; it carries you along. It's like a big wave. It's like love, which "until it is awakened in you, you don't know what it is." The British scientist Rupert Sheldrake talks today about how the word *field* may be today's parlance for the word *soul,* which has lost so much of its meaning of late. Your talk about vocation being "in this field" resonates well with his insight.

I think it is also important to acknowledge, as you say, that vocation is not a fixed thing. It is always evolving. Vocation is a verb. When I look at my life and my vocation, originally I thought my vocation was to be a Dominican priest and preacher in the Catholic Church. And then, in trying to be that, the whole thing exploded, and what can I say? I was exploded out of the Catholic Church, but I'm still responding to the same call, it's still the same vocation, it's still the same wave that I'm on. I am doing it in a much larger field, however, than the narrow boundaries of contemporary Catholicism allow.

ADAM BUCKO: Bill says that each generation has a new dream, and that our dreams, our vocations, affect and transform the world. The cyclical can affect the linear; growth is spiral in shape. I feel that that is what happened in your life. Your dream exploded you out of the church to create new models for spiritual living.

That is the beauty of vocation as a primary spiritual path. It is transformative and life changing, both to the person answering the call and to the world around them. In addition, vocation as a primary spiritual path resolves the question of contemplation versus action, which our traditions struggle with. Vocation tends to reconcile the varying aspects of contemplation and action, resulting in a life that is embodied, well integrated, and connected to the world. Vocation always involves creativity and the use of one's unique gifts in service of compassion and justice. It enriches life. This is a path that could really contribute a lot of good to the world and avoid some of the damage that our traditions have done in the past.

Before we go further into it, however, let's talk about two things: It seems to me that most people arrive at this inner creative impulse in their hearts, what we think of as "our calling," through both falling in love, the so-called Via Positiva, and through emptying and suffering, or the Via Negativa. I was wondering if you could talk about the Via Positiva and Via Negativa in the process of finding one's calling?

MATTHEW FOX: In many respects I would classify vocation as the Via Creativa, it is a creative call that we respond to creatively and generously and, as you say, it is always evolving and often surprising us by the directions it takes us. I love what Joseph Campbell says: "None of us lives the life we had intended." That has certainly been my experience—I thought I was going to be a Dominican preacher until death. I am still a preacher (mostly as a lecturer), and I surely draw on my Dominican tradition daily (and great spirits from that tradition), but I have moved out of the literal mold, or as I said above, I've been exploded out of it. Evolution happens.

So while our vocations are eminently creative, as is our response to them, the Via Positiva and Via Negativa are stepping stones to the Via Creativa. So your question to explore both in light of vocation makes a lot of sense. Often when I meet a scientist and we talk a bit, I ask them, When did you first know you wanted to be a scientist? They usually scratch their heads, pause, become pensive, and say, "I fell in love with a bush when I was six years old." Or "I fell in love with a worm when I was five years old" or "I fell in love with a star when I was six years old." Look what they are saying—their whole life and work and voca-tion derive from a falling-in-love experience! From the Via Positiva.

Of course, the Via Negativa plays a big role as well in at least two ways. First, once one commits to following one's vocation, there are obstacles—it might be one's parents (many artists have to struggle in that regard, as parents, often with good intentions, feel art does not guarantee a secure living—which, of course, is often the case). Just to get trained in one's field can be demanding and expensive and slow, a very uphill climb. A vocation is not the same thing as an ego trip or a narcissistic plunge. And that's why it's not superficial—it demands that warrior energy that is often developed from strife, which helps to purify the motive, the intention, and even the developing of the crafts and skills required. Imagine, for example, learning a language—that's work, it's not all fun and games. Learning any discipline takes sweat and blood and tears. And, as you said, it even takes breakdown at times. You went through some breakdowns that resulted in breakthroughs. Lessons of letting go and letting be are deep and often painful. Hearts sometimes get broken in the process.

A second way in which the Via Negativa enters the vocation jour-ney relates to others and to the world. Vocation often derives from the brokenness one sees all around one in the world—this brokenness itself calls one to respond generously, to commit one's life to a calling of healing. Take your example of meeting the homeless child in India and holding her hand—that changed your life forever. She awoke you to your vocation, which you are still playing out in the streets of New York now, with young adults rather than with children. But here too we encounter the Via Negativa in our vocations. It is the prophet Isaiah's call to heal the sick and instruct the ignorant and feed the hungry, a call that inspired Jesus surely to his vocation as well.

Just as there is a special relationship between the Via Positiva and the Via Creativa, so there is a special link between the Via Negativa and the Via Transformativa. A vocation is not a call of the ego—it is a call to serve the greater community.

ADAM BUCKO: In some Native American tribes, when young people were sent on their vision quest, they were not allowed to come back until they knew what their vocation was. It was a way for them to find their unique place in the cosmos. Sometimes they had to stay out for years before coming to a place where they could embrace the truth of their life. Vocation is not a game; it is not easy. It is a serious task that, at times, requires us to risk our lives, to go into the inner abyss, and to trust that there will be something there that will give us life and sustain us.

MATTHEW FOX: It gives us life and sustains us, and it gives our lives meaning.

ADAM BUCKO: One example of this type of courage and surrender is the story of Bisan Toron, an extraordinary experimental world music vocalist whose art bridges voice and soul.[5] She had a very deep impact on my life and work. My understanding of her journey is as follows:

Bisan was trained as a classical singer, and she mastered the technique. However, the classical way didn't really reflect what was awakening in her soul. As a result, she stopped singing for seven years. Yet she had a sense that something was there, longing to be voiced, but she couldn't voice it. She had to undergo the "dark night" of silence. Not being able to sing was very tragic for Bisan. It seemed she had lost her very soul, her very way of expressing herself in the world. During these seven years, she spent much time in contemplative silence, listening to her inner life.

Amazingly enough, a series of creatures, images, archetypes, and sounds began to come to her. She felt that she was being asked to paint them with her voice. Through listening and then embracing what was arising in her, something happened. She began to feel this spirit emerging in her and starting to work through her. That's how she developed her music and what her music is now. When she performs now, she searches with her voice for that place where her soul and God meet, and then brings that place down and offers it to her listeners. It is an extraordinary experience, and her music has a tremendous effect on people. Every time I see her perform, I feel like I am being transported to the holy city of Varanasi, where ancient saints like Mirabai and Kabir are still mysteriously present.

And that's what happens when one takes the time, undergoes the pain, and says yes to this love that is our vocation. It always has a transforming effect on people. It creates a certain kind of electricity and presence that changes us and allows us to offer our lives as a prayer to the world.

Bisan's story is a story of deep silence, of initially not being able to give voice to life, so that eventually life could have a voice of its own, so that her soul could have a voice, so that God's silence could have a voice.

MATTHEW FOX: That is a beautiful and powerful story about the role that letting go and the Via Negativa plays in our vocation. Notice how she first went through formal training and then let it all go, but no doubt she is also incorporating it into this larger field that is her vocation, a field that embraces the spiritual (which is so often missing in our music conservatories and art institutes, which are so often dedicated more to technique and commerce than to spirit and vocation and service).

ADAM BUCKO: Sam Keen said that "a society in which vocation and job are separated for most people gradually creates an economy that is often devoid of spirit, one that frequently fills our pocketbooks at the cost of emptying our souls."[6] It is for this reason, I believe, that Bill Everson said that having a vocation doesn't mean that you have a profession. We live in a world that often requires us to sacrifice our calling just to be able to make a living. So in today's world, having a vocation is not the same as having a career!

MATTHEW FOX: That's so important, yes. And it's so important to make that distinction in our culture, as you say, at this time. Also, since so many careers are just dying on the vine anyway, it's not as if a university or anyone else can promise a career anymore. There are all kinds of lawyers who are unemployed, for example, all kinds of professionals who can't get work in their field.

ADAM BUCKO: What I like about you, as an elder, is that when you speak to the youth, you don't hesitate to tell them, "Well, if you don't like the world you live in, it doesn't mean that you have to be stuck in it. Create your own." This helps young people to trust the intuitions that they might have, both for their lives and for the lives of their communities.

MATTHEW FOX: The first time I lectured in Ireland—I guess it must have been about twenty years ago—Ireland was in an unemployment crisis. It was before the dot-coms set up shop in Ireland, and there was a lot of unemployment, especially among the young, many of whom were emigrating, leaving Ireland. I spoke at a college, and I said to the college youth, "Look, if you don't feel part of this culture, because you can't get work here, then go start your own culture. And that's what the Celtic monastic tradition was about, monasticism was really about an alternative culture." In an alternative culture, you create your own food, your own relationships, your own values, your own economy. The Desert Fathers were originally young men who fled the dominant culture, when Christianity married the Roman Empire, because they didn't want to go around killing people in the name of Jesus and an empire.

It turned out that there was a nineteen-year-old in the audience who took me up on my challenge. Two years later, when I visited Ireland, I learned that he had started a monastery, so I went up to visit it. He had acquired some abandoned property, an old fort up on the ocean in Northern Ireland, right on the water. He had gathered there a number of participants ranging in age from their twenties to their fifties, Protestant and Catholic—and this was when there was still the Protestant-Catholic struggles going on in Northern Ireland—so that alone was a miracle. The community included married people, unmarried, single, gay, and straight; children; dogs goats, and sheep; a lot of plants; music—all of it going on. They were doing exactly what I talked about—they created their own culture, including their own entertainment.

I suspect in America today, given the bad economy, especially for young people, there will be more and more need for communities like the one I am describing.

But again, the key is that we're not stuck. If you honor your powers of creativity, that's the way out of stuckness and the way to living new and deeper values than the culture might be offering.

ADAM BUCKO: This is where elders like you come in. Elders who can be trusted companions on this journey and can encourage young people to take the next step.

Elders are needed to help create a world based on new values. A world in which vocation and life don't have to be separated from a job, and in which, as Dorothy Day used to say, "it is easier to be good and just." A world that can reflect Satish Kumar's translation of an ancient Hindu saying, *So Hum*, "You are, therefore I am."

This takes us beyond individualistic dictums and into an emergent worldview in which what matters is the collective community, but which also says we all have our unique part to play. It properly situates our individuality and all the gifts that it brings, not by diminishing it, but actually accentuating it toward the well-being of others. This is always a creative process, a dance really. Speaking of creativity and its role in birthing a world that works for all, bell hooks said that "the function of art is to do more than tell it like it is—it's to imagine what is possible." As we mentioned before, finding one's calling is always connected to creativity. Personally, I am convinced that finding one's vocation always results in a marriage of creativity and prophetic work. Can you speak more about the relationship between finding one's calling and creativity and prophetic work?

MATTHEW FOX: As I said above, the deep journey that vocation entails necessarily incorporates all four paths of the spiritual journey, and the Via Creativa and Via Transformativa naturally and organically spring forth. But remember too that part of the Via Creativa is the role of wildness. Adventure matters. Generosity matters. Thomas Berry calls wildness the source of our creativity in a wonderful passage that I cite in my book on creativity. He says, "Wildness we might consider as the root of the authentic spontaneities of any being. It is that wellspring of creativity whence comes the instinctive activities that enable all living beings to obtain their food, to find shelter, to bring forth their young: to sing and dance and fly through the air and swim through the depths of the sea. This is the same inner tendency that evokes the insight of the poet, the skill of the artist and the power of the shaman."[7] Without wildness we have no creativity. No species does.

Dr. Clarissa Pinkola Estés, in her brilliant book *Women Who Run with the Wolves*, develops at length the archetype of the wild woman, and she too connects wildness to creativity when she says the wild woman is "patroness to all painters, writers, sculptors, dancers, thinkers, prayermakers, seekers, finders—for they are all busy with the work of invention, and that is the wild woman's main occupation. As in all art, she resides in the guts, not in the head. . . . She is the one who thunders after injustice."[8] Estés calls us to "practice our Wild Woman." Notice how she too links the Via Creativa to the Via Transformativa (art to justice). All the prophets—including Jesus—were in touch with their wildness.

Clearly, if we're talking about the importance of creativity for vocation, then we have to bring in wildness. Where is the room for wildness in education, in religion, in media, and so forth today? Everything gets anthropocentrized. Even God loses its wildness; God gets tamed.

ADAM BUCKO: You can't be prophetic without being wild. It doesn't mean that you have to scream and shout. It just means that you are making a statement with your life that . . .

MATTHEW FOX: That doesn't have an insurance policy.

ADAM BUCKO: That doesn't have an insurance policy, exactly! So there's this wildness, but I think courage is also required. If I'm given a new dream, if you're given a new dream, that means that no one else has lived that dream in the way that we are called to live that dream. And that's really scary.

MATTHEW FOX: But it's scary in the sense that awe is scary—it's exciting, it keeps you on the edge, it keeps you alive, it keeps you alert and alive. It invites you to adventure. Isn't every vocation an adventure? And that's part of the warrior thing.

ADAM BUCKO: But I think that you can only experience the excitement component after you've done some inner work.

MATTHEW FOX: Well, that's right—you also need to find allies, find support groups.

ADAM BUCKO: Find support groups and have practices that can help you to cultivate courage, so you can fully receive the truth of your life and so you can incarnate that truth in the world.

Is it possible to say yes to your vocation without having a practice that can help you do that? Is it possible to say yes to your vocation without having a community?

MATTHEW FOX: I would say it's not possible to sustain the vocation without it. So part of vocation is to go hunting, to become a hunter-gatherer, to find whom your allies are. Some of them may have been dead for hundreds of years—maybe a Rilke or a Rumi or Meister Eckhart or Hildegard or Dorothy Day or Jesus or someone like that.

ADAM BUCKO: Well, certainly Meister Eckhart was your ally.

MATTHEW FOX: That's right. I always said that when I got in trouble with the Vatican I got more support from dead Dominicans than live ones—or supposedly live ones, is how I used to put it.

ADAM BUCKO: So you have to become a hunter-gatherer.

MATTHEW FOX: You have to become a hunter-gatherer, yes. And we all have that in us. Our species, for 90 percent of its existence, was hunting and gathering, so don't sit around feeling sorry for yourself. Go hunt and gather. This imperative is part of the healthy masculine, the Sacred Masculine, that is so often lacking in our patriarchal cultures, which overidentify masculinity with war and with winning and being on top. I develop this archetype and nine others in my book *The Hidden Spirituality of Men*. These masculine archetypes are not just for men but for women also (just as the goddess is for men as well as women). They are essential for overcoming fear and putting one's vocation into practice.

Hunting and gathering is also about finding a lineage that will support you and then finding allies. Especially at a time like this, when young people are feeling—and appropriately so—a "spirituality deficit" as far as a healthy planet, healthy jobs, healthy education, and healthy religion. But they can band with each other, become a tribe and a community of support for one another, in their wild vocations. Solidarity Matters.

ADAM BUCKO: It's what we say to our street youth who come to us, especially gay kids who have been abused by their families. Sometimes they feel really broken, because their parents are not really there to support them or even to know them. Not having that acknowledgment from the key figures in their lives sometimes prevents them from wanting to have a life. So, we often encourage them to create their own families and to find a new mother or father, people who will acknowledge and value them.

MATTHEW FOX: And does that happen?

ADAM BUCKO: It happens and it works. In a time when the institutions that are supposed to be there for us are falling apart, when the church—the mother—is no longer there to nourish and support our journey, it is time to create new families, to find new mothers, and to start new institutions.

Going back to the question of vocation, if vocation is a call, who's doing the calling?

MATTHEW FOX: Certainly—and we can all agree on this, whether we are atheists, theists, panentheists—the future is doing the calling. The unborn children, our great-great-grandchildren are doing the calling. A mere seventy-five years from now they're going to be saying, "What did you do, Daddy, when the Earth was collapsing and when militarism was where you were putting so much of your money, and when empires were still the mode of the day, and when religions were at each other's throats and Christianity was collapsing? What did you do? How did you interfere and say no?" So I think we could all agree that the call is from the future.

Now, the call is also—and Bill Everson would emphasize this—from the collective, from the species. He calls it a *race*, but I think *species* has a little more palatable tone. But it's not just our species, it's the other species that are calling today too, and I think more and more people are waking up to this.

ADAM BUCKO: It's the whole creation.

MATTHEW FOX: All of creation is calling, yes. And the ancestors—I mean, they care. They went through a lot to get us here and nourish us and do it the best they could. So the ancestors are calling. I like that image from the Middle East, where they see history as a caravan—a train of camels. The ancestors aren't the caboose. They're actually the engine;

they're out front, calling us and pulling us. That's a very different way of looking at history. Ancestors are not of the past—they, too, are of the future. I think that's beautiful. So the people we honor—like Martin Luther King or Jesus or Buddha—they're calling.

ADAM BUCKO: All of them are calling. And then God is also calling!

MATTHEW FOX: We can adapt Aquinas's words that I cited earlier by saying Spirit "hovers over the mind and heart of the young person seeking his or her vocation." So that hovering, that stirring of creativity, the creative life of a person, of a young adult, that's God calling. That's the Holy Spirit. Hildegard of Bingen says that "the Holy Spirit awakens everything that is." The Holy Spirit is the Awakener. The Holy Spirit calls us to our vocation and keeps us on track. That is why vocation is a verb and not a noun—it is never finished and never boring. When you are in your "vocation zone" or "vocation field," as you talked of, you are constantly being awakened. It is never finished; it only changes its clothes from time to time, and its address.

That wonderful passage in the Hebrew scriptures from Jeremiah, that "I have called you from womb—from the womb I called you." A very parallel thing. That text in many ways might be a classic text for vocation. It suggests that the universe had a purpose in bringing us forth, through over 13.8 billions years of labor pains. Every one has a purpose and therefore a calling.

A theology of the Cosmic Christ is talking about the Word and the prophetic call—the Word of creation and the Word of vocation. Both are *logos*, and in the Christian tradition that's the Christ, it's *logos*, the Word behind the words. I would think Buddhists too would talk about a call from the Buddha nature to the Buddha nature so that we live lives of right livelihood and of responsibility and balance.

ADAM BUCKO: This calling . . . it is a very intimate thing.

MATTHEW FOX: Intimate, yes. So let's talk about that, the intimacy of voca-tion. One thing that comes to mind is the uniqueness of one's vocation. Bill Everson has this in his book—he emphasizes how there's never been another you. Of course, that's good science: in fourteen billion years there has never been another you. Or, in theological terms, there's never been another Christ or Buddha like you. And so, becoming that Christ—now this is turning more theological again, but I think Chris-tians have to hear this, and maybe some non-Christians too. This is Eckhart too: that we're all the Christ doesn't mean we're all the same. It means we are unique and we have a unique expression of the Christ work and Christ awareness and Christ person. And so we're all sons and daughters of God, but in our ways, in our different ways, and we have different work to do on the Earth, different vocations.

ADAM BUCKO: I remember the time you said that in the end there is really only one vocation.

MATTHEW FOX: There is really only one vocation: that's to be mystic-prophets, to be lovers and defenders of what we cherish. What form it takes, how it is incarnated in history and culture, of course, will vary. However, we really do all have a common vocation. If we could begin to think like that, whether we're Muslim or Jewish or Native American or Buddhist or Hindu or Christian or atheist, it would create an incred-ible bedrock of commonality for service to community. You know, I've always been struck by the word *community* itself. It's really based on the words *cum munio*, "to do work together." Maybe it really means to do vocation together—to gather our vocations. Again, that's what worship should be. Worship should be the gathering together of the wonder and joy and pain and suffering we encounter while attempting to live out our common—though unique—vocations.

ADAM BUCKO: Absolutely! I like what you are saying here. For me, when I think of our work with youth, there's this element of coming together and witnessing what is emerging in each other; a way of being present with each other that encourages and supports what is being born in everyone. The community is about doing vocation together. If vocation is really both mystical and prophetic, which we said it is, then doing vocation in community is a way to give birth to a healthy world.

MATTHEW FOX: Yes, it's a way to living fully in the service of compassion and justice.

I would like to conclude with a quote from Bill Everson. This is something to reflect on: "In some way, the whole mastery of your vocation is a mastery of the mystery of death. It is an approach to that mystery, because in death all our purposes are subsumed into another dimension; we achieve in death what we opted for in life. From one point of view you might say that vocation, in teaching us how to expend ourselves, teaches us how to die."

6
Spiritual Practice

Touch Life and Be Changed by It

I feel that anything that makes us feel more alive and more connected is essentially a spiritual practice . . . whether that is swimming in the sea, running in the woods, surrendering to laughter, or experiencing moments of deep intimacy and connection with another individual.

K.R., Female, 28

"Work is love made visible." So if we really love our work and we're really pouring ourselves into it, that in itself can be a spiritual practice. So there's an emphasis on spirituality being an everyday component of our life.

P.P., Male, 28

Love making is very much a spiritual experience for me. It is a holy time.

N.B., Male, 33

My strongest sense of the divine is definitely in nature. . . . Probably the greatest spiritual practices that I resonate with are, I'd say, four things: Hiking—just being in the elements is very spiritual for me, and just realizing my context within the world and what provides for me. Dancing is another place of getting out of the mind and really being free to connect with other elements. My work is definitely a spiritual practice for me—not one that I preach, not one that I would ever define as such formally, but it is. Just the creative process in general is very spiritual. And there is a fourth one . . . Meditation, which I'm not very good at, but I do try to practice at least a few minutes a day, when I wake up and go to sleep.

C.K., Female, 32

It's really easy to have a yoga practice that can be a place to get away from the world, but yoga for me also—as an entire system, not just, of course, as the physical practice—really gives me a place to come back into the world and have a practice within every step of my day.

A.N., Female, 22

Doing massage, sometimes, I feel a certain connectedness.

S.O., Male, 34

I find that I struggle with keeping disciplined to only one kind of practice, a sign of my ADD generation, (lol).

K.R., Female, 28

Centering prayer and metta meditation are two of my daily meditations.

N.B., Male, 33

I do experience love making as a spiritual experience. I have practiced alternate breathing before and during sex which has transformed the experience to the point where the universe was breathing through us and all boundaries melted away. This was one of the most spiritual experiences of my life.

S.W., Male, 28

You might call my experience while running meditation because it is the most common way that I interact with Being (in the ontological, Heideggerian sense). I see the poetic nature of the world.

Anonymous

My biggest spiritual practice is acting (I am a professional theater actor). Acting is my primary spiritual practice, and as such, it is my main way I find myself in others, others in me, God in me, and me in God.

N.B., Male, 33

Working with the poor, working with the homeless, working on the margins was really where I was encountering God, where I was having a sacred experience. I had that sort of paradoxical experience that I was meeting God in the broken and desolate places. . . .

J.M., Female, 35

I do love to dance, but I don't know if one considers that a "spiritual practice." It does sometimes feel like you are in a trance, feeling the music through your body, forgetting everything else, moving with the beat . . . and the next day usually is when I feel that "connectedness" especially if I am so very tired . . . my mind just numbs out . . . you're so relaxed . . . just sit and see the world "play" itself out.

Anonymous

I view my sexual energy as being part of the life force that has created me and moves through me. I'm inspired by Brian Swimme's expression of sexuality as the universe's own deepest allurement and the urge to merge built into our being. It is linked to my ability and desire to connect deeply with the feminine energies that make me feel whole and complete. This activity can take on many forms such as deeply receiving the flow of nature or feeling the deep expressive moan of a cello. Sexual activity is a deeply sensitive act in which it is important to be conscious

and aware of the emotional and physical consequences. Holistic sexu-
ality is about exploring deeply and honestly my own relationship to
the pull of attraction within me, softening it and opening to the space
around it. At times it has been more fulfilling for me to give all of the
energy and passion and desire for sexual activity back to the divine.

S.W., Male, 28

I have no altar but I have prayer beads, a prayer rug, books of prayers
and scriptures, but I don't always use these things. Fasting during
Ramadan means a lot to me because it teaches me to rely on God. Just
sitting and meditating makes me feel very at peace and close to God. I
do a kind of centering prayer. I try to sit and let thoughts/feelings go
by. If I start thinking too much, I remind myself that for this time God
is taking care of everything and I don't have to worry. I am usually a
very anxious person, and I can feel my whole body relax when I do this.

K.C., Female, 28

I have created several altars. I collected pictures of my ancestors and
made an altar out of that. I also have collection of special items—like
rocks, seashells, and stuff like that. I give myself self-massage in my
room. This means a lot to me. Coming into my body and my sensual-
ity. I practice yoga and gentle movements on my own in my room. I
have a bunch of movement tools I experiment with and make up my
own stuff with. This practice helps facilitate the flow of my emotions.
On my own, I freely express my emotions. I was taught to hold in my
emotions when I was younger (which contributed to the anorexia), so
this is a challenging practice for me.

L.Y., Female, 22

In order to really allow the spirit to emerge, you need to fast sometimes,
just like Jesus fasted. There's a secret that comes from that, that you
only get by going through the experience of fasting. You need to pray
sometimes. You need to know what it feels like to put your head on the

ground and submit to your Lord, and to leave the whole world behind you, whether it's five minutes, seven minutes, or an hour, however long you pray—to take a time-out from your day to say, "I'm just going to turn to God and talk with him, and have a relationship with him."

J.S., Male, 31

One of the goals, of course, of meditation is to get to stillness. That's the value of stillness, to try to create space, or to realize that there's space there already. One of the things that living in a place like New York, as busy as it is, is that space is always at a premium. . . . Stillness is also the place, with a lot of traditions, where they say that the Divine resides. That God is in all things, of course, but at the same time to experience God, to experience the Divine you need to go into stillness.

K.K., Male, 32

We must spend a couple of hours each day in receptive silence—any silent spiritual practice that brings awareness and equanimity to our hearts and minds—and put the inner revolution and the outer revolution together. . . . Sometimes the most radical thing to do in a polluted violence-based system, is to be still. The mud settles to the bottom and we then have a clearer vision about our next steps—for example, facilitating the growth of the communities we want to live in or realizing that the most efficient tools against a system based on greed, fear, hurry, and violence, are generosity, courage, slowing-down, and loving-kindness.

Pancho Ramos-Stierle, 26 [1]

ADAM BUCKO: Andrew Harvey, in his book *The Hope: The Guide to Sacred Activism*, quotes Jungian analyst Marion Woodman, who once said to him that "continuing to do pioneering sacred work in the world as crazy and painful as ours without constantly grounding yourself in sacred practice would be like running into a forest fire dressed only in a paper tutu."[2]

So, if we are really serious about being authentic and living our lives in service of compassion and justice, if we are really serious about what Woodman calls "sacred work," we need to get serious about spiritual practice.

MATTHEW FOX: What practices do you find helpful in your life?

ADAM BUCKO: I was socialized into a spiritual system that taught that meditation is all that is needed in one's spiritual journey. It was common for my teachers to say, "Just meditate and all will be taken care of." I no longer subscribe to that kind of a theology of inner life. In my experience, it is only when I've included practices other than meditation that I've been able to experience real breakthroughs. One practice that was extremely important to my development was psychotherapy. It really changed my life and convinced me that in order to make real progress on a spiritual journey, a more integrated toolbox of practices is needed to help us address and develop all the dimensions of who we are. Ken Wilber's *Integral Spirituality* was extremely helpful. It helped me to understand the complexity of our self-system and its multiple intelligences, our capacities, and what it takes to have a spiritual practice that can actually engage and transform all dimensions of our being.

MATTHEW FOX: What did you find most helpful in Andrew Harvey's book that you referred to earlier?

ADAM BUCKO: You mentioned that we can no longer afford to hide our contemplatives in comfortable monasteries and that we need to reunite contemplation and action and mysticism and prophesy. In the book that I mentioned, Andrew Harvey shares something that I think is really instrumental. He talks about five kinds of spiritual practice that one needs in order to become a well-integrated and wisdom-driven healing presence in the world:

- "Cool practices" are things like simple meditation, walking meditation, and saying the name of God peacefully in the heart as a way of staying grounded and clear sighted in transcendent peace in the middle of the storms of our world.
- "Warm practices," such as Sufi heart practices, Hinayana Buddhist practices of loving-kindness to all beings, and passionate kirtan and devotional chanting as measures to keep the heart open and pulsing with fire energies of compassion for the world.
- "Sacred body practices," such as yoga, *t'ai chi*, and *qi gong*, to help us sustain the intensity of service required of us in order to truly incarnate and embody the truth of our calling.
- "Prayer practices" to help us rely on God for guidance and life-giving energy and to enable us to face our betrayals and defeats with unconditional trust and courage.
- "Shadow practice" or psychotherapy to help us see and deal with all the unconscious, repressed, undeveloped, and denied parts of ourselves that we tend to externalize and project onto others. It helps us reconcile all of our own inner conflicts, thus avoiding reactive behavior and, instead, acting with wisdom and integrity.

MATTHEW FOX: This is a helpful listing of ways and categories of practice. It is important to recognize how diverse our needs are and how diverse our various traditions are in assisting us with those needs. An example I like to use is how the Buddha lived a full life and died serenely at about eighty-four years of age, but Jesus got himself killed at about the age of thirty. To me, this instructs us all that we need, on the one hand, the serenity of the Buddha, but also the moral outrage of Jesus. This is one of the gifts of East and West coming together in our time; a healthy person and a healthy culture (and healthy religion, too) need the dance and dialectic between holy patience and holy impatience.

At the same time, we don't want to get literal about the differences between East and West. After all, over forty Buddhists lit themselves on fire the past few years to protest injustice in Tibet, and Jesus often retreated into the wilderness for contemplation and refreshment. The prophet is the mystic in action, as William Hocking put it. An integrated and solid toolbox of practice undertaken with a healthy theology can lead to such a sacred marriage of action and contemplation.

What does your spiritual life look like in practical terms?

ADAM BUCKO: I have several practices that guide me. These practices are my lifeline. They help me touch the state of "receptivity and listening." They help me be in the presence of God and say yes to God's guiding impulse in my heart. I don't do all of these practices all the time. When I'm on a silent retreat, for example, I might focus on one particular practice. Other times I might mix my practices, depending on the needs of the day. I also sometimes follow Thomas Merton's advice; he apparently said, "I don't pray on my days off." Taking a short break from practicing at times might be a very healthy way of resting in natural openness to God and thus deepening one's spiritual life. So, here are some of my favorite practices. All of them have helped me so much.

The first practice that is really important to me is Conversational Prayer. Brother Lawrence, a seventeenth-century Carmelite monk, encouraged people to simply talk to God every day as they go through the tasks of their day. The Hasidic master Rebbe Nachman of Breslov said, "Talk to God as you would talk to your very best friend. Tell The Holy One everything." And, so I follow their advice. I try to begin my meditations with a conversation with God. I try to open every single corner of my heart and life to God. I try to invite God in, so all can be seen, acknowledged, and related to this all-accepting and reassuring presence that I feel as a result. I speak of my joys, my struggles, and at times of special difficulties I just sit there and cry until there are no more tears to shed. Sometimes I also invite some of the saints that I feel close to. I talk to them, I cry with them, and I rejoice with them. This practice usually leads to a receptive silence in which I can simply say yes to God and what may be, where I can let go of my ideas about what's right and simply surrender to God's will.

My second practice is a practice of silent meditation or contemplative prayer. The method that I practice is inspired by Centering Prayer. This prayer, as Fr. Thomas Keating puts it, is "a very simple method in which one opens one's self to God and consents to his presence in us and to his actions within us." This practice has been really life changing for me. It helps me to sit in silence in the presence of God so the "Divine Therapist" can do the work of healing and renewal on me. This practice usually fills me with a great deal of trust. It helps me to bear witness to and to respond to all the tragedies that I see daily in the lives of the homeless kids that I work with.

One of the practices that I love the most is the Prayer of the Name. My early mentor Sr. Vandana Mataji, who had a small hermitage at the foothills of the Himalayas and who was both a Catholic Nun and Hindu Sanyasini, emphasized the role of this prayer as a spiritual bridge between religions. This prayer is truly universal and, with some variations, it is practiced by Sufis, Hindus, Buddhists, and Christians.

I love the words of a Sufi mystic al-Ghazali, who said, "Dear Friend, Your heart is a polished mirror. You must wipe it clean of the veil of dust that has gathered upon it, because it is destined to reflect the light of divine secrets." This practice really helps me to clean the dust of my heart and live in the "remembrance" of God. Another Sufi said, "It is said that remembrance of God begins with the repetition of God's Names by the tongue. Then, the repetition of the tongue descends and becomes the remembrance of the heart. Finally, the remembrance of the heart deepens and becomes the remembrance of the soul. At first, you chant the Divine Names, then they chant themselves, and then God chants through you."[3] So I aspire to live in the presence of God every day by carrying my prayer beads with me and repeating the name of God. I do it whenever I walk around the city, when I am on the subway, or when I am doing something that does not require my full concentration. This is one of my favorite practices, and I have been practicing it since I was nineteen years old. At times, I also combine this practice with a conversational prayer. I simply love this practice. What a beautiful and simple way to touch God.

Lectio divina is another practice that I incorporate into my life. It is an ancient practice that was first established as a monastic practice in the sixth century by St. Benedict. *Lectio* is a prayerful way of reading a sacred text for inspiration, not information. I often carry with me short sacred passages that I like to revisit. I approach them with my heart and I try to be present to them with all of my being. In the process, I often feel like the "soul" of the text touches my deepest core and opens my whole life to God.

Sacred Body Practices, while very challenging for me personally, are also a part of my spiritual life. I find things like yoga, A.I.M., Thai yoga massage, and hiking extremely useful. These practices open and strengthen my body, reintegrating it, making it possible for the Presence that I experience during my contemplative prayer to truly descend into my body. Lately I have been blessed to work with a seventy-one-year-old friend and mentor, Anthony Macagnone, who after spending the last forty years studying yoga, martial arts, and other mind-body systems, developed A.I.M. (Alchemy in Movement), which is a truly life-changing method of working with the body.

Spirituality is a whole-person enterprise, and as such, I would like to again mention the importance of psychotherapy and shadow work. In my view, contemplative practice needs to be supplemented by psychotherapy. Many practitioners are victims to what John Welwood calls "spiritual bypass," in which we use spiritual ideas and practices to avoid facing unresolved emotional issues, psychological wounds, and unfinished developmental tasks.[4] Speaking of this need for an integration of good psychology with contemplative practice, Welwood says that "we need a larger perspective that can recognize and include two different tracks of human development—which we might call growing up and waking up, healing and awakening, or becoming a genuine human person and going beyond the person altogether." Stressing the importance of this, he concluded that "we are not just humans learning to become buddhas, but also buddhas waking up in human form, learning to become fully human. And these two tracks of development can mutually enrich each other." In my life, psychotherapy is one of the biggest gifts that I have ever received. It has completely enriched and transformed my journey into Life and into God.

Finally, the last practice that I would like to mention is a practice of spiritual friendship. Brother Wayne Teasdale, in his book *A Monk in the World,* quotes a well-known story about the Buddha and his student Ananda, who once asked the Buddha about the importance of spiritual friendship. "Master, is spiritual friendship half of the spiritual life?" he asked. The Buddha replied, "No, Ananda, friendship is the whole of the spiritual life." So I find that spiritual friendships create a container and make our spiritual lives possible.

My friends inspire me when they share the gift of their presence and authenticity with me. They help me stay committed to my path and remind me why I am here in times of doubt and resignation. They speak truth about my life to me, when I try to avoid it. By doing so with love and acceptance, they help me look into difficult areas of my life and to have courage to work on them. Finally, they share my joys and my sorrows with me. This creates a tremendous energy of gratitude and celebration.

MATTHEW FOX: Do you consider your work to be your practice?

ADAM BUCKO: Yes, in fact, I consider my work to be my primary prayer. My work is an expression of my vocation. It is my way of touching

God and becoming an expression of what happens when I do that. All of those other practices that I just mentioned are there to help me be in my vocation and then to have the courage to live my vocation in the world—So my life can be an expression of God's presence and action in the world. In this way, my work can be my prayer, or to use Khalil Gibran's words, so my work can be "love made visible."

Matt, how about you? I feel like my practices are fairly traditional. Most of them have a monastic foundation and have been practiced in monasteries for centuries. In our friendship, my observation has been that your practices have been very creative and centered on life and creation. I would love to ask you about some specific practices that I observe in your life.

MATTHEW FOX: Well, first of all, I enjoyed learning from you there—the elements of your journey that you describe with candor and sensitivity and depth. Of course, my training as a Dominican was very formative for me, we had a structure that worked for me insofar as it combined— quite healthily, I believe—elements of *lectio divina,* of several hours of meditation and chanting and mantra chanting (i.e., the rosary) and worship (daily Mass), as well as deeply moving, aesthetic Gregorian Chant experiences especially on big feast days, along with community living, study, sports, spiritual friendship. I swam in that ocean of grace for a number of years.

I also spent several months in a primitive living situation in a colony of hermits on Vancouver Island, and that experience of deep solitude and silence gave me energy for years to come. Eventually I had to translate that into living alone in a large city like Paris, as well as on a farm in southern France for six months as I wrote my doctoral thesis. But silence and being in nature has always kept me grounded and supple. Even now, just walking in the woods or especially near water is a regular practice of mine, good for the body and good for the soul. During the years I was at Holy Names College and undergoing lots of attacks from the Vatican, my dog (who was my spiritual director) and I would walk in the wonderful redwood forests above the campus. Redwood trees absorb pain wonderfully.

I am glad that you mentioned psychology; I think that is an important contribution of our culture to spirituality. When I look back, when I was younger, I too had some psychological teachers who were important to me and who introduced me to studying many psychologists, so that eventually I was useful in helping others along their journey by employing some avenues for self-understanding. So psychology has been part of my path. Even recently I meet a couple times a month with a friend who's a Reichian and Jungian, a very wise old man who is also an Episcopal priest. We talk about a lot of things, and mostly what's going on in my life and in my work. He's been very helpful. It's very valuable to have a third party—someone who has objectivity and some wisdom—to bounce things off of.

But I've also found psychologists who have helped me, especially Otto Rank, who just blows my mind every time I read him, because he's just so much in tune to where I am in terms of the role of creativity and spirituality. To me, he has this profound, prophetic psychology. He is Jewish and he's conscious of the social dimension of psychology, not just the psyche. He actually says that *unio mystica* is the goal of life— mystical union. Again, I find him so compatible with my search that I continually go back to him. He died in 1939—thank God he wrote!

Rank talks about humans all being born with an "original wound" (as distinct from an "original sin"), and if Rank is right, then we see a powerful link between the very meaning of redemption and the work of the shaman. Rank also perceptively identifies our "original wound" as the separation from the womb that we all undergo, and that wound is triggered again whenever other profound separations touch us. He prescribes the medicine for this original wound as the *unio mystica*, the mystical union that love and art restore. So creativity is at the heart of my spiritual practice as well, and this is how I developed my pedagogy for spiritual education over thirty years and found such amazing results with our students—"art as meditation," we call it. It should not be underestimated as a spiritual practice. It leads directly to prophecy or social action, because every prophet worked in depth with issues of *moral imagination.*

Jung also has much to offer, and some of my best friends are Jungians. I was privileged to meet Rollo May on a number of occasions, and I love the work of Estelle Frankel, who has done such a wonderful job of marrying her Jewish mystical tradition with her practice as a therapist.

A lot of my practice is simplified as I get older. So I have an altar, and I try to spend a little time there daily. Walking—I like to walk by water, it empties my mind. And silence, finding silence.

ADAM BUCKO: You often talk of study as a spiritual practice. In your life, you have been inspired by many medieval mystics. When you talk or write about holy people like Eckhart, Aquinas, or Hildegard, I often feel like you have a real relationship with them. I sense that they are your real spiritual relatives and ancestors. Is study one of your primary spiritual practices?

MATTHEW FOX: Indeed it is. My study and my work, my writing and my lecturing and my research. They are all the Via Creativa at work. They are my prayer, my access to the Via Positiva, Via Creativa, Via Transformativa. I've always tried to integrate my study and my work and my practice. That's one reason I define prayer as a radical response to life. I think that when you're integrating your values with all areas of your life, the demarcation of what is prayer or what is practice isn't important.

Speaking of study as a spiritual practice, I learned this in two places. One is from the Jewish tradition: in the Jewish tradition the study of Torah, if you bring your heart to it, is prayer. But also in my Dominican tradition, the same thing. There's a story told of Aquinas, that he was visiting a monastery, and he was writing a book up in his room. A brother monk came and knocked on his door and said, "We're chanting the Office—come down for prayer." And he said, "No, I'm busy doing this." Then the guy came back a second time, he came back a third time. Finally Aquinas shouted at him and pounded his desk and said, "I *am* praying!"

So the Dominican tradition, too, is that the time you spend at study, *if* your heart's in the room—you see, you have to bring your heart—is prayer and meditation. It's about wisdom, not just knowledge. If it's really about wisdom, then also it's not just about the ego or about passing an exam or impressing people. It's about drinking truth into your heart as well as your head. And, of course, in the Jewish tradition, your intellect is in your heart, which is something that we've lost in the West since the Enlightenment, I think.

So all of that is extremely important to me, absolutely. And you can tell it's a spiritual experience to study and to learn, because, for me anyway, it makes me very joyful. I grow, and I feel less depressed or less bored or less ignorant after I've studied. Study leads you to contemplation; it leads you to quiet and to stillness. But it also leads you to want to teach or to speak that fire that Jeremiah talks about, the fire that the prophet has inside. Isaiah talks about that, too—that you don't want to keep quiet, because you feel you've discovered something really important, truthful, wise—some wisdom—and you want to share it.

ADAM BUCKO: I like that. It leads to a desire to share. It leads to wanting to birth something in the world.

MATTHEW FOX: Yes, that's right, Eckhart calls this giving birth to Christ in the world. As he says, "what good is it to me if Mary gave birth to the son of God fourteen hundred years ago, and I don't do it in my person, time, and culture?" So yes, it is a birthing, and that takes you to the creativity part.

There is another spiritual practice that I have developed over the years for myself that I would like to speak briefly about. It's called "praying the news." Just as Scripture and also Nature are proper subjects for meditation and even contemplation, so too are human nature and human culture. Just as a painting or music or a good book or a powerful film move us to ecstasy and insight, to silence and awe, to contemplation and action, so too can the daily news. We can pray the news and not just watch it or listen to it.

How do we pray the news? Take it in silently, like the *lectio divina* that monks of old meditated on and that you mentioned. The news is also part of human history and therefore universe history and, yes, divine history. Therefore, it deserves our heart attention as well as our head attention. This practice takes critical listening and disciplined response. And, of course, it includes the Via Negativa—all the bad news (and that often includes the media itself). The media itself, in what it chooses to tell us, in the way it chooses to tell us it, *and* in the way it leaves things out, is itself worthy of contemplation (and criticism). This is one reason I did my doctoral thesis on *Time* magazine; I wanted to explore in depth the messages hidden and not so hidden that the media feeds us daily.

ADAM BUCKO: You mentioned earlier that science and cosmology have played a very important role in your spiritual journey. How does cosmology help you to experience God on daily basis?

MATTHEW FOX: Another contemporary spiritual practice that is badly needed today concerns the new cosmology that we are learning from science—the latest findings about how we got here, how the Earth got here, how the sun and moon got here, where "here" is in the vast unfolding in time and space of our universe. This is news we ought to be praying also.

All the wonders that science has been uncovering, especially in the last century, in the post-Einsteinian discoveries of the kinship of all beings and how we all derive from a single über-moment of the big bang or the "flaring forth" of the original fireball—such information is not just facts. Meditate on the amazing pictures we receive daily from Mars or from the edge of the universe via the Hubble Telescope.

There is beauty there as well as information. It is also fodder for our souls, food for our imaginations, fuel for our sense of awe, wonder, and gratitude. An awakening of reverence can occur.

These findings feed the sacred imagination—but only if we invite them in and make them an important part of our meditation and awareness. No matter who we are and what human tribe we come from, or, indeed, no matter what creature we encounter, all of us boast a 13.8-billion-year existence. With this awareness we rediscover the sense of our own nobility and that of others. Original blessing has never meant so much. These new and sacred stories of our origins belong to all of us, regardless of our particular ethnicity or religion. Science is also unveiling our history as a species, as well as discoveries of medicines, for example, that healing and transformation too deserve our prayerful attention and gratitude. It also invites generous young people into vocations of healing. "A healing life is a good life," Meister Eckhart said.

ADAM BUCKO: You once said that the science of today offers us many opportunities to expand our souls. Can this view help us experience God in new ways?

MATTHEW FOX: We have to get over this notion, which many of us are taught early, that your soul is in your body. Because if your soul is in your body, it doesn't grow very much—your body is obviously limited in size. But if your soul's not in your body, but your body is in your soul, then your soul can grow as much as your heart and mind grow.

As a species now, we're on Mars with these little robot mobiles, so our souls are on Mars. Or, with the help of the Hubble Telescope, our souls are now reaching to the frontier of the universe, and we're reaching back to the beginning, we can pick up the sound from the original fireball over thirteen billion years ago. So we are expanding. But we haven't expanded very much at the level of relationship and self-awareness and consciousness. That's the problem; that's where we're at. But these are lessons that we can expand. And yes, I think all spiritual practice is about expansion.

Science itself, I think, today offers us so many opportunities to expand our awareness, our gratitude, our reverence for what is. For existence itself ("is-ness is God" said Eckhart). When you realize how special a species like the tiger is, or the elephant or the polar bear or the whale or, of course, the human being, that these are once-in-a-universe events. You're not going to find a polar bear or a human being on another planet, in another galaxy; you may well find some other beings. But if you love the beauty and the is-ness, the miracle, of a tiger or a polar bear or an elephant, a whale, or a human being, now's the time to sink into that. And what's more prayerful than that? Because that's about acknowledging the sacredness that's everywhere. And I just listed few things. What about species of trees, flowers? And then human accomplishments—architecture and music and theater and literature and poetry. . . . It goes on and on.

ADAM BUCKO: I love Martin Buber's idea of the I/Thou relationship. And it seems what we're arriving at is that spiritual practice helps us to have this kind of a relationship to life, where you can be touched by the soul of everything that you encounter, and that somehow releases more of *your* soul. And it's a dialogical relationship in which our souls just grow, where we sanctify the world and the world sanctifies us. And that somehow also, then, leads to action, which creates even more of that.

MATTHEW FOX: Exactly. Eckhart has this great line. He says, "God is delighted to watch your soul enlarge." So there again is an affirmation of enlargement.

But you hit on a key word there, which is *relationship*. And as you say, Buber named that so well. I think that, in many ways, our spiritual traditions have often underplayed that. I've known marriages, for example, that have been profound, that have lasted fifty, sixty years, and it's been a practice and a journey—it's been a mutual spiritual journey for those people together.

ADAM BUCKO: Underplaying the importance of this has often been connected to institutional power and a desire to govern and control people's spiritual life.

MATTHEW FOX: Exactly. And notice that it's all built on a philosophy of dualism.

ADAM BUCKO: Which has nothing to do with Jesus!

MATTHEW FOX: Exactly! And, as you said earlier, power—it's really about a power elite and keeping people in line, including celibate priests or so-called celibate priests. All that is blowing up in our faces at this time, so it's one more reason we want to talk about these things.

I just want to go back then to marriage as a spiritual practice, and work as a spiritual practice. And by "work" I don't mean the work of a priest—I mean the work of a lawyer, the work of an engineer, the work of a therapist, the work of an artist, the work of a mechanic.

ADAM BUCKO: That's what you've been talking about: the priesthood of all professions. When I was growing up and going into monasteries, I think I wanted my main spiritual practice to be meditation, because that was very sexy—and it was definitely related to the power framework that I embraced, even without recognizing it as such. But what I realized is that my life took me in a completely different direction. Most of my experiences of grace actually at first happened through service. It's through service that I feel that I touch God. And so service is my sacrament.

And it's closely connected to art and creativity. Some people make paintings; some people create music; I engage with human lives. I engage with the stuff of people's lives and help them create something that can start reflecting authenticity and beauty. That's my art.

MATTHEW FOX: Yes, you're creating mosaics, you're creating living stained-glass windows. But it's living, it's going on—and how exciting.

When you think about it, that's really what a teacher's vocation is, too—to bring alive the inborn wisdom of others, especially of the young. But, of course, the poor teacher at this time in history has to absolutely struggle and strive to be able to define his or her work that way, because, instead, they've been told to give exams and fill out papers and all this stuff. Finding the real heart of their art is something that's a real struggle. I would insist that struggle is spiritual practice, you see. That asceticism, that discipline, that struggle, is just as worthy as that of the hermit out in the desert in the fourth century.

ADAM BUCKO: To paraphrase a famous saying from one of the desert monks: one monk told his elder that he prayed that all of his temptations and all of his contradictions go away, so he could be at peace. And the elder said, "Well, that's a mistake. Pray that they never go away, but that you have the courage and strength to deal with them."

MATTHEW FOX: And why? Why don't you want them to go away?

ADAM BUCKO: Because then you're dead, right? There are no opportunities for aliveness, for expansion, or for creativity. And if those are the signs of spirit and also the ways into spirit, then you're lost.

MATTHEW FOX: The Native Americans have a wonderful teaching that you should pray daily for your enemies, because your enemies make you stronger, they purify your intentions, and—just like you said—they keep you alert and therefore creative. They force you to be creative.

ADAM BUCKO: I like the word *alert*, because, when I read the gospels, one of the things that I get is that, as much as we would like to think that Jesus gave us a very specific blueprint on how to deal with life, he really left us with a lot of questions. In the gospels there are, I think,

183 questions that are asked of Jesus and only three direct answers that he gives. It seems to me that one of the messages that he gives us is: pay attention, be alert, and approach life from this awakened perspective where you have to address each thing as something unique, where you have to approach everything with all of your life. Jesus doesn't really talk much about memorizing the rules—his followers do! And I think that being alert is a spiritual practice.

MATTHEW FOX: Absolutely. And again, that's essential to the warrior, isn't it? If the warrior's not alert, the warrior's going to die in battle.

ADAM BUCKO: And getting numb and beginning to live by rules—in a way, that's a certain kind of dying. Like, for example, when I meet fundamentalists—most of them, they're so simply dead, because they're no longer alert, because the security of their answers killed them.

MATTHEW FOX: That's a very powerful observation. Yes, the security of their answers killed them. That's very well said. They are trying to live inside not just a box but a coffin.

ADAM BUCKO: Can you speak more about art as meditation?

MATTHEW FOX: I have written extensively about this practice, because we have employed it in all our pedagogy for over thirty-three years now, and it really works. Clay as meditation, movement as meditation, painting as meditation, chanting, mask-making, photography, filmmaking, journaling, and so on. When you engage in these practices as meditation, the goal is not the product as such. The process is key—the way (as in "I am the way"). Yet you often learn a skill in the process, and that is a helpful thing. But the key is that, in honestly doing art, you have to enter your heart and find what is truly there and bring it forward, and there is great honesty in this, great insight often ensues, and you discover deeper places in your soul. I especially like the work of

M. C. Richards in her classic book, *Centering,* where she compares centering the clay on the wheel, as a potter does, with the inward centering of your own self. As she says, the greatest product the potter produces is not the pot—but the potter! M. C. was on our faculty for years at ICCS and UCS, and she was a formidable teacher and philosopher and presence. She practiced what she preached.

I often employ body prayer or circle dancing, such as dances of universal peace, but other dances as well, when I conduct retreats and workshops. They too were integral to our pedagogy at UCS and ICCS. Again, always with deep results. I profited personally from such ways of prayer, and still do. Our students did also.

ADAM BUCKO: Going back to spiritual practices. What are some of the other practices that you practice?

MATTHEW FOX: Reading the mystics and stopping when an insight strikes me—that is *lectio divina* also. I no longer pray the Christian mantra with the rosary very much, but I do often like to pray the "Ninety-nine Names of Allah" from the Muslim tradition. Sometimes I get going with some of the names, and then I soar into making up my own. It is a healthy mantra, and it allows you to focus, especially in times of stress or conflict. I try to swim regularly for my health, and I find that working out that way can also be a genuine spiritual practice, if you approach it with the right intention.

I find that many young people are hearing their deep vocation to be helping others with spiritual practice whether that involves righting our diets or practicing yoga or organizing protests. An example would be Skylar Wilson, who describes himself as "an ecologist and spiritual guide whose work is helping to restructure our culture from the ground up." He guides wilderness experiences that reinforce our profound connection with the rocks, earthworms, wind, stars, and the myriad flow of multivalent, interchanging forms of energy that make up our culture and our selves. His wilderness trips range from backpacking and canoeing expeditions to managing ecological restoration teams in damaged areas. He sees himself as a mystic, energy worker, and meditation teacher. His work centers on creating containers for transformation in which participants are welcomed to clarify and celebrate their cocreative role as human beings in a beautiful, evolving cosmos. Skylar, who is thirty years old, is committed to the process of becoming real by seeing and taking steps toward becoming one's "most alive" vision in the world. He advocates vision quests in the wilderness in the following way:

> It's often hard to gain perspective on one's life and relationships until one takes time to step away to reflect in the open spaces of earth and sky. I have been learning and developing a set of experiential, intuitive tools and practices that support the expansion of awareness necessary to see how inner and outer worlds correspond within the interpersonal, transpersonal, multivalent, embodied, inter-subjective relationships that move through us. These methods center upon slowing down so that the more subtle rhythms of life can speak to us. These activities range from mindfulness practices, ecological restoration, mind-body integration practices, flow-inducing practices, trust and surrender practices, fasting, opening to nature, and sharing your truth. There are underlying wounds and subsequent dysfunctional patterns in us all that have led to our social and ecological crises we are now experiencing on such a vast scale. We each have the ability within us to make the changes necessary to create the most beautiful, joyful, and sustainable lives imaginable and this may help change our world for the better.

What kind of practices do you find helpful for the young people you work with?

ADAM BUCKO: What I have observed over the years is that homeless youth, or more accurately, youth from all walks of life, are products of a post-religious world. This is even more acute for homeless youth —who often grew up in a religious household but were abused or abandoned by so-called religious parents. For lesbian, gay, bisexual, and transgender-identified youth who were turned out of the home because their sexuality didn't mesh with their family's religious beliefs, identifying as religious or spiritual doesn't feel safe. That is why a post-religious approach is much more appropriate for youth at the Reciprocity Foundation.

I have observed that spirituality is the only means for a homeless youth to deeply heal from their wounds. They can achieve a great education and have a successful career—but without spirit, they simply can't feel deeply fulfilled or make peace with their suffering. So we've learned *not* to start the conversation with theology or religion but, instead, guide youth into experiences in which they can be completely present. They might engage in yoga, meditation, acupuncture, walking meditation—all of these are great ways to help youth "go within." That's where they can't help but connect with spirit and notice the richness that exists within the space of their own heart. Then, after helping them experience basic contemplative practice, we will layer in contemplative mentoring or spiritual direction that invites youth to reflect on their own impulses and intuition about spirituality. The key is for the process to be exploratory and led by each youth's needs rather than by an agenda set by their mentor or by Reciprocity. They may choose a spiritual rather than a religious life—or they may return to their religion of origin. But again, it is extremely compassionate to begin with a post-religious framework and then let youth decide how to engage more deeply with spirit.

I remember the first yoga classes we held at Reciprocity—the youth were wearing baggy jeans and tight shirts and could barely hold a simple *asana* and yet were so hungry to practice so that they could touch an inner stillness. Even short meditation classes offered at our center seem to give so much rest and relief for homeless youth. They instantly fall in love with quiet, contemplative practice. They tell us "my mind is too active" or "I never really felt rested until I tried meditation." The impact of contemplative practice is instantaneous and powerful.

They also really gravitate toward "ritual," especially when it is embedded within a contemplative practice—reciting *Om* together after a yoga class, repeating a simple mantra during a meditation class or reciting prayers of gratitude at the end of a retreat. The experience of connecting to spirit in a shared context enables them to remember that they are spiritual beings but also that *everyone* is a spiritual being—even an ex-boyfriend or an abusive parent or a frustrated social worker.

In 2010, we began to lead three-day retreats for small groups of homeless youth in upstate New York. It was a chance for my co-founder Taz and me to expand upon the contemplative practices and rituals that we offered in our center in New York City. Obviously, the youth are nervous about leaving the city and entering a foreign environment—such as a Zen monastery or an interfaith retreat center. For the first day, youth retreatants are usually wary of the vegetarian food and rustic surroundings. They are scared by the silence and the forests and even by other spiritual practitioners. But after twenty-four hours, the youth begin to open—to themselves and to each other—in a way that isn't possible in New York City. Retreats serve as a "quick path" for youth to reconnect with their spirit—and it is clear that homeless youth desperately want to have this experience but haven't had the right opportunity or mentors or felt safe enough to tiptoe toward developing an inner life. Taz and I see them dropping their masks and fears and blossoming into such gentle, loving, and playful human beings. It is almost like witnessing a miracle. It gives me faith that spirit is available to absolutely everyone—no matter how deep or bitter our wounds.

On our most recent retreat, we focused on "forgiveness"—teaching youth how to cultivate compassion for their perpetrators and to step out of victimhood and into a more empowering mind. The youth engaged in many simple rituals to initiate themselves into the retreat—such as finding objects in nature that represented the people they wished to forgive—even if they didn't believe that forgiveness was possible. After two days of reflection, journaling, and discussion about how and why we need to forgive each other, the youth gathered at the edge of a lake. Taz and I invited each youth to step into the water—and to release the objects (representing the people they were ready to forgive) and to describe how it felt to let go of their pain and anger. Then, to deepen the healing, we also invited them to describe how their suffering had helped them to grow. We felt they needed a ritual to remember that pain wakes us up and reminds us of the ways in which we need to grow as human beings.

I was in awe as I watched each youth step into the lake and offer their forgiveness to people who had committed atrocious acts of violence upon their bodies and spirits. Their capacity to forgive was astounding—and they seemed to grasp the ways in which their suffering was also a blessing in their lives. Being able to create rituals in which youth participate as individuals but also share in a collective process—and integrating their body, speech, mind, and spirit with nature—is a powerful way to open the gateway for transformative experience. It is this kind of post-religious but deeply spiritual work that resonates with young people from the Reciprocity Foundation.

We closed the retreat with another ritual—the act of thanking each person, in turn, for having the courage to forgive. Youth need ritual to express their pain, to engage in healing, but also to find ways to connect with other youth. So many homeless youth believe that they have to be tough and closed to survive on the streets—but they are human beings, and they also need to feel the embrace and admiration of a friend. Homeless youth are all looking for ways to support their hidden needs—their need for loving connection and support; their need to feel seen, to express compassion and forgiveness, and to remember the humanity of absolutely everyone that they encounter.

MATTHEW FOX: I see ritual as the inner work of the tribe, the inner work of the group. And that's just as important as the inner work of the individual—you need both. So in many ways, ritual is what makes tribe possible. As I mentioned before, I love what Malidoma Somé says about ritual. He's a spiritual teacher from an ancient African tribe, a real expert in ritual. He says, "there's no community without ritual". And when you look at today's broken world, it's all about loss of community, isn't it? We've lost our pattern of connection with the soil, with the forest, with the animals, with other human beings.

ADAM BUCKO: That's why it's so easy for us to participate in structures that actually are hurtful to people and the planet, because we're not connected to those that we're hurting.

MATTHEW FOX: Yes, thinking of the bomber pilots in Iraq who dropped bombs from forty thousand feet—they were not connected to the objects of their work and wrath.

ADAM BUCKO: So what makes ritual possible and what makes ritual successful?

MATTHEW FOX: An African American theologian said to me over thirty years ago, when I was living in Chicago, "I think 95 percent of white ritual and worship is dead." And I asked, "how do you define dead worship?" "Dead worship is where you walk in, and you walk out the same person—where no transformation really happens."

ADAM BUCKO: You have certainly created rituals that really do transform people, especially your Cosmic Mass.[5] It not only speaks to young people but also brings different generations together.

MATTHEW FOX: Each of our rituals has a different theme. We pick topics that are universal, archetypal, and that appeal to the spiritual needs of all human beings today. One particular Mass was a "Mass of the Angels" in San Francisco, held at a big hotel during an Earth/Body conference, so about 1,200 or 1,300 people were there. Afterward, three young men in their late teens came up, and one of them said, "I've been going to raves every weekend for five years. What I look for in raves, I found here tonight. I look for deep prayer, I look for community, and what you had here tonight that we don't have in rave is you had multiple generations. In rave it's one generation." And he said, "That's what I've been looking for." That was really amazing. Imagine five years of raves! That's five times fifty, that's 250 raves, and he found something in that Mass that he'd been looking for that he hadn't found yet. And he was able to find it without drugs.

People are hungry for ritual. Why wouldn't they be? It's in our bones. Humans and other animals do this, but church is ineffective at it at this time in history, because its forms are modern, but we are living in postmodern times. And the synagogue isn't much better, frankly, and for the same reason.

ADAM BUCKO: It seems to me that a lot of youth scenes, such as the rave scene, hip hop scene, Deadhead scene, punk scene, Burning Man scene, or Phish scene, are all about global experience of community and ritual.

MATTHEW FOX: Just as the Grateful Dead scene was several decades ago. Now, of course, the shadow side is that in many cases those scenes have been hijacked by drug dealers—not everywhere, but in many places. But that's not its real purpose. I always said, if you can plug rave and what happens at those other scenes into a liturgical tradition, you're not going to need drugs, because you're going to get high. And we have proven this in sixteen years of doing the Cosmic Mass, and that's what that young man was telling me. He got high completely. What he was looking for in rave he found in this experience, without the drugs. And we make explicit from the start that no drugs are welcome.

One woman, who is a drug counselor with youth, brought a van full of her clients to one of our Masses in Oakland. On the way home, they said to her, "this is the first time in our lives that we've gotten high without drugs." And that's the whole point—that ritual and worship are about getting high (or ought to be). And what does that really mean? It means moving to another realm, it means transfiguration. This is what happens at a sun dance and, for me, even in a sweat lodge. You're in a sacred space that is nowhere like your daily routine. And it's shamanistic. It takes you into another world, but then it puts you back in, but it transforms you and transfigures you. And I think your homeless kids experience it during your retreats.

We have not only the right but we have the need, and elders have the responsibility, to invite the younger generation into realms of transcendence. Other tribes have always known this. Our ancestors knew it. It's just taken for granted in indigenous people that you have these dances that put the whole tribe, all generations, into altered states.

ADAM BUCKO: Yes, but the problem is that very few of our elders actually know what those states are about or how to get there. As I mentioned before, the mark of eldership in our culture is being in Florida and playing golf. That's not much of an accomplishment, if you ask me.

MATTHEW FOX: Well, those are not elders. Those are just old people. An elder is not just an old person. An elder has a spiritual life. And I'm afraid that, unfortunately, a lot of our older people, including our so-called ordained ones, do not have spiritual lives. Our seminaries have failed to turn out mystics, prophets, or ritual leaders, for the most part.

ADAM BUCKO: Perhaps that's why most of our organized religions are becoming so irrelevant.

MATTHEW FOX: I would like to talk about how to make ritual real again. I think the young people have an absolute role here of leadership, because in my lifetime new languages have grown up out of youth culture that I am absolutely convinced are totally practical for reinventing worship and ritual and ceremony. And among them are the technological advances of things like VJing and DJing and rap and even B-boy dancing and more. All this needs to be and can be integrated into worship today. It's today's language; it's postmodern language, which, of course, is closer to premodern language, because all of our ancestors danced when they prayed. It's only in the modern era that you sit and are read to, and we call that prayer—or you read out of a book, fumbling through the book to find the right page. And that's so debilitating, because we have other chakras that want to worship too, and they're not allowed to.

ADAM BUCKO: This seems to be in line with what Andrew Harvey recommends, namely that we need spiritual practices that can activate all of our chakras and not just some!

MATTHEW FOX: When you worship by dancing, first of all you're connecting to the Earth again, and you're getting into your lower chakras, and that's where the beginning energies really are. Kundalini begins there—it doesn't begin with the head or the eyes. It begins with the feet and the genitals and your guts, which is where your anger and your grief reside, among other things. All that has to be stirred up in an authentic worship ceremony or experience. And, of course, that's what we've been doing in our Cosmic Mass for sixteen years, and we've gotten some wonderful results. There's just no question in my mind that this is a very useful pattern in which to recover worship again. We have now created a complete manual and are sharing it on our website for others to develop cosmic masses. But it is also important to get instruction and to know the Creation Spirituality theology behind the Masses to get the best results, so we are also training others to do them sometimes in classes and sometimes online.

ADAM BUCKO: I find that when we create rituals that speak to young people on our retreats, it results in real miracles. Things that normally would take years to heal and process get taken care of in one ceremony.

MATTHEW FOX: That is vital information to share. I've seen healings happen in our rituals—physical, but also psychological, emotional, spiritual healing, a lot of it. And yet that's not been our primary intention, so to speak, but it happens.

I think it's one reason that psychology is such a big industry today. Our rituals are so anemic. They're not doing the healing job that they should be doing and that they used to do in tribes around the world, because we've lost the real connection to the symbols and the languages that can get to what you call the deeper depths in ourselves. But we're in a place where this could come back, and we could put a lot of young people to work today making rituals. It's fun and it's community building, just the making of it. And it's memorable. Ritual is the "art of arts," for it brings out many forms of art from the community: music, visual arts, poetic arts and spoken word, dance, even the art of grieving.

Ritual is not just the ceremony that's going on. It's all the preparation for the ceremony—that, too, is part of the ritual. An Aboriginal woman once said to me in Australia, "Well, in our culture we work four hours of the day, and the rest of the day we make things." I asked, "What are you making?" "We're making ritual." So there you have it. Well, that's interesting, because a lot of young people today only have four hours of work a day, and that's all they're going to get. So why not spend the other four hours a day doing something really important and creative, such as putting on rituals. Wow, there's a thought! That ritual is an "industry," that there's a need for it, a much greater need for it than Diet Pepsi or Marlboros. Much healthier—better return on your effort.

ADAM BUCKO: With all the unemployment among young people, this could also be a nice way to give people meaningful work.

MATTHEW FOX: My dream is to see ritual centers, just like now we have all these entertainment centers around with jumbo theaters where you can see twenty-four-hour movies or what have you. I'd like to see ritual centers in every city, where we can be honoring one another's stories, because everyone has stories to tell. The Latinos have their stories, and the Native people have their stories, the blacks have theirs, the Celts have theirs. We honor one another by sharing our stories, the Via Positiva and Via Negativa stories, in a ritual context. The stories include great beauty and joy and courage but also great pain and suffering and grief. And these are spiritual things—these are in our bones and our hearts. We act out if we have not done this kind of inner work. So like you say, ritual and ceremony are one of the deepest and most fun and important ways to heal and to bring community alive and real.

ADAM BUCKO: I think it would be nice to finish this chapter with some practical tools that people can use as they embrace their journey toward spirit-centered living and keep hope alive in such chaotic times like ours.

MATTHEW FOX: Buddhist activist Joanna Macy, together with Chris Johnstone, speak to the spiritual and activist needs of our times in their recent book, *Active Hope: How to Face the Mess We're in without Going Crazy.*[6] Among other things, they offer a practice of "Visioning" that is important for our actions. They name three stages to Visioning: what, how, and my role. (1) What would you like to see happen? (2) How do we see this coming about? What are the steps needed for the larger vision to come to fruition? (3) What is my role in helping the vision come about?

They caution against the "static thinking" that invariably leads to cynicism and presumes reality is fixed, solid, and resistant to change. Static thinking boasts slogans such as "you can't change the system" and such. In contrast, "process thinking" views reality more as a flow, "each moment, like a frame in a movie, is slightly different from the one before." Existence is understood as "an evolving story" that states

(1) this is how things are now, (2) choices I make influence what happens next, and (3) how can I be active in moving toward that. This they call "Active Hope."

Some spiritual practices they recommend are the following:

1. A practice for empowerment. Use these opening sentences in self-reflection or journaling or as a partnered listening exercise with someone else:

> I empower myself by . . .
> What empowers me is . . .

2. Developing a partnership with Earth. John Seed recommends writing a letter that begins, "Dear (insert your name): This is your mother Gaia writing . . ." This way the Earth writes through us. We are instructed to continue the letter, just letting the words flow, not editing or thinking overly much.

3. Developing a "wider sense of self." This can be assisted by the following exercises from Joanna Macy and Chris Johnstone:

> Imagine a stranger asks you: "Tell me, who are you?" Write your response down and then ask the question again. Try to respond a different way each time. Do it again and again for at least ten different times.
> Do the same with a partner. Taking turns, each of you take five minutes to answer the question, "Tell me, who are you?" and exchange roles. Repeat again and again.
> Then do the same exercises (alone and/or with another) answering the question: "What happens through you?" many times over.

4.   A practice for honoring the pain in the world. Sit in pairs with one person acting as speaker; the other as listener. Begin with the following opening lines and the speaker speaks for two minutes. Then switch roles.

> When I think about the condition of the world, I would
>   say things are getting . . .
> Some concerns I have include . . .
> Some feelings that come up when I think about these
>   are . . .
> What I do with these feelings is . . .
> One of my worst fears about the future is . . .

5.   A gratitude practice. Complete the following sentences either alone with yourself or with a partner devoting several minutes to each sentence. Return to the beginning of the sentence and offer fresh answers as you move along.

> Some things I love about being alive on Earth are . . .
> A place that was magical to me as a child was . . .
> My favorite activities include . . .
> Someone who helped me believe in myself is or was . . .
> Some things I appreciate about myself are . . .
> A positive thing happened the past 24 hours and it
>   pleases me—let me share that with you.

6.   For maintaining energy in the struggle, Macy recommends the following exercise. Complete these opening sentences, journaling either alone or within a group:

> Things that drain, demoralize, or exhaust me include . . .
> What nourishes and energizes me is . . .
> The times I'm most enthusiastic are when . . .

Macy's definition of an activist is this: anyone who is active for a purpose bigger than personal gain. Active Hope involves being an activist for what we hope for in the world.

ADAM BUCKO: Perhaps it would be best to end this dialogue with a testimony from Pancho Ramos-Stierle of Occupy Oakland. It speaks to the power of spiritual resistance. He was asked about what happened during his actual arrest:

> On Mondays we practice silence, and the police officer who arrested us thought that we were deaf because we were not speaking. So he got a notebook and a pen. It was very considerate of him, and I could feel his energy shift a little, and so when he gave me the notebook I wrote, "On Mondays, I practice silence, but I would like you to hear that I love you."
>
> When he read that, he had this big smile and looked me in the eye and he said, "Thank you. But, well, if you don't move, you're going to be arrested. Are you moving or not?"
>
> So I wrote back, "I am meditating."
>
> He said, "OK, arrest them one by one."
>
> That was one of my favorite moments from the whole ordeal.[7]

7
No Generation Has
All the Answers

Elders and Youth Working Together

*I've had a mentor since we were "matched" when I was fifteen and I
believe she was God sent. She's now in her sixties and has retired back
home in Birmingham, Alabama. She is so much of what I needed then
and what I need now. She believes in me like no one else, including my
family. She is the example that has let me know that it's okay to be me,
to take risks, to not know the answers but to trust myself. I don't know
what my life would be like without her. I would be okay, I am sure.
But I see all the ways that she enriches my life and I am so grateful. I
am so lucky to have met someone who believes in me so and tells me.*

C.M., Female, 35

*I have a few mentors that I've chosen over the years to serve as my
life-inspiration based on my admiration for their way in the world.
They have changed the course of my life by serving as examples of
mindful and compassionate living, people who take risks to live a life*

of authenticity and passion. They have guided me beyond my own patterns of which I was often not even aware with their precedent, attentiveness and direction.

C.C., Female, 35

I have never had a spiritual mentor, though I long deeply for one.

V.H.K., Female, 30

One mentor who has meant a lot to me is Father Micah. After I finished with my undergraduate engineering degree, I spent 6 months living at a contemplative monastery in Snowmass, Colorado. I met with Micah weekly to check in and discuss anything on my mind. At that time, I was processing my new interest in contemplation and how my path was conflicting with the anti-contemplative, anti-pluralistic tendencies in Christianity that I'd previously been exposed to. He encouraged my questions and searching without trying to give me black and white answers—exactly what I needed.

E.B., Male, 30

I've yet to have a mentor in the classical sense. . . . I have often wondered if my ego has kept him/her at bay by believing our cultural myth of isolation and false strength through independence. The more I exist outside my ego, the more I reach to my brothers and sisters, the more I realize that everyone is my mentor and I theirs. We share mutual mentorship with one another.

R.P., Male, 32

I haven't had a spiritual mentor. There are a few older "wiser" people I have in my life (my acupuncturist, a couple of teachers from acupuncture school who I interned with, my dad). I've also had a yoga teacher but not an ongoing one on one relationship. All these form a conglomerate "mentor" of sorts but honestly it's not the same as having a mentor . . . not really the same at all. I've craved having a real mentor!

M.C., Female, 35

I have had many mentors. They have all changed my life immeasurably. In all these relationships, the keynote has been friendship: deep, palpable, human friendship. We often fear in the West that in order to maintain our individuality we have to be "equal" to everyone else. The truth is that all of us are "above" or "below" others in different areas of life. To be mentored one needs to recognize this, one needs to learn a certain humble stance, a way of interiorly bowing to another. This doesn't entail giving away one's responsibility, but rather taking on one's responsibility. Eventually it is transformed into a beautiful experience of being able to bow to all beings in friendship.

R.M., Male, 35

Other than my husband and friends, I don't have a spiritual mentor. I have been looking for one. . . . A lot of Muslim elders come from different cultures and don't understand my experience of Islam. They tend to see the religion differently from me.

K.C., Female, 33

My mom is my mentor. She is a reformed Catholic and now a Wiccan who believes I should make my own choice through knowledge and experience. She has taught me about Christianity, Paganism, and other world religions.

J.H., Male, 17

I have several people who inspire me. In general I am inspired by those who define and express their deepest convictions and creativity and have done inner work on themselves. Those who are emotionally intelligent, physically healthy, humble, open, flexible, powerfully in their own vulnerability. Brian Swimme, Matthew Fox, Stephan Goodman, Craig Chalquist, Eric Bloch, Martin Luther King Jr., etc., to name a few.

S.W, Male, 28

My parents are my mentors. I'm the daughter of Jesuit hippies. They are completely spiritual in their own ways. They taught me about many religions when I was young. My mother had a "home church" my whole adolescence, with people from many faiths that came together to talk about life and share. Being part of those times with a group that really tries to connect and question, was unusual for sure.

A.N, Female, 31

MATTHEW FOX: I would like to begin with a statement from one of the older Egyptians commenting on Arab Spring. He said,

> My generation is a cowardly generation. We were the ones who created this mess. We lived in fear. We never imagined that these young people could bring down with their hands one of the most notorious regimes in the Middle East. It was a miracle, I tell you, exactly the kind you read about in the Bible. But they were prepared to face death. They didn't learn the old-fashioned rules that they were supposed to respect their elders. They broke out of our shell because they had this wider world that is strange to us. Now the country is going to be theirs, which is good, because we are in the past, they are the future.[1]

ADAM BUCKO: "They didn't learn the old-fashioned rules that they were supposed to respect their elders."

MATTHEW FOX: Yes. Elders have to earn respect. I've often said that you're not an elder just because you've got white hair. You've got to have done some inner work as an elder. Just because you sat in front of the television for fifty years doesn't make you an elder. It's not just about age; it's about wisdom.

ADAM BUCKO: What do you think should be a balance there? Because I think that young people can also at times be arrogant, and I know that when I was seventeen, I thought I knew everything.

MATTHEW FOX: Well that's right, and that's why there does have to be a balance. And elders ought to have something to teach. But most of what that older Egyptian fellow was saying was that his generation sold out and lived in fear, and they didn't do anything about their fear. So people who live in fear are not developing their wisdom.

ADAM BUCKO: So would you say that one of the marks of an elder is that they've dealt with their fear?

MATTHEW FOX: Right. They've done some inner work. You've got to do some inner work. How else would you have wisdom? And if you've spent your life succumbing to and going along with negative powers, you're certainly not qualified to teach the next generation. So intergenerational wisdom means, I think, that both generations have to work at the level of wisdom, including resisting an immoral system.

ADAM BUCKO: One of the complaints that I hear is that many of our spiritual leaders and ministers and priests are not capable of offering anything to the new generation. They simply miss the mark. Young people are not inspired by them, because what they are offering is somehow not relevant to what young people feel, long for, and struggle with. Why do you think that is?

MATTHEW FOX: First of all, because of the training the priests, ministers, and clergy get. The training they get is not about spirituality, frankly.

It's rarely about bringing the mystic or the spiritual warrior alive—it's not. It's much more about church rules and religion and a theological system that they're trying to shove down people's throats. It's a system that again young people have outgrown, if you will. And that's just one of the elements. And then there's church itself and the complicity with powerful forces and other things that young people see through—the hypocrisy. In addition, the new generation is a postmodern generation. They see life differently from those raised with the modern worldview.

ADAM BUCKO: When I was nineteen, I heard Rev. James Morton speak at an interfaith gathering. He talked about training ministers by sending them to the streets to live with homeless people. Later on, I also learned about Zen Master Bernie Glassman, who did street retreats with his students in which, by living on the streets and experiencing homelessness firsthand, his students would begin to see their prejudices and boundaries, and eventually they would come to recognition of interconnectedness of all life and the responsibility that they had. I was very touched by that.

When I joined the ashram in India and began working with homeless kids, that's what we did. Once a week we slept on the streets of Delhi. That experience changed my life. It changed how I work with young people and how I relate to them. That experience initiated me into a contemplative way of working with young people. It helped me approach them in a state of "curious not-knowing" and trust. It allowed my actions to be an expression of an inner impulse that arises in the heart when one is truly present in a prayerful and receptive way. The contemplative way doesn't impose top-down solutions, instead it invites everyone into this presence so everyone can begin to sense the guiding movement of the spirit.

When Occupy Wall Street began and spaces around the world were being occupied by young people standing up to greed and power, seminaries remained open with their students tucked safely inside. Shouldn't they have instead been closing down and sending their students to the streets to live with the Occupiers? Isn't that where Jesus would have been?

MATTHEW FOX: Your question reminds me of the specialness of my mentor, Père Chenu, with whom I was studying in the spring of 1968, when the students were protesting all over the world, but especially in Paris, where their rioting actually did bring down the government of President Charles de Gaulle. Most of life was shut down in Paris at the time, but my university was still in session. After class, Chenu, who was seventy-five years old at the time, shut his notebook and said, "We have been studying twelfth-century history—here is your chance to make it. Do not come back next week; come back in two weeks and tell me what you have contributed to the revolution." This was the same spring of student protest that turned a professor named Josef Ratzinger (later pope Benedict XVI) into an archconservative in Tübingen, Germany, and the founder of Communion and Liberation into the same in Italy.

In the West, the seminaries have sold their souls, I think, to the academic system, which is thoroughly polluted and which includes, of course, a distinct resistance to mysticism, to experience, to spirituality. It's built into it. And they've sold their souls to these accrediting-body institutions, which are all about numbers. It's not about soul expansion or development. That's why I developed an alternative pedagogy and for a number of years even stepped out of accreditation for our doctor of ministry program, because 95 percent of our students didn't want it. They felt it would suck the juice, the soul, the creativity out of our unique pedagogy—that we'd have to sell our souls to get accreditation. I think they were right.

Who accredits the accrediting bodies? I can assure you (I have worked with many)—they are by no means mystics. And they aren't prophets either. Even within their own profession, the education profession, they're not raising the right questions. That's what really gets me angry. I knew theology professors with big names, who sell good books, blah, blah, blah. And they could preach Marxism and all this other stuff, but they couldn't critique the system that was paying their paycheck. They could not critique—and by "could not," I don't mean just financially, I mean psychologically—they did not have the courage to risk their jobs by raising questions about the system: whether this whole system that we call academia is not part of the problem. Because it is—it produces the Wall Street people. Everyone who works on Wall Street went through some university; they all have degrees. Thomas Berry says 95 percent of the destruction of the planet is happening at the hands of people with PhDs. Einstein says that rationality and intellect do not give us values. Values come from intuition and feeling, he insists (i.e., the right brain or mystical brain). Academia is afraid of the mystical brain and the result is that we graduate people with the power of knowledge but rarely the gift of wisdom.

ADAM BUCKO: Usually some of the best universities.

MATTHEW FOX: And the best, right. Someone recently said to me that two-thirds of Harvard graduates go to Wall Street. So there you go. The system is not being critiqued. One thing that gets me angry is that even liberation theologians in North America who are so gung-ho about revolution in South America don't apply the principles to their comfortable status in the ivory tower of tenure and the other ways that they may have sold their souls.

ADAM BUCKO: That's why we live in a world that is so messed up, because most of us go along, simply because going along is connected to our paychecks. And that's what we've been taking on with the homeless youth system. The system doesn't work. In my estimate, 70 to 80 percent of homeless kids who graduate from shelters and residential programs go back to the streets or go back to their abusive homes, or whatever the situation was that essentially put them on the street. Yet—

MATTHEW FOX: No one's talking about that.

ADAM BUCKO: Well, yeah, because first of all, the system is divided into compartments, so it's very difficult to see it, because no one sees the big picture. And second, everyone wants to get paid. It's more and more difficult to make a living nowadays, and no one wants to challenge the system, because their paychecks are connected to it. Yet everyone is frustrated, and I believe that deep down everyone has to sense that something is really wrong. At Reciprocity, we have been talking about it for many years. Only recently have we seen some changes in the conversation.

MATTHEW FOX: Well, that's what's so special about Reciprocity. You've developed a model that is much more transformative than what's passing as a model. So you're getting results that they don't get, because you're treating the whole person. You're treating young people's spiritual needs, if you will, and you're listening to their powers of creativity. And that's not happening in those other shelters, youth development programs, or schools. You're a voice crying in the wilderness there.

ADAM BUCKO: At one point you said that young people are struggling with discovering who they are and how different they are from their parents. And I feel that our spiritualities and our institutions are not necessarily set up to help people individuate. Because when you individuate, there's a good chance that you will actually start questioning the institution that you're a part of. I feel that this new spirituality, this new way that is emerging, should have practices in place that help people do that. The question that I like to meditate on in my life is, am I incarnating my truth in the world? I feel that few of my spiritual trainings encouraged me to ask that question, let alone begin to live that question. It took some years of working with courageous mentors and a good psychotherapist for me to finally build the courage to want to incarnate my truth in the world. Meditation didn't help me with that. The religious institutions that I was a part of didn't help me with that—it was too dangerous, because what if my truth is a questioning truth?

What I admire about you is that courage and truth telling have always been such an important part of your journey and your spirituality. To me, your life truly embodies what Henry David Thoreau advised when he said, "Be yourself—not your idea of what you think somebody else's idea of yourself should be." When I, as a student of theology, read your autobiography, it had a liberating effect on me. It gave me what Richard Rohr calls a "dangerous permission" to examine my soul, claim my truth, and begin to incarnate that truth in the world.

There is a beautiful poem of Rumi that says,

> There is one thing in this world that you must never forget to do. If you forget everything else and not this, there's nothing to worry about; but if you remember everything else and forget this, then you will have done nothing in your life. It's as if a king has sent you to some country to do a task, and you perform a hundred other services, but not the one he sent you to do. So human beings come to this world to do particular work. That work is the purpose, and each is specific to the person. If you don't do it, it's as though a priceless Indian sword were used to slice rotten meat.[2]

MATTHEW FOX: That advice from Rumi is a wonderful way of talking about the importance of vocation and our generous response to it. We all have a calling or a vocation and that underscores everything else we do.

ADAM BUCKO: This is also echoed by Viktor Frankl, who, after surviving a Nazi concentration camp, concluded that the most important lesson for any young person to learn is that everyone comes here with a very specific mission in life. He said, "Everyone must carry out a concrete assignment that demands fulfillment. Therein he cannot be replaced, nor can his life be repeated. Thus everyone's task is as unique as his specific opportunity to implement it."[3]

This is very important, because what happens if we don't investigate what's in our souls? What happens if we are not lucky enough to have mentors who model to us what authentic life looks and feels like? What happens if we don't have elders who can give us permission to question and help us find tools to recognize our truth? What happens if we never individuate and grow up spiritually? Well . . . we simply miss life. We miss the opportunity to truly be alive and give birth to what we are here to give birth to. And that's a tragedy!

When I was twenty I saw a documentary film about dying. It was a very simple film made in a hospice. The film focused on weekly interviews with people who were terminally ill. The film essentially chronicled the last few weeks of their lives and eventually showed them dead, in a black plastic bag, being taken out of the hospice. The tragedy of the film was that every single person that was interviewed was upset and angry because they felt like they missed their life.

MATTHEW FOX: In other words, they died with regret.

ADAM BUCKO: They died with regret. They said, "All my life I wanted to travel. I never did—I thought I didn't have time. All my life I wanted to do this; all my life I had these dreams. I never addressed them." And so an interviewer would be like, "Oh, you're looking so much better this week." And they would be raging, "Don't lie to me. I'm dying. Can't you see I'm dying? And I missed my life, I missed an opportunity to be alive."

Watching that film was a very important part of my spiritual training. It showed me that this "game of life" is not really a game. It's a very serious task that requires real commitment and courage. And unless we make that commitment, unless we surround ourselves with mentors who can help us find our ways, unless we work on building the courage to follow the longing of our souls, we simply miss life. We miss the opportunity to incarnate what we are here to incarnate.

MATTHEW FOX: That sounds like a really powerful movie. Well, again, spiritual practices from many traditions around the world have always recommended meditating on death.

But, you know, there are two ways to look at that meditation on death. One would be, I think, what I would call the fall and redemption: the words about sin and guilt and penance and fear of hell—"what comes next?" The other is really what you're talking about, and that is, "hey, life is short—get ready to live it fully, and persevere in that full living." Again, this is what I mean by "a radical response to life"; this is meant to be a prayerful person, in that sense, a spiritual person. But notice that, in a way, I would say toxic religion has hijacked death and the meditation on death and made it extremely sour, whereas it really ought to be a way to meditate on the opportunity of life, what life really offers.

And once again, that movie, even in your brief description, shows the power of art. The people who made the film, who had the concept and so forth; the people who were in the film, honestly telling their regrets at the end of their lives and then dying; and the people watching the film—watching, participating in art is itself a form of meditation. It is an art form. Whether you're admiring painting or music or theater or film, you are a participant, and that's an art form in itself. Gabriel Marcel, whom I like very much, a French philosopher, used to say that the participants in art, the observers, if you will, are themselves artists. Otherwise, the artist would not have an audience, and the artist has to presume an active audience. Shakespeare had to presume that there are a lot of souls out there who are alive and intelligent and seeking, and, therefore, he had something to say to them.

Let me go back to a personal thing. When you were talking about my own story and just preceding that, you were talking about finding one's identity. I was thinking about my own freedom and how my own work, in many ways, began in France and thanks to the French. And by that I mean that when I was doing my doctoral studies there, I was not weighed down like friends of mine were in the German doctoral system—with a ton of papers to write and footnotes and all this. The system at the doctoral level in France was such that you had freedom to do your own searching. And they trusted you, because they felt that by then you had mastered some kind of methodologies and ways of thinking and research; it was a matter of trust. That's very rare in academia, to be blunt. So I was able to really listen to my soul. And of course, this was the late 1960s, and there was all the turmoil going on in America and in Europe and all over the world. I wanted to explore more deeply spirituality in culture. So I was freed to do it my way—I was encouraged, and that's rare.

Then I had a lot of solitude, because I went and lived on a farm in the Basque country to write my thesis, and so I was in nature too. But it was just an unusual confluence of opportunities. I had friends who were very courageous, who were involved in the student protest movements in Germany and Spain and in the anti-Franco movement in Spain. My best friend had a ten-year sentence on his head—to return to Spain, he had to sneak across the border, because if Franco caught him, he would be imprisoned. He was involved in the union movement in Spain, which was, of course, forbidden under the fascist Franco. So I was with courageous people, and I think that's a very important part of my education.

Also, being in France, I was with artists. You can't live in France without breathing the appreciation of art. And that's not so in America. It's the opposite—art is essentially a consumer enterprise in America, unfortunately. That's not what it really means to the soul of the French, for example.

I realize that a lot of my freedom and self-identity came at that time. And I remember the moment when I was at my typewriter, working on the thesis, and I realized that I was a writer—I said it out loud, as I mentioned earlier—and I realized that this was going to be the way I was going to give a gift to the world and at the same time enjoy myself, which is what a vocation is, I think.

Ever since, I've always tried to surround myself with or be around people I could admire, people with courage in their own field. And the faculty that I gathered around me for over thirty years were that way, in many respects: many of them rebels in various ways, whether scientific heretics like Rupert Sheldrake, religious heretics like Jeremy Taylor and Starhawk, and many artists and so forth. These people have always attracted me, because I know they have something to teach me. And it's not just knowledge—it's also courage and how to survive on the edge.

ADAM BUCKO: Matt, what you described is very important. You're really talking about the importance of having mentors, friends, and a tribe that can inspire us to have courage to say yes to life as it manifests in us. I know this from my life; some of my friends tell me that I've been very lucky to meet some really great mentors. I agree. I have been extremely lucky. But I also worked very hard at it.

MATTHEW FOX: Yes, you seek it out.

ADAM BUCKO: Yes, because I take my life and my calling seriously. I intuit my mission. I intuit the dream that I am here to give birth to. And I know that I can't do this on my own. I need support. I need the wisdom of the elders. I need their spiritual guidance. I need their support and their prayers. So I try to surround myself with people who have taken a similar journey, people who chose to live their lives with courage, people who can be honest with me about their life experiences and encourage me to look honestly at my life, people who can ask me difficult questions in a loving way. I feel that this is something that we need to encourage young people to do as well. It's very difficult to get anywhere on your own. We are not meant to do things on our own. We become who we are through other people. Giving birth to who you are is meant to be a community enterprise!

And that's what we try to tell our kids at Reciprocity. We encourage them to seek people who inspire them. We say to them, "Every time you read something that moves you, every time you see a work of art that inspires you, find the person who authored it. Get in touch with them." And we live in exciting times; nowadays you can find people within few minutes on Facebook, Twitter, and LinkedIn. Find them! Write them! You might never hear back. But the person you are writing might also turn out to be your new guide, your best mentor, and your lifelong soul friend.

MATTHEW FOX: Just this week I got a letter from a woman in a theology doctoral program in San Antonio; she was going to present a paper on my ninety-five theses at a religious congress. She wrote and said, "I just want you to know that I'm doing this." Well, I was real excited—I wrote back and encouraged her. And then she wrote back and said, "Would you like a copy of my talk?" And I said, "Absolutely!" So there's something cooking there.

ADAM BUCKO: Will you speak more about those ninety-five theses?

MATTHEW FOX: When Cardinal Ratzinger was made pope in 2005, I had deep concerns about the future of the church, having known Ratzinger and having been in a battle with him for over twelve years. I was invited to lecture in Germany at Pentecost time, and I was thinking of cancelling the event, since Pentecost represents the "birthday of the church" and I didn't feel there was a lot to celebrate. I asked for a dream and sure enough I woke up at three in the morning realizing that Ratzinger was the first German pope in hundreds of years and that, of course, Martin Luther was German, and he pounded ninety-five theses to the church door in Wittenberg to protest papal corruption in his day. So I got up, sat in a rocking chair, and drew up ninety-five theses of my own before the sun rose.

I translated these into German, and when my lecturing was finished in Germany, I took a train to Wittenberg and pounded them at the door where Luther had pounded his. A blog in Germany had over ten thousand people on line debating (1) do we need a new reformation today, and (2) which of the ninety-five theses are the most pressing? I published these theses in my small book *A New Reformation,* and they are also available online on my website.

More recently I translated them into Italian and pounded them at the basilica in Rome that is overseen by Cardinal Law, the archbishop of Boston who was "elevated" to run that basilica when the attorney general of the state of Massachusetts came after him for his role in covering up for pedophile priests (one of whom had abused 150 boys). I pounded the theses there on a Sunday morning, as people were coming to church in Rome. I think it is important not to dwell in denial. The Vatican Police were there and among other friends they beat a friend of mine who was filming the event.

But I love what you're doing in Reciprocity; it's so important. You know, every writer, every artist, appreciates their work having an impact, especially on the younger generation. And again, young people inspire older people. I'm very inspired by what's happening in the world. I'm inspired when I watch dancers dance, and you have to be young to do that—your body can only do that for so many years. Or even I'm inspired when I see a good football play or baseball play. One thing that youth bring to older people is inspiration, especially around beauty. And beauty is not just physical beauty, although that's part of it too, but when you're older, there's a deeper appreciation for beauty.

Again, it's about patterns—you see the pattern, for example, that a young person has moral outrage and is finding effective ways to express it. It's very important that the older generation sees this, feels it, and tastes it. Otherwise they become cynical old goats, and they die with regret. But if you can see that younger people are also tapping into visions analogous to those that you had in your twenties, that's very heartening. If you have something to teach them—which you probably do, especially if you carry some wounds yourself—then there's a mutual learning that goes on. It's not one-way by any stretch of the imagination. It's a beautiful thing.

I think parents also have this role. Neither of us is literally a parent, but I think this is probably one of the most exciting and delicious parts of being a parent: having children who are carrying authentic values with impact into the world. Look at the example of Bernard Amadei, whom I was with a few weeks ago. He's got fourteen thousand people in his movement Engineers Without Borders, and when he talks about his students in their twenties and how committed they are, how 97 percent of them have spent time in other countries with the poor, his whole face becomes young again. He is an incarnation of what authentic eldership is. He has handed something on that they've run with. He doesn't want a carbon copy. That would be an ego problem; that would be a psychological problem.

ADAM BUCKO: Speaking of this being not a one-way street, I remember you talked about Fr. Bede Griffiths and how, when he discovered cosmology and new science, it gave him twenty more years of life.

MATTHEW FOX: Right. When he and Rupert Sheldrake met, Rupert was a young man—I'd say in his late twenties—and Rupert had given up on Christianity. He had called himself an atheist for years, although in northern India, where he was working as a biologist, he was practicing yoga and really getting into some of the Hindu practices. And then a yogi said to him, "Well, you're a Westerner—you should go meet this Christian in the south, Bede Griffiths." So he went there, not knowing what to expect. And they fell in love in the sense that Bede, I was told, was ready to die—he was in his young seventies, I think, and he thought his life was kind of over, and he was packing his bags to leave. When he met this young man who had all this knowledge of new science, cosmology, and other things, it awakened him and gave Bede twenty more years of life.

ADAM BUCKO: And it really transformed his spirituality, his theology, right?

MATTHEW FOX: Absolutely, absolutely.

ADAM BUCKO: It really moved him into more of a prophetic consciousness.

MATTHEW FOX: Yes, definitely. It gave him courage. But it also gave him a vision. But the conversion was mutual. By that I mean that Rupert was equally awakened by Bede, and Rupert became a practicing Christian. To this day he and his wife, Jill Pierce, are practicing Anglicans, and it was Bede who opened the door of a deeper Christian tradition and practice to Rupert. So there you have a fine story of intergenerational grace and blessing. Rupert as a scientist blessed Bede with new life, and Bede as a contemplative Christian blessed Rupert.

But I love your point about teaching the young, encouraging the young to connect to their mentors, especially now that it's so much easier with the internet.

ADAM BUCKO: Absolutely, it's so much easier. And we teach them how to do it, how to find people on Facebook, how to find people on LinkedIn, how to find people on Twitter, because nowadays all of that information is public information. You can't control whether someone writes back or not, but it doesn't matter, because you're reaching out. And I encourage them to do that every time they are moved by something, to find the author of it and to get in touch—and to tell the author what their story is, to tell him or her about their dreams and how they were influenced by what they just read or saw. In my view, this is the spirit of reciprocity.

And I see what's happening as a result. I see how empowering it is to our kids when they connect with some of those people. I see what happens when they connect with people who listen to their story, who sense and acknowledge their potential. It has a liberating effect on them. It literally moves them from dreaming about life to saying yes to life and to living life in their unique way and expressing their unique gifts.

I know that in my life one of the biggest gifts that I received from my mentors and spiritual directors was that—through their presence and through the questions that they asked me—they helped me touch the essence of my calling. They helped me touch that special impulse in my heart that was carrying an important message for my life. Once I touched it, they named it for me. That gave me permission to be at home with that experience. It encouraged me to deepen that experience and build my life around my calling.

MATTHEW FOX: That is such an important point. What you're naming there is the role of the mentor. That's what a mentor does. All kinds of studies have shown that young people who find mentors have their lives transformed. I experienced that also when I found Père Chenu in Paris. (And I found him because I contacted an author—the monk Thomas Merton—and asked him for advice about where to study spirituality; he told me to go to Paris. So I thank him for that.) Chenu became my mentor. He named the Creation Spirituality tradition.

And having Chenu as my mentor gave me courage. First of all, his life gave me courage, because he was silenced by the pope for twelve years, forbidden to write; he worked with the worker-priests movement and Marxists; he contributed substantively to Vatican II; and he helped launch Liberation Theology. This guy did so much, but he kept his humor, he kept his love of life, and he was not bitter or anything like that, right up to the end. At the end he was asked, "Aren't you depressed by what's happening in the Church today?" And he said, "Oh, if you're going to have omelets, you've got to break the eggs." He said that Vatican II was prophetic, so it's already obsolete anyway. He said now is the time, when everything's in chaos, this is when the Holy Spirit loves to go to work. He said now is the time for theology to really happen. He was about ninety-two years old when he said those things. So he maintained his youthfulness and his love—not an ounce of cynicism in him. And the way he treated young students taught me a lot—he was always respectful of them and their ideas. I never heard him put down a question or a questioner. No sadomasochistic one-up-man-ship games, which are so common in academia.

ADAM BUCKO: That's beautiful. And the beautiful thing about mentorship is that an authentic mentor always shares his or her life, love, and wisdom with the student, which means that it's very integrated and all-encompassing. The experience affects all domains of life. It's not just spiritual direction, it's not just educational help, it's not just advice on how to accomplish things in the world, and it's not just encouragement to work for a betterment of the future. It's a certain kind of presence that affects all of those domains of life and more.

One of my mentors, who is a rabbi, once said to me that in his particular lineage, a rabbi is never a guru. He said you move in with the rabbi, you become part of his family, just to make sure that you can see all the problems in the household. And, to me that's really what mentorship is about. It's about authentic sharing of life. You are transparent with your mentee. You don't hide behind titles and accomplishments. You don't need the mentee to project some kind of a superhero mask on you so you can feel really good about yourself. Being a mentor is about sharing life. It's about engaging all of the ingredients of your life and using them in the service of your mentee's life and soul. And in the process, your life is changed as well. In fact, if this process works well, it's often not clear who is helping whom. It's just authentic life evoking more life.

MATTHEW FOX: That's right. Autobiography is a very important part of learning, especially at this time, because stories are more trustworthy than institutions. Individual stories are more trustworthy than the stories the institutions are trying to feed us, which are extremely tainted and uncritically examined—such as, for example, what is success, what is education, or what is religion. You have to step back and say, "what about hypocrisy, and what are the implications of this for sustainability," and so on.

So when institutions' stories are no longer credible, or at least are full of holes, where do we go for stories? We go to autobiographies. And that particularizes things, but really everyone's experience has a universal dimension to it. We're dealing with archetypes, after all. And these are the things that young people can connect with. I mean, again, a story is not a literal thing. You can connect to aspects of it, and you take what you need from the story.

ADAM BUCKO: Contemplative activist and teacher Mirabai Bush puts it well when she talks about the role of elders and today's youth in the following manner.

It is our experience that many young people today are not choosing to relate to elders in a hierarchical way of just listening.

There is a new self-confidence in young people. It is partly a result of empowerment by the digital world which has given them (all of us) access to so much information and such global reach. And since entering that digital world does not require age or experience or formal education, it is open to everyone, and often youth adapt to it more easily than their elders. Youth have also benefited from the liberating changes of the past forty to fifty years, including women's liberation, civil rights, mind-body health awareness, etc.

My son and his friends, born in 1972, started their lives in a world that was only a dream not long before. Since then the world has continued to change so radically that it *has* to be a dialog or conversation rather than a hierarchical passing of information or even wisdom. Youth know the world in a very new way. There is history and timeless wisdom to be learned from elders, but there is much about the world that youth know and can teach to their elders.[4]

MATTHEW FOX: It is my experience that youth bring hope and humor, laughter, and often joy into the room. Lama Surya Das talks well of the reciprocity between young and elders, how one gifts the other, when he says, "When I read or listen to the world news, it can be depressing and cause me to wonder where it's all leading. . . . But whenever I talk with a young person, I am irrationally filled with hope, optimism, certainty and delight."

ADAM BUCKO: I like the way Pir Zia Inayat-Khan emphasizes the individuality of each young person one mentors. He puts it this way, "In all ages, mentors have been most effective when they have 'worked with the grain' of their mentees. Every seeker is unique, hence every mentorship relationship must be in some degree different from all others. In my experience, spiritual mentorship means holding up a mirror in which a seeking soul is enabled to perceive the light of its own divinity."

MATTHEW FOX: I am in complete agreement. Each person's expression of Divinity, each Cosmic Christ and Buddha Nature, is unique and elders need to respect that.

There is one more point I want to bring in about mentorship relationships, and it comes from a recent scientific discovery. It seems that for years anthropologists have been arguing over what killed the Neanderthal branch of our family tree. Some people have theorized that there were wars between our immediate ancestors and Neanderthals, and that our ancestors won. But the truth is that we have found some Neanderthal DNA in some humans on the planet today, so clearly there was intermarriage going on. What scientists have now found is this: that the Neanderthals lived to be only about thirty years old, whereas our ancestors lived longer—this means that *Homo sapiens* had grandparents and elders, and the Neanderthals did not. That is what seems to have saved our species! That we had the wisdom of the elders. This is very important information, and both elders and young people should reflect deeply on it. It also helps to explain the great esteem for elders among ancient peoples and among indigenous peoples today. They remember how vital the contribution of the elders was to their very survival in the past. And, of course, good communication among generations. All that is part of the history of our species, and we are foolish if we block out the wisdom of any one generation. We are in this together. Let us learn from one another and learn mutually.

8
Birthing New Economics, New Communities, and New Monasticism

I'm stressed out and depressed. I feel trapped. The American Dream is dead for my generation. WE ARE THE 99 percent!!!

A.N., Female, 24

There are many people who long to live a fully integrated spiritual life and many who are doing it now. By necessity they have to operate outside of the current systems, which are not based on a holistic approach to life. I aspire to build a life that is true and whole and deeply satisfying; to feel connected to the Earth, to myself, and to others; and to be fully and fearlessly engaged in the world in a way that will help to build new systems that support an integrated life.

V.H.K., Female, 30

I can't speak for my generation. I don't want to speak for my generation, actually. I do however want to say . . . I see much that is unequal in society and I decided long ago, when I was a teenager, I think, to try to do what was right. To use the education that I have to help or speak on behalf of those who can't.

C.M., Female, 35

I believe that nine out of ten actions must be creating the community that we want to live in—we're talking about permaculture, independent media, restorative justice, gift economies, free currencies, and preventive medicine. By doing all that, we make ourselves stronger.

If you ware creating true alternatives to the collapsing, rotten system then you will naturally come into conflict with the power structure. Then the political action becomes necessary. So I think one out of ten actions should be obstructive—that is boycotts and protests and marches and nonviolent civil disobedience.

But when we cultivate inner awareness, it's easy to see that what we need to do is spend most of our time creating the communities that we want to live in.

Pancho Ramos-Stierle, 26[1]

Lost my job, found an occupation.

Female Protester, Occupy Wall Street

Many people in my generation are yearning to find a career and path that is fulfilling—one that makes a positive contribution to humanity and the world. Although this is true of the youth of many generations, I wonder if this feeling is not becoming more common and even urgent today. There is still a lot of pressure to make money and be "successful," but we want something more meaningful than that. I'm encouraged by the growing strength of interfaith and interspiritual movements, Rory McEntee and Adam Bucko's New Monasticism, the New Monasticism of Shane Claiborne and Jonathan Wilson Hartgrove, intentional communities focused on environmentalism and justice, and the growing permaculture movement. All of these reflect a growing desire for a new economy and way of life that is environmentally, economically, and emotionally (quality of life) sustainable.

E.B, Male, 30

Look mom. There's no future.

Sign of a seven-year-old child protesting at Occupy Wall Street

If voting could change anything, it would be illegal.

Female Protester, Occupy Wall Street

When I place my fingers on the pulse of my generation I feel the awareness of a profound profanity we've created. Deeper than that I feel an unstoppable desire to turn the profane sacred again through bold love. A love so bold it saturates every aspect of our lives. For it's through bold love that the profane becomes sacred again. Of course, nothing other than our perspective actually changes and we are really transforming ourselves through the use of bold love.

R.P., Male, 32

Stop believing in authority, start believing in each other.

Male Protester, Occupy Wall Street

For the young people who are [part of the Occupy movement] day in and day out, . . . what is getting them out there is pretty visceral economic hurt. . . . Many of them are . . . people who have college degrees. . . . They have a huge amount of loans and they have found themselves unable to get jobs, and that's why they can find time to spend in Zuccotti Park or wherever they are protesting.

Noreen Malone, Female, 27[2]

"If you want to affect any real change, you have to work inside the system." There's not a self-identified occupier who hasn't heard these

words or something to their effect. I would almost guarantee it. Being one of those "occupiers," I don't agree with this assessment of the situation, not entirely at least. . . . We must work inside the system—since that is what we have—to reclaim our democracy, we must also take the fight into our own spaces, out among the stars, where we can shape the new possible.

Brian Perkins, Occupy Baton Rouge[3]

I think my generation aspires to find a new "meaning to life." In the past, traditional religious myths filled this void, but currently the western myth of unending materialistic progress is creating a huge void in the world. We feel it is toxic to our souls, and we know that no myth from the past will be able to fully capture what we are looking for. We need a new myth, a new story, which can hold the eternal truths of Life but can also give us an orientation in the modern world, one around which we can build a world that "works for all." We don't need a lot, we aren't looking for materialistic debauchery or lazy lifestyles . . . we want a society where we can live meaningful, spirit-filled, creative, independent and self-sacrificing lives of service. We believe that this is our birthright.

R.M., Male, 35

Violence Against Women is a major problem around the world and too often undocumented. . . . With a background in documentary film making, I decided to put media at the center of my work with displaced women in Northern Uganda. Most women I talked to mentioned the fact that they feel completely silenced, both within their communities and their households. Many said they had no voice and never had a chance to discuss the traumatic events they survived. . . . I believe young activists should support local initiatives and assist in giving a voice to women. Sharing life stories through photography and video may promote critical dialogue within the community, while, at the same time, help to reach policy and decision-makers.

Naomi Freotte[4]

Talents of many young people are wasted, especially young women who often end up in abusive relationships and early marriages due to cultural biases against female children. . . . I have been longing to be in a group of inspiring youth who can rally themselves to promote, empower and play an important role in creating human rights awareness among rural youth, work to find solutions to emerging human rights problems such as HIV/AIDS, to build a network among us young people as future leaders with an interest in the field of human rights and, lastly, to hone the skills and expand the knowledge relevant to human rights practice.

Joshua Oswago, Kenya[5]

Many of the people behind these inspiring, powerful revolutions were citizens who are the same age as me, some even younger. This fills me with pride and hope that problems such as media censorship and control, as well as the oppression of vulnerable groups, such as indigenous peoples, may be eradicated in the future. Although these are very serious problems, they are being tackled one movement at a time by proactive and engaged young people: from the Arab Spring, to the Occupy Wall Street movement, to the Red Shirt demonstrations in Thailand. Young people are leading the way in the Information Age. Generation Y will soon become the backbone of society, and we are already seeing young journalists, bloggers and activists transform world events. . . .

We, the youth, as the next generation's leaders, must vow to move toward an open world with fairness guaranteed to all. Such a profound move starts first with knowledge.

Manuel Ibanez, Peru[6]

MATTHEW FOX: In our first chapter, we introduced this book with Howard Thurman's distinction between the God of Life and the God of Religion. In this chapter, we will be discussing the distinction between the God of Life and the God of Wall Street and other false gods that dictate our civilization to us.

David Korten, one of the important figures on the planet in new economics, says, "The old economy of greed and dominion is dying. A new economy of life and partnership is struggling to be born. The outcome is ours to choose."[7]

We feel this choice has everything to do with the communities in which we choose to live and the values that we bring to our community life. So in this chapter we'll be discussing the values in the communities that we are capable of giving birth to at this critical moment.

ADAM BUCKO: Elsewhere, David Korten says, "Imagine an economy in which life is valued more than money and power resides with ordinary people who care about one another, their community, and their natural environment. It is possible. It is happening. Millions of people are living it into being. Our common future hangs in the balance."

MATTHEW FOX: David Korten, at the time of the latest Wall Street collapse, which brought down economies all over the world, said that it was a teachable moment. And we have to ask, have we really been taught, have we really learned something deep from this, or are we still just providing band-aids to a system that is intrinsically feeble and increasingly immoral? He calls the system as we have it today, the economic system symbolized by Wall Street, a "predatory system," a "dangerous financial system . . . devoted to reckless speculation that produces nothing of real value." That is his definition of Wall Street. It is very important that we meditate on what he is saying. He has real credentials and has been studying (and often teaching) economics for decades.

Korten says Main Street, in contrast to Wall Street, is about real wealth, because it is "local businesses and working people engaged in producing and exchanging real goods and services," while Wall Street is not. He says, "As it now exists [it] is a world of pure money in which the sole game"—notice it's a game—"is to use money to make money for people who have money—a world of speculative gains and unearned claims against the real wealth of Main Street."

So given these understandings, obviously there is a choice. We don't have to take the dictatorship of economic powers that be, including Wall Street. We have a conscience and we can choose what direction we want to go. And that's where community comes in, because communities can reinvent systems they are part of.

ADAM BUCKO: You speak about this as being a teachable moment, but from where I stand, it seems to me that very few people in our society are actually seeing it that way. Most people are still in denial and think that somehow things are not as bad as they seem. It's as if they believe that all we need is a temporary fix to hold us over until things eventually get better. They don't believe that anything really needs to change.

Some of the only people who are truly seeing it as a teachable moment are young people, particularly the young people who are part of the Occupy Wall Street movement. And, of course, they are demonized and mischaracterized by both the liberal and conservative media, mainly because they refuse to get involved in politics as we know it. They refuse to essentially get involved in the system that the media and all the power structures so desperately are trying to preserve.

Many people are frustrated with what the kids at Occupy are doing. Even people who support the movement tend to miss the essence of what the movement is about. They say that in order to fix the system and to be relevant, a specific list of demands is required. But the kids at Occupy are questioning the very logic of what makes things relevant in our society. Occupy at its best is not about fixing the existing system or imposing a new fixed rule. It's about something much more powerful than that. It's about pioneering a new way of living that is based on a daily practice of putting aside our egos and figuring out what it means to create a community and world that works for all.

Speaking of this new way of living, one New York City minister named what he observed at Occupy a "rehearsal of a Kingdom of God." That was my feeling too. When I witnessed what was happening in Zuccotti Park for the first time, I wrote down in my journal, "This is our new holy ground, church, temple, mosque, synagogue. God is where moral courage is!"

MATTHEW FOX: Speak more about your experience with Occupy participants. I have learned from visiting sites in Boston, New York, North Carolina, Colorado, San Francisco, and Oakland but I am sure the youth you work with in New York City are important allies of Occupy also.

ADAM BUCKO: Some of the homeless youth that I work with, who have been living on the outskirts of our society for some time, without much chance of building a sustainable future for themselves, have decided to join the Occupy Wall Street movement. They have left the shelter system and gone back to the streets to be with the Occupy folks, and they have been truly transformed and empowered by the experience of participating in a community dedicated to a daily practice of direct democracy and mutual aid. In that community, they have begun to see themselves differently, to trust their "original goodness." They have begun to relate to each other in a way that has enabled them to help each other discover their unique talents and what kind of contribution they can make to this world. As the movement changed its strategy from occupations to issue-oriented actions for liberation, some of them are now talking about building small communities where they can grow vegetables on the rooftops of their apartments, feed the hungry, and live simply, in a way that is healthy and life enhancing. Some became activists and got much media exposure standing up against police brutality against young people of color in New York City. Others, who are still connected to the shelter system, are talking about organizing homeless youth and holding public ceremonies of forgiveness in front of some of the social service organizations and shelters that claim to be solving homelessness but instead are dehumanizing the people they serve. By publicly forgiving those who dehumanize them on a daily basis, they hope to awaken the humanity of the people who run those organizations and bring it to the forefront of social services and life at large.

MATTHEW FOX: It sounds like they have learned lessons from Mahatma Gandhi, Howard Thurman, Martin Luther King Jr., and Nelson Mandela.

ADAM BUCKO: In all cases, what all these kids are really talking about is this new impulse of creativity and goodness that is emerging in them. They are saying, "This is a truly *teachable* moment, and when we pay attention to what is happening in the world and what is happening in us, we feel that we are experiencing an inner impulse to start to create a community that could embody our inspiration for a different kind of world, a world that is based on principles that are completely different from Wall Street and from some of the other power structures that we were born into." So, for them, it's a real movement from a false life, in which they are asked to become someone they are not just to support the system that doesn't even work for them, to an authentic life, in which they can truly become who they are. These communities become a place to celebrate that and to support others in the same process. So it's really about authentic communities that can birth authentic people and generate more authentic life.

Some people say that focusing on building these small communities and "autonomous zones" is not enough—that we also need to work on changing the system. I agree that in order for any change to be sustainable and all-encompassing, it needs to include what Integral theorists call "I, We, and It zones." We need to work on ourselves, and then incarnate those personal changes into our relationships. But our lives and relationships don't happen in a vacuum. They happen within institutions, which often have their own logic and tend to dictate rules, behaviors, and possibilities. So, institutions do need to change. Having said that, we cannot underestimate the transformative power of small communities and the profound impact they can have on individuals and the world. They can also model what future institutions will look like.

MATTHEW FOX: Can you give some examples of what you are talking about?

ADAM BUCKO: Two examples come to mind. One about the change, on a personal level, that can happen in this kind of a setting, and one about how the small-community method of resistance can help birth a new system.

The first example comes from my time working on the streets of Orlando with teenagers involved in sex work and prostitution. It was a real war zone, where violence, abuse, and the crack epidemic were destroying many communities. While there, we would essentially try to create these emotional or spiritual autonomous zones around our outreach van. This would give both the abused and abusers a chance to take a break from their identities, to enter this caring environment, and experience something authentic and human. As a result, I noticed that those authentic and caring interactions transformed how they interacted with each other outside our zones. While this didn't solve the whole problem, it was a first step toward bringing heart to a world that was very harsh and violent. Later on, some of the abusers and pimps who participated in our autonomous zones actually helped us find and protect some of the kids who ended up on the street and were in danger of getting killed.

MATTHEW FOX: That is a powerful and very real story based on the real world. What is your second example?

ADAM BUCKO: The second example comes from Poland. When you look at the Poland of the 1980s, you realize that probably more than half of the country was part of the resistance, with our own ways of exchanging information through underground publications and media, with alternative networks to get food and other necessities, and with very strong human bonds and relationships, often called "solidarity." In many ways, what we are talking about was an alternative network of friendships and small informal associations, which led to the creation of a country within the country. As a kid, I was very inspired by that. Later on, as a teenager, when I joined the anarchist youth movement, it was that same inspiration that I embraced. It was based on building small communities of friends and a network of loosely connected communities, and then eventually moving the center of life from the official system to this new network of communities that emerged. So, as the majority of Poles began to live outside of the mainstream system that did not support or enhance human authenticity and life, the big mainstream guys became so irrelevant that they had to pack their bags and leave. And while what happened in Eastern Europe was more complex than this (with United States' support and other factors) and while this alone did not cause the collapse of the Eastern Bloc, I truly believe that this was the soul of the revolution, and this was what made it possible.

I think that both of these examples show how reclaiming our authenticity and building communities around it can become both a life-enhancing and world-changing enterprise.

MATTHEW FOX: You used the phrase "life enhancing." It's interesting, in the two quotes that we have from David Korten, the word *life* is prominent in each of them, just as that word is so prominent in the words of Howard Thurman in our first chapter. The idea that we're in a box manufactured by Wall Street is something we have to educate each other about—which is hard to do with the mainstream press, because the mainstream press is thoroughly a part of that system. Again, though, the alternative press, the internet, and social media, are great ways to take advantage of this teachable moment and elicit alternatives.

Korten says that the Wall Street business is creating money and playing financial games using deceptive practices. That is what brought about the crash in the first place. So the point I would just make is we can do better, and I think that's what the young are saying. We have to do better, and by putting community first, we're also including the ecological destruction that is intrinsic to the present financial system. We can no longer afford to leave this ecological accounting out of our accounting books. And the young know this—the young absolutely know this.

So it will take strength—it will take spiritual strength and it will take the strength of communities—to build alternative ways of living in the world, including alternative economics.

ADAM BUCKO: What are some solutions that Korten proposes?

MATTHEW FOX: David Korten points out that what he calls the New Economy 1.0, that we are stuck in now, "leaves unchallenged the implicit assumption of the old economy, namely that life exists to serve the economy," and it creates what he calls a "magical high-tech fantasy world of limitless growth in mindless consumption." So it does not critique the whole consumer addition. Remember that 72 percent of our current economic system in America is built on consumption. Part of today's teachable moment would be to cut that in half. Why should the economy be about greed at both ends—the greed of those who want to make infinite amounts of money, on one hand, and the greed of those who want to do an infinite amount of shopping? You see? It's all fantasy. It's not what life is about. Life is not infinite, and obviously our time on this Earth is not infinite, and the planet itself is very finite. So life must be about something else.

In contrast, Korten's New Economy 2.0 "begins with a recognition that we humans are living inhabitants of a living Earth and that creative, conscious living in strong healthy communities with strong and healthy families is the foundation of human happiness and well-being. It further recognizes that the economy has no other legitimate purpose than to serve life"—so life is not here to serve the economy, the economy is here to serve life—"all life, including all the world's people. It calls for a radical reinvention of our defining economic culture and institutions to create a New Economy that serves all the people all the time."

So that, to me, is really the number one question in economics today. Can we create an economy that serves, that benefits everybody? And "everybody" being not just the two-legged creatures, but all the other creatures too, because we're here together. This kind of reinvention has to happen at ground level, in small communities.

ADAM BUCKO: That does seem to be the number one question—and the media dares not give it even a voice. But the Occupy movement is doing so.

MATTHEW FOX: As Korten points out, in September 2008, "trillions of dollars of phantom financial wealth vanished in the blink of an eye. The corruption of [our] economic system . . . was exposed for all to see." That's the teachable-moment part that we haven't picked up on very much yet. But as you say, these are the questions the young people are asking. And there are more and more communities that are living out these questions.

Another dimension to his teaching is he actually talks about the reptilian brain and how militaristic, consumerist capitalism appeals to the reptilian brain. It's win/lose. You can kind of sense this in a person like Donald Trump. Korten points out, of course, that this is no way to survive. The reptilian brain, as applied to humans, in only one-third of our brainpower. Yet notice what he's saying: our economic system runs on that brain, that third of our total power. Our mammalian brain, is the compassionate brain; it is the brain of kinship; it is the brain of community. And that brain needs much more attention economically. What is an economics for the mammalian brain, as distinct from an economics for the reptilian brain? Here's where the medial cortex brain can enter the cognitive-intellectual-creative brain. We have the power to move from an exclusively reptilian economic system—survival of the fittest—to much more of a maternal, mammalian, community concept of mutual enhancement in which everybody lives and everybody wins. You don't have winners and losers, and you don't have this extraordinary gap between people making hundreds of millions of dollars a year, while others go without food.

So I think this contribution he makes feeds very much into issues of spirituality, because I believe that we can tame the reptilian brain through meditation and other spiritual practices. Without that taming, we're always ripe to be seduced by reptilian economics. Which is, in fact, a great detour from our objective, which is community. Community too requires the taming of the reptilian brain, and living it can be a practice that contributes to taming the reptilian brain.

ADAM BUCKO: What I like about Korten is that he understands the complexity of the situation and the real purpose of the economy: life is not here to serve the economy; the economy is here to serve life. Our present system does not serve life; it doesn't even really take life into consideration. It is here to serve the stability and expansion of the system, and the system, of course, is not neutral. Someone is definitely getting rich from it and, to use Occupy's language, it's the 1 percent that is profiting. What we need is a democratization of this enterprise, so everyone can benefit and live. We need a framework that can begin to serve, nourish, and enhance life as it manifests in each person with their uniqueness and value. What we need is a framework that can make it possible for us to actualize our potential and grow our souls.

What will this new framework look like? Korten talks about a network of small, decentralized, and localized economies and communities. In doing so, we could say that he talks about moving from imposed uniformity to diversity. Shane Claiborne, a Christian New Monastic leader, said that uniformity and sameness (homogeneity) are part of the empire. He said, "Caesar makes coins that are all identical. But our God is a God of diversity. Our God is an artist. The kingdom of God is a place where every person is unique, just like our fingerprints." So, for example, you look at the coin, and the "symbol of Caesar" controls all life, because all life has to be mediated through that symbol. But the Kingdom of God that Jesus advocated was very different. When Jesus called people, everyone responded differently, depending on his or her vocation and mission in the world. Some people sold everything and followed him; other people did other things. It seems that there was room for diversity in the kingdom that he advocated. Jesus gave very few answers, but he asked many, many questions. Questions that helped people discover their own sense of direction and sense of aliveness and identity in God. What they discovered oftentimes put them in conflict with both the political and religious systems of first-century Palestine.

MATTHEW FOX: No question there was plenty of diversity in those times and a lot of imagination was at work in standing up to the dominant empire.

ADAM BUCKO: Our present system is the opposite of that. It asks us to give up who we are and to leave unexplored our deepest longings. To help us deal with the meaninglessness of this, it gives us distractions that lead to an obsession with consuming, which creates a false sense of aliveness. Our lives become about shopping and consuming, and we slowly lose the ability to see what really matters. We lose the ability to ask important questions. And, as you said, we end up in a place where the greed of those who want to make infinite amounts of money feeds the greed of those who want to do an infinite amount of shopping.

Our God might be a God of diversity but the God of Wall Street is a God of uniformity, uniformity that ensures that the system as we know it will be reproduced and maintained. Unfortunately, this system only works for a few, and there is no room in what it produces for our most basic and essential needs.

MATTHEW FOX: Shopping is an addiction just like alcohol can be. Like all avarice, addictions "tend to infinity," as Aquinas says, and they do not satisfy.

ADAM BUCKO: We need to reject this system of uniformity and this system of life mediated through symbols that value *having* over *being* and that rely on addiction to keep it going. Instead, we need to reconnect with our spirit, with our life, listen to its guidance, and allow that life to live through us. In doing so, we will discover the real essence of who we are and why we are here. And then, through that direct intuition and in a dialogue and community with others (reminding each other of this experience and our authenticity) we will begin to build our lives around what emerges out of this process, with each community representing a different dimension of this dream that is trying to be born here. This is the way to transform our world from a world in which life is asked to serve economy to a world in which economy serves life.

When I think about the type of a future world that I would like to live in, I like what Korten says about the future being about small, decentralized, and localized communities and economies. The questions that I have are: Would it be possible to create a large frame that is big enough to hold many different subframes? Is it possible to have a very general system that can hold many different subsystems that somehow operate according to different philosophies? Some of them could be perhaps more cooperative and based on anarchist principles, some could be more capitalistic, some of them could be more socialistic, but all of them would be small and in relationship to each other. The fact is that capitalism and socialism, when done on a face-to-face level, are not actually that different.

MATTHEW FOX: Done on a face-to-face level—that's key.

ADAM BUCKO: Talking about Christianity, I think that for a very long time we were fed the story that there is this original church that we can discover, that it's uniform and it has certain structures and its original teaching. But through all the new historical research, what we're discovering is that, in fact, there were many different churches, almost like house communities, and all of them operated according to slightly different rules, and probably different disciples got a different kind of transmission from Jesus. And it was just a network of . . .

MATTHEW FOX: Of very diverse communities, absolutely. It's clear that Paul had his kind of churches. And even there, even within Paul's expression, there were different versions—there were storefront churches, there were home churches, and so forth. But James has his, as you say, transmission, his version; Peter his; and so forth. That's right—the origins of Christianity are not at all uniform. That is very clear from today's scholarship.

ADAM BUCKO: It's also very clear that different disciples got different teachings, based on their needs or perhaps based on their vocation.

MATTHEW FOX: And their gifts. And a good example is Mary Magdalene, who, according to today's scholars, such as Bruce Chilton, was entrusted by Jesus with the whole ministry of anointing and healing, which developed into the sacramental system. But, unfortunately, it has become more system than sacrament. And healing goes often underplayed in the process.

But as you say, the story that Christianity was uniform, and we just have to call on that all the time, is a false myth. That story of uniformity, of course, developed in the fourth century, with the empire. It's imperial thinking: uniformity, get in line, obey. And obviously the inheritance of the empire by the Christian church was a huge detour from the teaching and the spirit of Jesus. So that's part of what we're wrestling with today, to deconstruct an imperially based Christianity in favor of something truer to the values that Jesus preached.

ADAM BUCKO: And, for that matter, all religions, because all of them seem to have . . .

MATTHEW FOX: Yes, eventually religions do get used by other forces, political and military. Yes, so they all need, well, *semper reformanda*, continual reformation.

ADAM BUCKO: It's interesting when you mention that, because I think it takes us into the conversation about monasticism and New Monasticism. When I look at the development of monasticism within the Christian tradition, I see it as a protest movement. Essentially, when Christianity hooked up with the empire in the fourth century, a bunch of people rejected this partnership. They moved to the desert to protest their religion being corrupted by the system and used to build something that had nothing to do with Jesus.

MATTHEW FOX: To kill in the name of Christ.

ADAM BUCKO: To kill in the name of Christ, absolutely. And that's when diversity ended, because diversity was seen as too dangerous. Everyone had to subscribe to the same principles. Interestingly enough, in his last speech that he gave, in Bangkok in 1968, Thomas Merton compared some of the elements of the countercultural youth revolution of the 1960s to those first monks. In his article "Raimundo Panikkar on the Monk as Archetype," Francis Tiso said that in Bangkok, during Merton's last speech, just moments before his tragic death, when Merton began to praise radical poets of the 1960s and American hippies as the "true monks of our times," it became obvious that the monastic leadership wanted nothing to do with these ersatz "new monks."[8] But Merton did. And I think that he perhaps envisioned a possibility for a new monasticism, a new movement of small communities of resistance that could combine elements of what, in our own day, the kids at Occupy Wall Street are doing, with a deep spiritual and contemplative practice and life. This movement could enable people to be together in a way that awakens their authenticity and helps them transform their lives. It could help them discover their unique sense of purpose and nourish their souls and talents, and, as a result, it could build a counterpower to our present system, of which Wall Street is a big part. And if this movement is to be successful, it needs deep, transformative spirituality because, as you said before, democracy needs spirituality, community needs spirituality, and ultimately, economy needs spirituality, or else we will keep coming up with solutions that eventually will be hijacked by our reptilian brains and used in service of aggression and greed.

MATTHEW FOX: Speak now about your experience with the New Monasticism movement.

ADAM BUCKO: Now, when we talk about New Monasticism, especially in the United States, it's mainly known as an evangelical movement. I think that there are many good and beautiful things that are happening within the evangelical New Monastic communities. I have felt personally indebted to and inspired by the New Monasticism advocated by Shane Claiborne and Jonathan Wilson-Hartgrove. I see them as real prophetic figures who are expressing new impulses of the Holy Spirit and *re-visioning* the Christ path. Having said that, I have also come across evangelical New Monastics who are very fundamentalist in their approach to both their faith and their relationship to other faiths, as well as to issues related to homosexuality. As we enter what Br. Wayne Teasdale called an Interspiritual Age, characterized by our ability to move beyond our sectarian understandings, we need a broader New Monastic movement, one that moves in the same Spirit, but that can be more embracing of all people, no matter what their traditions are. We need one that can offer all people tools for a deep contemplative path for personal and social transformation.

In order to achieve this openness, we need to reevaluate our religious traditions in relation to the contemplative experience that lies at the source of each tradition and in relation to other wisdom traditions, modern science, and new cosmology. This reevaluation will slowly lead us into a new understanding of ourselves and our traditions within the context of the whole of the human history and the human family.

There are many different models for what this new movement could look like. Two models that I personally really like are present in Sufism and in the Christian Base Community movement.

Let's start with some inspiring examples from Sufism. In his essay "The Universality of Monasticism and Its Relevance in the Modern World," Frithjof Schuon describes Sufism as the monasticism of Islam.[9] He states that the contribution of Islam to the universal monastic culture is the possibility of a "monastic society." Unlike other forms of monasticism, which imply withdrawal from the world and exclusion of things like marriage, family, and career, Sufism aims to carry the contemplative life into the very framework of society as a whole. Things like regular daily contemplative practice; connection with a spiritual community, or *dargha;* and spiritual direction from a Sheikh or a Pir create an internal structure for a deeply contemplative life in the world. So while many people would say that there is no monasticism in Islam, Sufism is a form of monasticism, according to Schuon, a monasticism that happens within the world rather than in a monastery, separated from the world. This has tremendous implications for New Monasticism, because it offers a tested model for how to bring the spiritual perspective and experience into every domain of life and society and how to transform the world from within.

There are many examples of this kind of transformative power in Sufi communities. One example of a community that I really love is a group of young people from the Sufi Order International.[10] This group is an international circle of friends who don't necessarily live next to each other, but whose friendships embody the deepest meaning of community. They truly exemplify what it means to have a community and communion on the level of the soul. Their lives are rooted in a contemplative and spiritual depth that I rarely see in young people. Their relationships are based on authenticity, honesty, integrity, and real knowledge of each other. In fact, I have never met another group of friends who respect each other so much. And yet their respect is not based on some kind of illusive projection. It is based on real knowledge of who they are, on real mutual acceptance of their gifts, difficulties, and struggles. It is based on real love, which allows them to be present to each other in an unconditional way and to give each other permission to be who they were born to be. This empowers them to be committed to the truth that is emerging in their souls. It gives them courage to incarnate that truth in the world and lead lives that are rooted in the authenticity of their calling, employing their gifts and talents in the service of life, compassion, and justice.

I personally have been deeply touched by that community, and I have learned a lot from my Sufi friends who are part of this community. Oftentimes, when I witness communities like this one, all I can think of is that this is what Jesus meant when he used the phrase "the kingdom of God." This kingdom exists where relationships in which "love and not power" are at the center. These relationships make God "happen" in our midst. They evoke a certain kind of electricity that transforms what's possible in life and in the world.

MATTHEW FOX: Speak more about the history of this movement. It sounds so important and useful for us on so many levels today.

ADAM BUCKO: Speaking of this particular group of friends, it is important to mention that this transformative quality that they embody didn't just happen by accident. Their relationships, and the fact that now they are such a healing presence in the world, unfolded as a result of a very specific training, spiritual practice, and guidance from mentors and elders. All of the people I am talking about are part of a very transformative lineage that today is guided by Pir Zia Inayat-Khan. This particular Sufi path was brought to the West by Pir Zia's grandfather, Pir Hazrat Inayat Khan, who was an Indian-born musician and mystic, often cited as the first teacher to bring Sufism to the West. He founded the "Sufi

Order in the West" in 1910. When he came to the West, he spent sixteen years traveling all over the Western world, performing classical Indian music, lecturing on the spiritual dimensions of the problems and opportunities of the modern world, and training students in the inner culture of Sufism. Hazrat Inayat Khan was a true pioneer, who offered people something extraordinary. He offered an all-encompassing path that included all areas of life and gave a new and modern expression to the universal wisdom of Sufism.

There are many people who have been touched and transformed by this path. After the First World War, his movement sought to transform the cultural assumptions that had created the monster of militant nationalism. Part of this response was an interfaith service called Universal Worship, which, through lighting of candles and readings from scriptures of the world's great religions, portrays at a single altar the sweeping vista of the human encounter with the Divine. During the Second World War, Hazrat Inayat Khan's daughter, Noor Inayat Khan, served heroically as the first woman wireless operator in Nazi-occupied France. Betrayed to the Gestapo, she was executed at Dachau in 1944 and was posthumously awarded Britain's George Cross and France's Croix de Guerre. Later on, Hazrat Inayat Khan's eldest son, Pir Vilayat Inayat Khan, continued his father's work and drew extensively on the world's mystical heritage, as well as on music, science, and psychology, founding the Sufi training center and spiritual community called the Abode of the Message, which is a spiritual home to many Sufis all over the world. He also inspired the founding of the Omega Institute, known as the largest training center for holistic culture in the world, pioneering a unique brand of American spirituality that marries deep contemplative wisdom of the East with insights of Western science and psychology.

MATTHEW FOX: How else is the movement operative today?

ADAM BUCKO: Today Hazrat Inayat Khan's grandson, Pir Zia Inayat-Khan, continues this tradition in a deep, transformative, and powerful way through founding such initiatives as Suluk and Seven Pillars House of Wisdom. Although Pir Zia Inayat-Khan is a practicing Muslim (just like his grandfather), the Sufi order is open to people of all religious and spiritual persuasions, thus helping people to deepen their own unique sense of God and life in God. Today it is common for Christian, Jews, Muslims, Buddhists, Hindus, and others to be part of this Sufi lineage in a way that is life changing and yet does not necessarily take them away from their own traditions.

Suluk, in my view, is one of the most comprehensive spiritual formations and training programs that I have seen. It is able to actually transmit this ancient spiritual knowledge within the context of the twenty-first century and to change modern lives. The brilliance of the program is that the training marries the deep, intellectual formation based on the writings of Hazrat Inayat Khan and a profound contemplative practice with deep psychological process, one-on-one spiritual guidance, solitary retreats, small group work focused on presence and authenticity, and a profound sense of celebration and joy. In addition, the guides of the program are composed of an intergenerational group of senior teachers and practitioners. It is a truly all-encompassing path that many spiritual organizations and churches should be learning from.

Pir Zia is a spiritual director and guide to the group of young people I mentioned from the Sufi Order International. Many of them are now participating in and are collaborators with the Seven Pillars House of Wisdom, which offers deeper ways of knowing and serving life, through the application and integration of contemplative wisdom, new cosmology, the need for enlightened action, and wisdom of the Earth. It is dedicated to both synthesizing knowledge from the past and advancing new paradigms. This organization is truly an outward manifestation of the spiritual heritage and practice of Pir Zia and all the collaborators. In my view, it is a way for the Sufi order and their friends to share the fruits of their inner lives with the world in practical and culture-shaping ways. It simply recognizes that we live in a world in which, to use Lama Surya Das's phrase, wisdom is an endangered species. Our world needs a drastically new vision for life and development. While we as a species have reached the height of our powers, our might has outpaced our wisdom, and, as a result, life on planet Earth is withering before our eyes. Seven Pillars is a direct response to this crisis.

This is just one example of a wisdom-based approach to life and society that New Monastics could draw from. They could learn from this community how to be a pocket of light in our world and how to build a kingdom of God one friendship at a time. They could learn the true meaning of community, where relationships have a deep, soulful quality and are based on life and soul-enhancing presence and commitment. They could learn how to share prayer and how people of different religious and theological persuasions can meet in silence and celebration of the prayerful and receptive heart. They could learn how to combine a deep spiritual life and practice that includes the whole person with an outward expression that has a culture-shaping effect on our world.

Clearly, this is a very specific outward expression. The beauty of this movement is that all communities can discern their own calling and vocation as individuals and communities. Then we can connect our communities in a network of dedicated friendships that can begin to shift what matters in our world and shape a new way of being. This network can begin to help us move from a false aliveness, mediated and inspired by symbols that value *having* over *being*, to a true aliveness, in which life evokes more life, and in which our gifts are used in service of compassion, justice, and mutual empowerment.

MATTHEW FOX: You talked about another model that inspires you today.

ADAM BUCKO: The other model that is truly inspiring is the model of Base Communities in Latin America. You once said that, in your view, the Base Community Movement was one of the most authentic Christian expressions that you had ever seen in your life. I was wondering if you could talk about your personal experiences with Base Communities and what could New Monastics learn from this movement.

MATTHEW FOX: I had read about the Base Communities and the liberation theology that spawned them after the Second Vatican Council, but my opportunity to visit Central and South America came when I was silenced by the Vatican for a year. I took that opportunity to visit Nicaragua, Brazil, Costa Rica, and Ecuador. In my journeys I had the privilege to spend quality time with Leonardo Boff, the most prominent of the liberation theologians of South America; with Cardinal Arns, a true hero, insofar as he stood up almost alone to the military dictatorship of Brazil for years; and with Bishop Casigalida, whose diocese was the rainforests of Brazil. I also attended large and small political gatherings in Brazil and Nicaragua and lectured in Costa Rica.

The Base Community movement took seriously the teaching of Vatican II that "the people" are the church, not just the hierarchy. Unfortunately, this put the movement on a collision course with forces in Rome who wanted it otherwise (and still do—see my book *The Pope's War*) and also with the CIA, who linked up with Rome to split the Latin American church. The methodology of Base Communities was to let the peasants and the poor people speak about their relation to and implementation of Gospel values. I was most struck by the courage of these groups, as many of them were taking on multinational corporations (who were, for example, destroying the rainforests and the indigenous people who dwell there), as well as government interests. They were willing to pay even the ultimate price for standing for values of justice and compassion; many of them were tortured, imprisoned, or murdered. One has to admire such a spirit as that. They were taking Jesus's teachings seriously. (One of the reasons the Vatican silenced Bishop Casigalida was that he called his friend Óscar Romero a "saint" after his martyrdom at the hands of the right-wing death squads of El Salvador. So you see the Vatican itself took sides, but rarely took the side of those fighting the battles on the front lines, such as Romero, whom they opposed fiercely.)

The emasculation of this movement and killing of the grassroots invigoration of Christianity that it affected has been almost complete during the past forty years of Roman Catholic history, in alliance with the CIA and German right-wing groups, as I detail in my book *The Pope's War*. So what is happening today in the Latin American church? On the papal side, Opus Dei flourishes and is taking over more of the hierarchy everywhere—that is Rome's goal. (Opus Dei is an extreme right-wing movement that is very secretive and was founded by a fascist Spanish priest). But the church of the people is moving beyond the church. As one ex-bishop put it, "I used to serve the church, now I serve humanity."

Leonardo Boff has recently written about the movement in this way,

The Church . . . was never the object of the preaching of Jesus. He announced a dream, the Kingdom of God, in contraposition to the Kingdom of Caesar; the Kingdom of God that represents an absolute revolution in relationships, from the individual to the divine and the cosmic. Christianity appeared in history primarily as a *movement* and as *the way of Christ*. It predates its grounding in the four Gospels and in the doctrines. The character of a spiritual path means a type of Christianity that has its own course. It generally lives on the edge and, at times, at a critical distance from the official institutions. But it is born and nourished by the permanent fascination with the figure and the liberating and spiritual message of Jesus of Nazareth.[11]

And he points out that people of many faith traditions—including atheists—admire the values that Jesus stood for and died for. "Many people say, 'if there is a God, it has to be like the God of Jesus.'"

ADAM BUCKO: Do you know of any communities in the United States that reflect what Boff is talking about?

MATTHEW FOX: One marvelous community to be found in Oakland, California, is the Canticle Farm, modeled after St. Francis of Assisi's teachings and values. Currently consisting of five houses with gardens and more in the Fruitvale (largely Hispanic) area of Oakland, the homes boast names such as "Sister Water" and "Brother Sun," taken directly from Francis's poem "Canticle of the Sun." Its visionary and founder, Anne Symens-Bucher, worked with Dorothy Day as a young woman and currently works with Buddhist activist Joanna Macy. In between, for many years, she was mentored by Fr. Louis Vitale, an eighty-year-old Franciscan friar well known for his courageous stands in favor of peace and justice (and who has gone to prison to bear witness to those values numerous times).

Included in the community are young and older adults. Pancho Ramos-Stierle, who has been cited in this book, is a community member, along with other activists and spiritual warriors trying to heal the planet while living lives of witness. They attract other seekers from Dorothy Day's Worker House movement and more. This is just one of many examples of communities being born in our time where young adults are finding a life of simple but healthy living and of dedication to values and principles worth living for.

There is a movement called "Creation Spirituality Communities," which has grown from students who have studied with me.[12] They are committed to putting principles of creation spirituality into practice through courses, rituals, blogging, learning experiences of many kinds. Let me also say that Sister Dorothy Stang, who was assassinated in the Amazon for her work among base communities there that were committed to saving the rainforest from corporate logging, was a graduate of our creation spirituality master's program. She stands as a hero to many for her generous witness to justice and compassion, and she regularly wrote back to our program direction that it was her work in creation spirituality that kept her in her vocation, even though she was aware of the danger involved. She was originally from Ohio.

ADAM BUCKO: Also, I heard you say that the Alcoholics Anonymous movement, in your view, is an example of a Western base community.

MATTHEW FOX: In my book *Creation Spirituality: Liberating Gifts for the Peoples of the Earth,* which I wrote after my visits to South America, I try to name the "base communities" that we have given birth to in North America, movements that will be different from those of South America, for obvious sociological and cultural reasons. And one of those that deserves to be highlighted is Alcoholics Anonymous, along with its many spinoffs, because clearly addiction is one of the greatest oppressions that we deal with in our culture. We have touched on this above, in discussing our addiction to shopping, for example. The words *addiction* and *dictator* are closely related, obviously. An addiction is a kind of inner dictator. It interferes with full living, with our freedom, with the emergence of our authentic wisdom and beauty. And it spreads evil to others. Think about the damage, for example, that an alcoholic father rains down on his family, damage that can persist for generations of woundedness. Alcoholics Anonymous addresses some of those issues, and it is, like Base Communities of Latin America, not about hierarchy but about the authentic stories and experiences of everyday people. It is also about service and compassion, for the real healing that goes on there is assisted by those who have been through the darkness of alcoholism. It is compassion in action.

Addressing our other addictions, such as shopping, is equally important at this time, if true community is to emerge. But we cannot be naive: the truth is we have an *entire economic system based on rendering us addicts from the time we are young children*—that is the deep shadow behind consumer capitalism and its trillion-dollar advertising industry. It feeds on human weakness: greed and avarice. That is why we need a new economics. We do not live to shop. We live to live. Don't we?

ADAM BUCKO: In a recent program that we did on young people and inter-generational activism, you mentioned that it might be useful for the New Monastic movement to go back to the traditional monastic vows and reimagine what they could mean for the twenty-first century. I was wondering if you could offer your interpretation of the three traditional monastic vows in the light of your theology of Creation Spirituality, which, in my view, combines the incarnational spirituality present in Sufism with the prophetic and social justice spirituality of the Base Communities?

MATTHEW FOX: Yes. So let's talk about the traditional vows of poverty, obedience, and chastity. First of all, poverty: we've been talking about alternative economics. So what this vow is really about, I think, if we step back from it, is human nature. Human nature is driven this way and that by economics—we all have financial problems, one way or another. If you're part of the 1 percent, your problem is holding on to your wealth and multiplying it, but if you're like most of us, your problem is just paying your bills every month or ending up on the street, literally. So obviously the issues of economics are everybody's issues.

Second, the vow of obedience. The issue of government, of politi-cal power, is what the vow of obedience is really addressing in some rather narrow way. But who makes decisions? How do we make deci-sions? Whom do we allow to make decisions for us, about our own self-expression or our own values, and so forth? Is government truly of the people, for the people, and by the people? Or is it by the few for the few?

The third vow addresses sexuality. Very simply, if you're in the Buddhist tradition, it's just a question of what is responsible sexuality. But the vow of celibacy is really saying, "okay, here's one way of deal-ing with sexuality—it's kind of unusual, but it's doable." It's kind of an extreme thing, the idea that you can sublimate sexuality and still be healthy. And your sexuality will come up in other forms—that kind of energy can be focused for other purposes.

Another dimension of celibacy, which I'm convinced is what really made it significant in Europe in the Middle Ages, is that, obviously, it's a form of birth control. And I think that was very important because the growing season was so brief—it was only a few months long. In the twelfth century, Europe warmed up, because the currents in the Atlantic Ocean shifted. That made a huge difference; you had a longer growing season and a larger population as a result, larger families. But the point is that celibacy served a very social need, and that was birth control. Today modern medicine offers rather simple forms of birth control. Now, of course, each of these has its shadow side to it, too.

But let's just go back a minute. Regarding economics: we've been talking about the alternatives to the economics of today. So a modern version of the traditional vow of poverty in these new communities might be a vow to work toward an economy that works for all. I, we, will commit ourselves to doing what we can to build alternative economics, not this rapacious, reptilian economics of Wall Street, but an economics of community and Main Street—that seems to me like a very worthy vow. A vow, of course, is a sacred promise; it's a way of clearing your mind so there's no doubt, "Oh, this is what I'm about. This is part of my vocation, that I commit to this," however I do it. I may do it as an artist, as a filmmaker, as a teacher, or a preacher, and certainly as a politician, certainly as a citizen.

What is classically called the vow of obedience in these new communities is really, I think, a promise to work democratically—to look for the consensus of the group and to try to work from the realization that wisdom does come through a circle of sharing and decision making, and to commit to that rather than to vertical, hierarchical dictates. So that would be, I think, an appropriate promise, an appropriate sacred pledge. We might rename the vow of obedience the vow of democracy. I think a perfect example of a vow of democracy being put into action would be to take on the awful Citizens United decree of the Supreme

Court and get a constitutional amendment passed as soon as possible to overturn it. The notion that corporations have the same rights as individuals is no where found in our constitution, nor in common sense. It obviously opens the door to the complete corruption of an already failing democracy, one in which a billionaire corporate head has far more influence with his or her vote by flooding the electoral process with excess of cash. It is a real scandal that needs correcting as fast as possible.

Another issue today that democracy faces is the fact of voices of the more-than-humans. The fact that forests and oceans, fishes and four-legged ones, and soil and plants have no voice is no longer sustainable. We have to move beyond the anthropocentrism of the modern consciousness to include other species and ecosystems in our decision making on this planet.

Then the third vow, the traditional vow of chastity, is, I think—not to be overly complex or nuanced—simply about living lives of sexual responsibility. Today that includes, first, intelligent birth control, because our species has plenty of people—we're not short on people. So it takes both intelligence and a decision not to bring undue numbers of more human beings into the world. Second, there's the issue of transmitted diseases, which is part of responsible sexuality as well. Third and finally—I don't think there's a lot more to the morality of sexuality—sexual responsibility requires us not to be promiscuous and go around breaking people's hearts or bringing babies into the world who will not be loved and cared for. Love and lovemaking takes focusing and takes commitment and takes time, and it really is a serious thing when we go around breaking the hearts of those we love or parenting children with little future to offer them. So commitment, when there's commitment made, it needs to be kept. Of course, we make vows of marriage and commitment, so we're already kind of working in that arena.

A fourth area of the issue of sexuality, which has come to a crescendo in our time, is that of recognizing the sexual diversity that is out there. I am speaking, of course, about replacing homophobia with recognition of the rights and responsibilities of homosexual people. The fight for gay rights and gay marriage is another dimension of the vow of responsible sexuality in our time, as I see it. The emergence of gay rights may also be Gaia's way of lessening somewhat the human population explosion, because many (certainly not all) gay and lesbian couples choose not to bring children into the world, but express their creativity in other and alternative, often artistic, ways of giving to the culture and the greater community. Science teaches us that 8 to 10 percent of any human population is gay or lesbian (and over 484 other species have gay populations as well). It is time to get real.

So that's how I would kind of rename the traditional vows. Again, I think there's archetypal wisdom there—and power. The issues of money, finance, economics; the issues of government, political power, decision making; and the issues of sexuality are universal. But in this context, there are diverse ways of fulfilling these vows. For example, of responsible sexuality, there's responsible gay sexuality and there's responsible heterosexual sexuality.

Of course, there's responsible parenting, and the parenting obviously should not be restricted to literal parents; all adults have a role of parenting in our culture. And parenting includes the whole issues of education, obviously, because we're always teaching young people. Of course, the media too—media is a form of education. It's instruction, it's information, it's how children and young people receive so many of their values. So the responsibility of adults to not use something as powerful as the media to manipulate children, it seems to me, would come under that vow of responsible sexuality and parenting, if you will.

Maybe that's what it should be called, not just a vow of responsible sexuality, but of parenting as well. And that would shine the light on a lot of issues. We often don't include the children when we're making the decisions. An obvious example is putting sugar into children's cereal. Is that responsible parenting? Of course not. And schools that are only giving exams—is that responsible parenting? No, it's not. And then agribusiness—is that responsible parenting? We're pumping chemicals into animals and into the soil that are not going to be healthy for future generations. Or tearing down trees—how can that be responsible parenting? So whole areas of values light up with the kind of beacon these three vows shine on culture.

ADAM BUCKO: So the monasticism of the past had some very positive dimensions to it.

MATTHEW FOX: The high monastic era in Christianity in the West was, of course, during what we call the Dark Ages, so extending from around the fifth century up through the twelfth century. The monasteries were the center of education, culture, and so forth during a difficult and very cold period of Western history. But then it did become fat and lazy and overly identified with the economic system of the time—the feudal system—and that's why it became fat and lazy. They needed a revolution to shake it up. And that is exactly what Francis of Assisi represented, as did Dominic, his peer, and the new university movement, which literally took education from the rural monastic system into the new cities.

Now, there is something parallel to those problems today. In this instance, religion in the West has overidentified with capitalism. Indeed, sociologists have pointed out the intrinsic connection between Calvin and the Protestant movement and the rise of capitalism in the modern era. Today we are questioning the kind of capitalism we have. And, of course, Marx questioned it, as did Dickens 150 years ago. Now we have a new version of capitalism, which, of course, has had no peers since the Soviet Union collapsed. Capitalism has been running practically unfettered for thirty years and has shown its shadow side.

So the decoupling of religion from consumer capitalism and casino capitalism (Robert Reich's term for Wall Street gamers) is the issue today. That, I think, is what Occupy Wall Street is about. And that is what we're talking about when we talk about a New Monasticism, one that is not rural exclusively, and yet is not anti-rural. So this New

Monasticism can be in cities, it can be in towns, it can be in the coun-
tryside. It's not partial to one occupation, profession, or setting. It can
be in multiple settings. What unites it is a common commitment to
creating an economic system that works for everybody, and, therefore,
is not Wall Street or consumer capitalism, it's not appealing to greed or
to the reptilian brain. Its effort is very mammal-like: it's to create communities that nurture and that make joy and justice easier to come by.

ADAM BUCKO: I truly feel that a new impulse of the Holy Spirit is knocking on our hearts today. In my view, this new impulse is asking us to
combine the prophetic energy of the young people from the Occupy
movement with a deep and contemplative spirituality. If we respond
to this impulse properly and if we truly pay attention to what is being
asked of us, this could lead to something amazing, a new society based
on the principles and practice of spiritual democracy. I was wondering
if, as an elder, you had any final advice for people who are part of this
new movement?

MATTHEW FOX: I think all our dialogues in this book and all the surveys we
took and the filming we did of young leaders for this project speak to
the intergenerational wisdom we need to come to grips with what you
say is "a new impulse of the Holy Spirit knocking on hearts today." In
our concluding chapter, we can hopefully bring these thoughts together.

Conclusion

Occupy Generation and the Practice of Spiritual Democracy

We believe that the movement, from Cairo to New York, from San Francisco to London, that is being called "Occupy" is a movement of spiritual democracy. We want to give credit to those young people around the globe who, often in the presence of real and present danger, are standing up for others, are taking stands for spiritual democracy.

In discussing the exciting topic of spiritual democracy, we want to give credit to a spiritual ancestor, Walt Whitman. Whitman used this phrase on many occasions, as when he said, "I say to you that all forms of religion, without excepting one, any age, any land, are but mediums, temporary yet necessary, fitted to the lower mass-ranges of perception of the race—part of its infant school—and that the developed soul passes through one or all of them, to the clear homogeneous atmosphere above them. There all meet—previous distinctions are lost—Jew meets Hindu, and Persian Greek and Asiatic and European and American are joined—and any one religion is just as good as another."[1]

This is a very important quote, because essentially it describes the climate that many young people find themselves in today. It's this climate that Brother Wayne called our "interspiritual age," or what Matthew Fox has called "deep ecumenism." More and more people (and especially the young) are realizing that essentially, while they drink from traditions or a specific tradition, in the end the teaching—even though sometimes it comes through the tradition—is really about going beyond the tradition itself, going into that space that is beyond all religions. The late Catholic monk Thomas Merton talked about the need to "discover an older unity. My dear brothers and sisters, we are already one. But we imagine that we are not. So what we have to recover is our original unity. What we have to be is what we are."

When Adam was growing up in Poland, he felt he was born into a specific tradition, but now he knows that he has been nurtured by a variety of traditions with mentors from several different traditions. "Even though I tend to identify as a Christian, I realize that most of my teachings actually come from life directly, and then I relate it to Christianity because this way it gives me context. But the transmission itself comes from life, so to speak."

Matthew too comes from the Christian tradition and remains in it, but not at all in an enclosed way. He admits that his sharing of prayer in sweat lodges, sun dances, vision quests, and more with indigenous people, for example, have been essential to his spiritual growth and well-being, as well as Buddhist encounters and practices, *t'ai chi,* Taoist readings, Jewish rabbis, and much more, including in-depth psychological thinkers and practitioners. We are already living in a time of deep ecumenism. Therefore, a time of spiritual democracy.

Life trumps religion. Life and existence in this universe are 13.8 billion years old and religions are 5,000 years old or 100,000 years old, when you include the oldest, which are the shamanistic and the indigenous. But the point is that, why would we be driven to put religion before life? And then, of course, go to war with other religions—take life, destroy life, in that name? Hopefully this is one element of human evolution, of consciousness, that is shaking down at this time. The young people aren't buying into this notion that my God beats up on your God or Goddess.

Another teaching from Whitman about spiritual democracy is this:

> There will soon be no more priests. Their work is done. They may wait awhile . . . perhaps a generation or two . . . dropping off by degrees. A superior breed shall take their place. . . . The gangs of kosmos and prophets *en masse* shall take their place. A new order shall rise and they shall be the priests of man, and every man shall be his own priest. The churches built under their umbrage shall be the churches of men and women. Through the divinity of themselves shall the kosmos and the new breed of poets be interpreters of men and women and of all events and things.[2]

It's interesting that 150 years ago, Whitman was calling for the de-clericalization of spiritual leadership. That is, therefore, for spiritual democracy. Again, he's not denying, it seems to us, the fact of people's charismatic gifts and the gifts of leadership. But he does not see that occurring in terms of a hierarchical priesthood, but rather in terms of the depth of the encounter with the divine that people find within themselves. And it's out of that kind of depth that leadership will emerge.

It is also noteworthy that he includes the "kosmos" as an integral part of his vision of a spiritual democracy. In the context of the universe, none of us lords over others. We are all citizens of the universe. None is in charge, yet all are responsible. Given the new creation story that science and the new cosmology present us with today, the implications of this are very great for all of our institutions, from economics to politics to religion. The new cosmology is also democratic, insofar as it is not "owned" by any one national, ethnic, economic, religious, or historical tradition but offers a common language about the origin and development of our planet, of the universe, of our very bodies—a creation story that is capable of providing an essential story that can help to feed spiritual democracy.

Like George Fox and the Quaker movement that influenced him deeply, Whitman is essentially democratizing the religious experience or the spiritual experience. He's taking it away from institutions and figureheads and saying we all have the divine right to experience it in our lives, and we can have access to it directly. The mystical experience of union is for everyone—as are the courageous and prophetic stand we must take. Thus the democracy that he envisions and the life that he envisions start from that experience. He is asking us: How should we be changing the world? How should we be talking about the future? We have to start with this experience, and then live from that. Matthew has written about the same for years, saying that every individual is born a mystic and every individual is called to be prophet or spiritual warrior.

Whitman is replacing religion with spirituality, with experience. He puts it very bluntly and memorably. "The true Christian religion," he says, "consists neither in rites or Bibles or sermons or Sundays— but in noiseless secret ecstasy and unremitted aspiration, . . . in the universal church, in the soul of man, invisibly rapt, ever-waiting, ever responding to universal truths."[3] When he is talking about a "noiseless secret ecstasy" he is talking, obviously, about the inner life. It is about the journey we can take within. His inner journey spilled over into his poetic work and vocation.

Carl Jung says that only the mystic brings what is creative to religion itself. In other words, it is people who have these experiences and are true to them who must reinvent religion. It's not going to be a five-year plan; it's not going to come down from the upper echelons of academia and seminaries. It's going to come from below, from the people, out of their experience of spirit. Just as it did with Buddha, Isaiah, Jesus, Muhammad, and others.

Another dimension to Walt Whitman's teaching on spirituality is his explicit connection to shamanistic traditions. Shamanism is the oldest religion on the planet by far. Buddhism is 4,000 or 5,000 years old; the Bible and the biblical people of the Jewish tradition are about 4,000 years old; and the Christian tradition is 2,000 years old; Islam is about 1,300 years old. So each religion has had its story and its beginning, its history. But shamanistic religion, which is that of indigenous peoples everywhere, is far more ancient than are the civilizations that housed Buddhism, Judaism, Christianity, Islam, and so forth.

Carl Jung said he never dealt with a North American at the level of spirituality when he didn't find a Native American inside—shamanism is not something we've outgrown. It's in all of us. Thus it is about spiritual democracy. Because of certain religious ideologies, we try to pretend that we've outgrown shamanism or that it's inferior to civilization or religions that have emerged since. But in fact, the shamanistic tradition has so much to teach us, including an ecological consciousness, since in shamanism the birds, the animals, the spirits of the land are all sacred and communicating with us. This sense of the sacredness of nature is something that we have lost in the modern era of humanity; we have been taking nature for granted and exploiting nature, not treating it with reverence and respect and gratitude. So for that reason alone, shamanism has something to teach us.

But also there are practices in shamanism that are available to all of us. They are very democratic—for example, the drum or dancing, especially within a community setting. Whitman considered his poetry to be a trance-inducing drumbeat, a spiritual practice; he talked of beating on his "serpent-skin drum" in calling the people to a new religious vision. He called the practice of his poetry "vocalism." It was democratic because it was available to all. Drum rituals, which are so very ancient, are universal. They still speak to the human heart and are still valuable; they do not depend on a hierarchical priesthood to lead you into such practices. And, of course, there's the vision quest and other rites that we have spoken about in a previous chapter. The shaman archetype calls upon the spirits of the animals, the winged ones and the four-legged ones, to inspire us. Many experiences people have with their cats and dogs are echoes of that shamanistic relationship, which is very ancient in our human experience—very ancient and very profound. Animal spirits and animal guides are coming to many persons today in dreams and in visions. There is good reason for this. The late Thomas Berry, one of the great eco-prophets of our age, used to say that we need fewer priests and fewer professors and more shamans.

The question of a direct relationship with the divine is primal in Whitman, and with it the question of democratization of spiritual experience and direct access to it. He developed his own very specific method of accessing that consciousness, which is the method of free verse.[4] Free verse is a way through which any person might experience Spirit, a way to achieve unification of body, soul, and spirit through writing. Poets the world over, including great Latin American poets, have picked up on Whitman's invitation to free verse. Free verse and vocalism were Whitman's contemplative practice.

It is important to recognize that different people access a direct inspiration and a direct connection with the divine in different ways. For example, for Adam it is through service. He says:

I relate what Whitman describes here very much to service, because for me when I work with homeless kids, for example, it's about being present with them without any kind of pre-conceived notions about what they need and what needs to be said, what needs to be done. It's about bearing witness and being there in the state of curious not-knowing, and sitting there in silence, in presence, awaiting the creative impulse to arise. And then once the impulse arises, then having courage to say yes to it, and becoming an expression of that. And some-times that means saying something to someone; sometimes it means crying with them; sometimes it means praying with them. It's different depending on the situation and depending on the impulse.

I know, for me, whenever I follow that, it always works. I feel like all of my gifts are being used, but I'm not using them. Something else is using them. So it's like the gifts that I have or the skills that I have are being reassembled in a way that I wouldn't necessarily assemble together.

In many ways I relate to Whitman's method of free verse because I imagine that his experience with that was what he calls "immortality," essentially something takes over and he becomes an expression of that something, and writing happens.

Whitman talked explicitly about the trance state he went into when he was writing. What Whitman and Adam are speaking of is the common experience of *creativity*, the experience the artist has from time to time. If one remains in the active state of "not-knowing" and not controlling, one gets taken over and used by Spirit or the power of creativity itself. All this speaks of the Via Creativa—the experience of spirit via art. Whitman's term "vocalism," as self-expression through rhythmic poetry, is about free verse. It does not follow a rigid form that restricts the imagination. His practice was first of all a revolution in poetry, but it is also a revolution in spiritual practices.

At the age of ten, when Whitman heard the Quaker preacher Hicks speak, who was half Native American and half black, he realized how powerful the beat behind words can be. He sensed that the power of the drum itself was shamanistic. Today's rap is very, very close. When its message goes beyond reptilian brain conquest to speak about truth itself, it carries a profound dimension of beat that is drum-like. It too is democratic, and rap has spread all over the world and from "the bottom up." It began where people are living at the edge, in the ghetto.

This is how Whitman put it 150 years ago: "Dancing yet through the streets in a phallic procession, rapt . . . beating the serpent-skin drum, accepting the gospels, accepting him that was crucified, knowing assuredly that he is divine."[5] It is interesting how he is wrapping together the ancient practices of a serpent-skin drum, the shamanistic practice, with the Christian story. It is amazing that he's at home with both, and that it assists the meditation, the Christ story, to be able to process with a drum as well. Speaking of his personal experience, Matthew Fox says, "the rituals I've attended with Native people have not made me less a Christian in any way. They've deepened by far the experiences of the story of Christ."

What is at the heart of spiritual democracy is a beautiful shift from relying on institutions to relying on your own inner teacher, and then living from there in a way that is uniquely your own. When we look at Jesus, for example, he was that kind of a guy who did exactly that. To live from that place includes a very strong prophetic component to it. So it's not just about being a "bliss bunny," as Andrew Harvey would call it, or being spaced out. It's about incarnating the truth that you discovered, incarnating it in the world, and expressing this quality of spiritual warriorship, which is also very shamanistic. It's about really taking on the dark forces, so to speak.

Here we want to give credit to Steven Herrmann, who's done such good research on Walt Whitman, including his shamanistic tendencies. Herrmann, who is also a Jungian analyst, explains how the American self-image lacked a shadow side with the Puritans. Being out of touch with their shadow side, the Puritans projected so much on the indigenous peoples and contributed to their being wiped out. "Whitman's fight for spiritual democracy helped to make the evil in the American self conscious. The Puritan myth was based upon an unconscious projection of evil onto indigenous peoples, the life ways of the two spirits [that is, homosexuals] and a bi-erotic image of the soul's wholeness. Consequently, the aim of bringing about a newly formed God image, patterned upon the principle of wholeness, failed miserably with the early settlers. There was no ecumenism, there was no deep ecumenism between the Puritans and the Native people."[6] What resulted, of course, was war and genocide.

This shadow needs to be addressed and wrestled with—otherwise it's going to run our history. This is part of acknowledging and celebrating the wisdom of the shamanistic traditions, not seeing them as the other or as an antithesis to, say, Christianity. In fact, we need to look into the Christian story for shamanistic aspects of Jesus's life. And these aspects are definitely there: stories about Jesus living in the wilderness during his apprenticeship to John the Baptist as a young man; Jesus's vision quest and his wrestling with the devil's invitations to power and vain glory; many retreats to the desert. There is his deep relationship to nature, such that it seems that he could quell storms on the sea, and so forth. There are definite examples of shamanism within the Christian story itself. And, of course, that's just about Jesus. Later you have Francis and his talking with the wolves and the animals and the birds. Meister Eckhart has a lot to say about animals and spirit as well, as does Hildegard. So there's not an absence of the shamanistic presence within the deeper aspects of Christianity. It's when Christianity is untrue to its own lineage, to its own roots, when militarism and avarice take over, that so much negativity gets projected onto the indigenous peoples, such as when the Spaniards and the Puritans came to the Americas.

Another aspect to spiritual democracy in Whitman is his complete acceptance of gay marriage 150 years ago. He was not homophobic and celebrated the diversity of sexuality in our species. He challenges, therefore, the sexual projections we make on each other from our unexamined inner fears.

Whitman calls us to reexamine our traditions and our relationship with our traditions and our life, and to envision a future that is based on a direct experience of spirit.

Spiritual democracy is a more horizontal way to celebrate religions and accept the splendid diversity as something positive, instead of relating to each other competitively. It doesn't use the reptilian brain to see differences, to look at who's on top, but uses a larger brain that knows and accepts and takes delight in the diversity of the universe in its multiple expressions.

Spiritual democracy encompasses all aspects of spirit and life and culture. It starts with deep ecumenism and a chance to drink from different wells in a unique way that is your own, and, at the same time, it gives us access to this direct experience that then spills over. It challenges us to a democratic economics as well—for how can you acknowledge the Godliness of all beings and all human beings and still lord over them in the name of economic tyranny? David Korten's ideas about economics, discussed in chapter 8, relate directly to the concept of spiritual democracy. It seems obvious that we can't have a democracy that is of the people, by the people, and for the people if we have an economic system that is of the few, by the few, and for the few—or of the corporations, by the corporations, and for the corporations.

Since economics and politics always go together, we cannot resurrect our failed political systems if we don't also resurrect our failed financial systems. The work of democracy is a spiritual discipline. It's a yoga. In this sense, spiritual democracy is a *practice*. It is a focused way of seeing the world and culture in its multiple images of kaleidoscopic beauty. It takes focus and a kind of meditation practice to follow through on these insights and put them into practice in society and institutions. The Occupy movement has reminded us that real democracy is a yoga or spiritual practice to be lived. It is demanding—consider those who are sleeping outdoors in good and bad weather to make their witness to the powers that be. Consider again how an elder talked about the courage of the youth in the Egyptian uprising that brought down Mubarak's dictatorship.

> My generation is the cowardly generation. We were the ones who created this mess, and we lived in fear. I never imagined that these young people could bring down with their hands one of the most notorious regimes in the Middle East. It was a miracle, I tell you. Exactly the kind you read about in the Bible. But they were prepared to face death. They didn't learn the old-fashioned rules that they were supposed to respect their elders. They broke out of our shell, because they had this wider world that is strange to us. And now, the country is going to be theirs, which is good, because we are the past, and they are the future."[7]

The Occupy generation can boast that one true sign of spirit: courage.

Life is to be lived not through the language of a frozen system but from the "shaman in us." Spiritual democracy challenges politics because it enables us to interact with other human beings and other beings in a way that is democratic and that respects that grace that is coming to all and through us and others. Circles rather than ladders demarcate the basic dynamic of spiritual democracy applied to politics. Leadership, yes. But preferably leadership in circle settings, not in a top-down hierarchy. And in the end, it invites us to build institutions and cultures that are based on universal principles. The principle that "all men [and women] are created equal" is not a bad beginning. The term "spiritual democracy" almost parallels a term that symbolizes what the future could be: the "Kingdom of God," in Jesus's words.

The topics we have dialogued on in this book all seem to speak to an application of spiritual democracy or a preparation for it. How to get from where we currently are to what we are yearning for. In chapter 1 and 2 we considered the movement from a God of Religion to a God of Life and the implications of that for compassion and justice. In the following two chapters, we covered our personal stories of vocation, contemplation, service, mysticism, and justice making. In chapter 5 we treated the pivotal theme that every young adult faces: vocation, how we find our calling in life and how we use our gifts in service of life, compassion, and justice. In chapter 6 we considered the personal practices that build up one's strength and courage to carry on one's vocation as well as the ritual practices that community building requires. In chapter 7 we discussed the relationship between young adults and mentors and elders and the intergenerational wisdom that flows from such healthy relationships. In chapter 8 we examined emerging movements of economics and new communities, including the "New Monasticism" movements, since community is so much at the base of the quest for a satisfying and authentic existence today.

What spiritual democracy teaches is that grace itself is democratic. Isn't that what Jesus was teaching? The Spirit is accessible to all. Moreover, the resurrection story teaches that immortality is democratic, none of us needs fear death any longer. It is time to get on with life. That teaching was a complete breakthrough in human consciousness. The idea is that grace is available to everybody, not just those who are preening themselves at the pinnacle of imperial success, whether financial or political or military or religious. So it is definitely a deconstruction of hierarchy, and no wonder it's been muted by the powers that be. Spiritual democracy doesn't only break the empire—it renders it irrelevant. It substitutes democracy for imperial politics, economics, and religion. Diversity is allowed and encouraged—it's not one-size-fits-all. It's not the imperial motif of unity equals conformity. But rather the model from nature that celebrates diversity in the midst of plurality. *Vive la différence!* Celebrate the differences!

> It seems fitting to the coauthors of this book to end it with wisdom from the Occupy generation. Below is a letter written to us all, young and elders alike, from an Occupy leader, Pancho Ramos-Stierle, after he was led away to jail while meditating at Occupy Oakland.

OPEN LETTER FROM THE OCCUPY GENERATION

Dear beloved sisters and brothers,

May this letter find your thoughts, words and deeds in harmony.
    This is a warm invitation to collectively step up our love, truth and courage. You could be within or without the system,

inside or outside a corporation, it really doesn't matter. We must appeal to our highest aspirations.

If you are not a religious person this means it is time to bring more integrity to your life to fully develop your potential as a compassionate, courageous, loving, kind and wise human being.

If you are a religious person this means that it is time to bring God, Allah, Yahweh, Krishna, Rama, Buddha, Jesus or whatever name you use, closer to your life. Acknowledge God in your heart and let it shine.

Photo: Noah Berger

Don't do it for you or me. Do it for your children and future generations.

In the next following days, when you look at the eyes of a child close to you, don't tell him or her that you are following the orders of your boss. Rather, tell him or her that you are following your heart and the Law of Love, it might or might not be aligned with the law of men.

Then, before going to bed, reflect on how your days went. How am I feeling right now, and how am I feeling after a hard day at my job? Am I loving me, my family and my children enough? Am I loving with no strings attached, purely, selflessly? Am I acting with as much integrity as I can? What am I willing to do if I'm fearlessly choosing to lose title, job and to not have fear of prisons? What will it take for me to follow my highest aspirations, my highest ideals? Is my job aligned with these aspirations?

If you look deeper, you will see that we don't need jobs. What we need are meaningful livelihoods. We need work that supports not an industrial growth society but a life-sustaining civilization.

It doesn't matter if you are part of the apparatus of the University of California (UC), BP (British Petroleum), Bechtel, Novartis, Syngenta, Monsanto, Wall Street, the army, the police, the FBI, the CIA or Immigration and Customs Enforcement (ICE). You could be asked to be a spokesperson of the so called 1% or to participate in violence you disagree with, that destroys families and the Planet. What cannot be denied is that nuclear weapons, deep ocean oil-drilling, genetically modified crops (GMOs), attacking urban agriculture—like the raid this morning [last Monday] at the ongoing farm at the Gill Tract in the East Bay—, privatization of learning, wars, police brutality and leaving children orphaned due to the deportation of their parents, all these facts are harming, in concrete and real ways, not only our present but also the future (physical and spiritual) environment we are leaving for our children.

A few weeks ago, a person who lived for twenty-three years with Mahatma Gandhi was asked at a UC Berkeley talk how to be non-violent and compassionate with an institution that is actively

proliferating hydrogen bombs—like the UC is doing as we speak—
by the development of "safer nuclear weapons." He responded,
"If you have 50% of Gandhi within you, you will stop cooperating
with this institution and you will start creating a new way of
learning, an alternative university."

It is time to pull out from institutions that are harming us.
What a great opportunity for a personal transformation to boost-
up your happiness and that of your loved ones! A wonderful opportunity to unconditionally serve others. For real.

Please remember you are not alone. Move from "me" to "we."

We are looking for a spokesperson of truth not for the 1% but
for the 100%. We are looking for officers who can enforce the Law
of Love. We are looking for intelligence balanced with the heart.
We are looking for entrepreneurs fully invested in the business
of kindness and generosity. We are looking for scientists organically supporting the magnificent web of life. We are looking for
students of creative love and gratitude. We are looking for lovers
of life.

We are waiting for you, with open arms, to join the greatest movement around selfless service humanity has ever witnessed.

It is time to pull out from institutions that are stopping your development as a complete and happy human being. It is time to make a wise decision. It is time to farm truth, love, courage, compassion and wisdom. At least, it is time to let farm truth, love, courage, compassion and wisdom. This is true security, security that involves all of us.

Look into the eyes of a happy healthy child. Then look within yourself. Connect with that inner wisdom we all have. There are no paths, the paths are made by walking. As you walk, please look around. You are surrounded by gifts. Your means are the ends in the making.

We trust you will follow integrity; as true happiness is when our thoughts, words and deeds are in harmony.

We are waiting for you.

We are the 99% facilitating the healing of the 100%.

May all become compassionate, courageous and wise.

Please receive all my love and universal blessings.

Undocumented and unafraid, in radical love,
your brother always,

Pancho Ramos-Stierle

Afterword
Co-Creating a Better World

Awaken the Mind, Open the Heart, and Nurture the Soul

Lama Surya Das

I believe deeply that we must find, all of us together, a new spirituality. This new concept ought to be elaborated alongside the religions like secular ethics in a way that all people of good will would adhere to it.

Tenzin Gyatso, The Dalai Lama of Tibet

We are the weavers of the fabric of modern society. We can weave love, truthfulness and peace or we can weave hatred, mistrust and war. We will have to wear whatever fabric we weave.

Vimala Thakar

As a young man, I worked for years in Tibetan refugee camps in the Himalayas, mostly in India and Nepal. Like many people, I've lived for decades on the margins of society. I know what it's like to be poor, although I have never been entirely hopeless, disenfranchised, or forgotten. I chose voluntary poverty, simplicity, chastity, and obedience in my Tibetan lama's monastery cloister. But tonight, there will be about 4,000 homeless kids forced to sleep in the hard streets of New York. They did not choose their circumstances and are disenfranchised and mostly forgotten by mainstream society. This is unacceptable to me in a great first-world city—or anywhere on this bruised and beautiful planet.

"Where is God?" Adam Bucko writes. "He is here on this street, lying naked in the gutter. He is here on this street, homeless. He is here on this street, in all the lonely and unwanted, waiting for our love."

Adam has said to me many times that I've told him repeatedly, "It's important to cultivate future mentors who could guide the new generation into their own sense of wisdom," for these are my hopes and intentions, prayers and resolute aspirations for the younger generations and the world so sorely lacking in spiritual leadership today.

Spiritual elders and mentors are few and far between, though not an extinct species. Perhaps their greatest talent and visionary gift is being able to empower and embrace others and to lift them up, helping each to see the world and themselves as equals and beloveds. Insightful wisdom cum self-knowledge is like a invaluable endangered natural resource in our world, which we overlook at our peril. It is crucial today, I believe, to reach deep inwards and exploit our own inner natural resources for a change, and give our depleted environment a break. This is the spiritual heart of sacred activism—wisening up while empowering, educating, and elevating. I bow to and praise gratefully our compassionate mentors and benefactors, the inspirational beacons and stewards of our collective inheritance.

I feel delighted and even honored to conclude this inspiring book by Matthew Fox and Adam Bucko, which challenges us to develop a profound sense of universal responsibility, to further common efforts in solving common problems, and to strive always to walk our talk. This is a significant collaboration, in the form of a friendly collegial dialogue between a wise elder and savvy younger, and augers well for our compassionate awareness and altruistic activities here at the intersection of past, present, and future.

Matthew Fox, a teacher and theologian, shaped his prophetic path by reclaiming the authentic Christian spirituality of compassion and justice, and re-introduced the Western world to Meister Eckhart, Hildegard von Bingen, and Thomas Aquinas. One of the most-read American Catholic Theologians, he was kicked out of the Catholic Church for his teachings emphasizing the "original blessing" of Creation Theology, a tradition of spirituality that was named for him by his mentor, the acclaimed grandfather of liberation theology, Marie-Dominique Chenu, with whom he studied theology in Paris. He was sent to Paris to study the intersection of spirituality and culture by Thomas Merton, another venerable maverick, original thinker, and homegrown American mystic. This original blessing I have come to lovingly call "our original goodness" over the years, as a loose translation of innate Buddha-nature or *tathagatagarbha*.

Be Buddha now. That's my message too. "We are all Buddhas by nature; it's only adventitious obscurations which veil that fact," as Tibetan texts tell us. Our main task is to recognize and awaken to who and what we are. We can practice *presencing* through mindful awareness and wonderment, *being there* while getting there, every single step of the way. This is the way with no waiting. One moment of total awareness is one moment of freedom and enlightenment. We can survive and thrive in difficult times, moving from the scarcity mentality to abundant contentment through genuine conscious evolution combined with an evolved and integral social conscience today.

Fox has skillfully integrated sacred vision with daily life, and reconciled mysticism and contemplation with the spiritually centered social activism of prophetic witness. "I feel passionate about the changes I call for, both personal and societal transformations, and I see them as deeply related. If you don't work on yourself then much of your politics is merely projections. We have to do the inner work that allows the outer work to be authentic and also effective. I get enough positive feedback (and negative too, such as the Vatican saying a major work by me was 'dangerous and deviant') to let me know I'm on the right track more or less."

Adam Bucko I have known during the last decade or so. Like a young Buddha—as a mentee and co-conspirator in fostering, facilitating, and serving youth and street people—he has impressed me as a hirsute younger brother of a kindred Polish spiritual bloodline. He grew up longing to discover God in the silence that monks and yogis talk about, eventually coming to the fullness of spirit in the broken lives of homeless youth and out into action via the heartfelt need to respond to their call. Old Hasids say we should look for God in the ashes and not just on mountain tops; Adam trenchantly calls us out on this verity with his noble work in the streets, as evidenced in writings such as "My God Lives on the Street."

These fresh and original voices summon us to radical action as well as to contemplate our conscience and follow its dictates in all things. Compassion in action must be guided by wisdom's insightful eye in order to avoid the pitfalls of proselytizing and looking down on others less fortunate than ourselves, while wisdom's open eye intuitively illumines the way for us. That is the mission of bodhisattva leaders and awakeners like Adam Bucko and Matthew Fox.

Buoyant and uplifting, relational and collective rather than insular and exclusive, these servant leaders are fomenting a consciousness movement and beloved community committed to witnessing and working towards social justice, peace, and harmony. Anyone concerned with global socio-economic problems, environmental depletion, anachronistic institutionalized religions, corrosive corporate politics, and the promise of the rising evolutionary consciousness will want to hear these clarion voices raised in support and praise of a unifying global spirit. An excellent antidote to the poisons of modern day stressors with their accompanying waves of malaise and cynicism, and to overwhelming feelings of powerlessness, here is a hopeful view of a new generation's egalitarian values congruent with the emerging interspiritual age of equality, interconnectedness, and interbeing.

We're all in the same boat; we rise and fall, sink *and* swim together. The religions of this world each arose principally as part of humanity's attempt to deal with death and mortality, grieving, fear, and continuity, however variously understood. Although we come into this world alone and leave alone, spiritual traditions as well as universal wisdom tell us that we do not stand alone in this uncertain, evanescent universe. We are totally interrelated, dependent upon powers of nature and society transcendent over and beyond any of us as well as immanent in each and all of us.

Contemporary American teacher and spiritual pioneer Ram Dass, author of *Be Here Now* in the sixties and, more recently, *Be Love Now*, believes that: "You and I are the force for transformation in the world. We are the consciousness that will define the nature of the reality we are moving into."

Andrew Harvey invites us to answer the call of sacred activism by accessing our inner compass and renewing our passion and hope. He suggests that from this deeper place springs our creative, inspired solutions to old problems. "All that we need is already there, in the currency of people, and it only needs to be tapped into," he says. I myself have taken the altruistic Bodhisattva (Awakener) vow and work at sacred activism, Engaged Buddhism, and spiritually centered social activism. I try not to fall into being merely an enraged Buddhist, although there's certainly plenty to be enraged about in these turbulent times. This I believe to be our true work—our real work, and true vocation; making a life and not just a living—growing ourselves while growing our career and family—and serving a purpose greater than ourselves and the community good we must co-create together in our workplace, homes, and society. This includes cultivating mindfulness of how we consume, what, when, where, and why, to help steward our planetary resources and be spiritually healthy.

These days, and especially since 9-11, the daily news seems conducive to sadness and discouragement, if not despair and depression. Yet whenever I look into the eyes of a young person today, I irrationally feel an upsurge of hope, excitement, and optimism. This augers well for the future of this, our world, and our society, community, and all beings—and the environment, too, endangered as it may be. I myself have been turning more towards youth in recent years, including the internet, developing social media as spiritual media, relational mindfulness, and other forms of outreach stemming from *inreach*.

May this work, and others like it, help seed, water, fertilize, and germinate the coming together of fertile young leaders and creative elders, generating a movement for a new spirituality and wisdom culture which can inspire new structures for a new world and a bright future—that future which begins right now.

Jesus talked about ushering in the great kingdom of heaven here on earth. I believe that we must be the ushers midwifing in the kingdom, part and parcel of the messianic age, and not wait and postpone it till some others energies bring it forth for the blessed benefit of all. We must become the enlightened leaders we wish to see in this benighted, fractured, and anxious world.

The best way for a ruler to reign over his country is first of all to rule himself. The Buddhist view is that a true leader is one who makes the right decisions. And making the right decisions depends on taking the Right View, which leads to the Right Action. Thinking the right way means making sure that every action is based on the right intention and the right motivation, compassion, and altruism.

The Dalai Lama

American Buddhas, saints, and sages, awaken! Throw off your chains, your limiting mental concepts, hang-ups, and fixations. Why be like a narcissistic thinkaholic? Intellect is a fine servant but a poor master. Let's live to love, to light-en up and enlighten up, to contribute and to serve. This is my prayer and my aspiration, embodying wise awareness as compassionate action for the benefit of one and all.

Noble-hearted friends, let's try to keep our eyes on the ball in preserving and realizing the vital essence of nonsectarian, post-denomination spirituality, without overly grasping to the local cultural forms and ritual traditions.

So much light! Even shadows are nothing but shades of light. I have circled the globe thrice in search of the Ultimate, only to find nirvana in my own backyard—in my heart center, like Buddha in the palm of our hands. This is true; help yourself.

Once upon a time I was no more. It lasted not, but one must live as if it were true, being there while getting there, every single step of the Way. I am a word, and the word is with, and the word is *was*. One moment of incandescent awareness is one moment of awakening, freedom and enlightenment.

Life is precious, fleeting, tenuous: handle with prayer.

With love,

Lama Surya Das

Notes

Introduction

1. Howard Thurman, *Luminous Darkness* (Richmond, IN: Friends United Press, 1989), 23–24.
2. Since the eviction from Zuccotti park and other sites, this work is continuing in many different ways and forms. As the movement changed its strategy from occupations to issue-oriented actions for liberation, some were inspired to work within the system for change, while others are pioneering new ways of building a new world, one community and one issue at time. One only needs to look at post–Zuccotti Park initiatives like Occupy Sandy, Rolling Debt Jubilee, and many other issue-oriented actions and campaigns to realize that, while not as visible as during the Zuccotti days, the movement might actually be stronger than ever.
3. Thomas Berry, *The Great Work* (New York: Bell Tower, 1999), 10.
4. Paul Buchheit, "Time to Get Mad: Three Ways the Super-Rich Have Cheated Young Americans," *Counterpunch*, July 9, 2012, www.counterpunch.org/2012/07/09/three-ways-the-super-rich-have-cheated-young-americans/.
5. Ibid.
6. Walt Whitman, *Specimen Days & Collect* (Philadelphia: Rees and Welsh, 1882), 279.
7. Sarah van Gelder, "Pancho Ramos Stierle: Nonviolence Is Radical," *Yes* magazine,

February 23, 2012, www.yesmagazine.org/peace-justice/pancho-ramos-stierle-nonviolence-is-radical.

8. Ibid.

9. Howard Thurman, *Jesus and the Disinherited* (Boston: Beacon Press, 1996), 55.

Is It Time to Replace the God of Religion with the God of Life?

1. Henry A. Giroux, *Youth in Revolt: Reclaiming a Democratic Future* (Boulder: Paradigm Publishers, 2012), 136.

2. Chris Hedges, "Real Hope Is about Doing Something," *TruthDig,* November 29, 2010, www.truthdig.com/report/item/hope_in_the_21st_century_20101128.

3. Excerpt from Dr. Howard Thurman's Baccalaureate Address at Spelman College, May 4, 1980, printed in *The Spelman Messenger* 96, no. 4 (Summer 1980): 14–15.

4. In Adbusters #102, July/August 2012.

Radical Spirituality for a Radical Generation

1. Philip Clayton, "Letting Doubters in the Door: Those without Religious Affiliation Aren't Necessarily Rejecting God," *Los Angeles Times,* March 25, 2012.

2. " 'Nones' on the Rise," *Pew Forum on Religion & Public Life,* October 9, 2012, http://www.pewforum.org/unaffiliated/nones-on-the-rise.aspx.

3. Philip Clayton, "Letting Doubters in the Door."

4. To learn more about Creation Spirituality and Four Paths, see Matthew Fox's *Creation Spirituality: Liberating Gifts for the Peoples of the Earth* (San Francisco: HarperOne, 1991) and *Original Blessing: A Primer in Creation Spirituality Presented in Four Paths, Twenty-Six Themes, and Two Questions* (New York: Jeremy P. Tarcher, 2000).

Adam's Story

1. The Chernobyl nuclear disaster happened on April 26, 1986, in Ukraine (then officially part of the Soviet Union). Chernobyl was located only 325 miles from where Adam lived in Bialystok, Poland. It released large quantities of radioactive contamination into the atmosphere, which spread over Europe. It is considered to have been the worst nuclear power plant accident in history, followed by the Fukushima Daiichi nuclear disaster in 2011.

2. Ton Snellaert, known in India as Ton Baba, established Sewa Ashram, which served as a rehabilitation center for the poorest of the poor suffering on the streets of Delhi. Ton was Adam's mentor, and much of Adam's work is inspired by his time spent at Sewa Ashram.

3. Taz Tagore, "Fighting Homelessness with Mindfulness," *Shambhala Sun*, September 26, 2011, http://shambhalasun.com/sunspace/?p=23152.

4. The manifesto is available on the HAB website (www.hab-community.com /HAB/New_Monasticism.html).

5. For more information on interspirituality and new emerging spirituality please see Kurt Johnson and David Ord's *The Coming Interspiritual Age* (Vancouver: Namaste Publishing, 2013).

Matthew's Story

1. Margot Adler, "Why We Love Vampires" (sermon, All Souls Unitarian Universalist Church, New York City, October 21, 2012). To listen, go to All Souls' website (www.allsoulsnyc2.org).

What's Your Calling?

1. See Jamie Manson, "Recognizing the Church that We Already Are," *National Catholic Reporter,* November 9, 2011, http://ncronline.org/blogs/grace -margins/recognizing-church-we-already-are.

2. Steven B. Herrmann, *William Everson: The Shaman's Call* (New York: Eloquent Books, 2009).

3. Desmond Tutu, *God Has a Dream: A Vision of Hope for Our Time* (New York: Doubleday, 2005), 109.

4. To learn more about Llewellyn Vaughan-Lee's Sufi approach, see his *The Face Before I Was Born: A Spiritual Autobiography* and *In the Company of Friends: Dreamwork Within a Sufi Group*, published by The Golden Sufi Center.

5. For more information on Bisan Toron's methodology see Toron's "Thoughts on Mysticism and the Voice" *Seven Pillars House*, February 7, 2012, http://www.sevenpillarshouse.org/article/thoughts_on_mysticism_and_the _voice, and "Dimensions of Voice," *Seven Pillars House*, February 7, 2012, http://www.sevenpillarshouse.org/program_audio/item/bisanonvanishing voice.

6. Sam Keen, quoted in *The Sun* magazine's Sunbeams section (August 2008)

7. Thomas Berry, *The Great Work* (New York: Bell Tower, 1999), 51.

8. Clarissa Pinkola Estés, *Women Who Run with the Wolves* (New York: Ballan-
    tine Books, 1992), 12–13.

Spiritual Practice

1. Sarah van Gelder, "Pancho Ramos Stierle: Nonviolence Is Radical," *Yes!*
    magazine, February 23, 2012, www.yesmagazine.org/peace-justice/
    pancho-ramos-stierle-nonviolence-is-radical.
2. Andrew Harvey, *The Hope: Guide to Sacred Activism* (Carlsbad, CA: Hay
    House, 2010), 133.
3. James Fadiman and Robert Frager, *Essential Sufism* (San Francisco: Harper
    SanFrancisco), 209.
4. To learn more about John Welwood's thoughts on spiritual bypass, see "Hu-
    man Nature, Buddha Nature: On Spiritual Bypassing, Relationship, and the
    Dharma" in the articles section of his website, www.johnwelwood.com.
5. To learn more about Matthew's work on reinvention of ritual and the Cosmic
    Mass, see his website on the Cosmic Mass, www.thecosmicmass.com.
6. For more practical tools and spiritual practices for activating hope see Joanna
    Macy and Chris Johnstone, *Active Hope: How to Face the Mess We're in without
    Going Crazy* (Novato, CA: New World Library, 2012).
7. Sarah van Gelder, "Pancho Ramos Stierle: Nonviolence Is Radical," *Yes!*
    magazine, February 23, 2012, www.yesmagazine.org/peace-justice
    /pancho-ramos-stierle-nonviolence-is-radical.

No Generation Has All the Answers

1. Bruce Feiler, *Generation Freedom: The Middle East Uprisings and the Remaking
    of the Modern World* (New York: Harper Perennial, 2011), 53–54.
2. Coleman Barks, trans., *The Soul of Rumi: A New Collection of Ecstatic Poems*
    (San Francisco: HarperOne, 2002), 150.
3. Viktor Frankl, *Man's Search for Meaning* (Boston: Beacon Press, 2000), 113.
4. Mirabai Bush, personal correspondence.

Birthing New Economics, New Communities, and New Monasticism

1. Sarah van Gelder, "Pancho Ramos Stierle: Nonviolence Is Radical," *Yes!*
    magazine, February 23, 2012, www.yesmagazine.org/peace-justice/pancho
    -ramos-stierle-nonviolence-is-radical.

2. Cited in Stacy Curtin, "Occupy Wall Street: The Youth Perspective," Yahoo! Finance, October 27, 2011, http://finance.yahoo.com/blogs/daily-ticker /occupy-wall-street-youth-perspective-152840699.html.

3. Bryan Perkins, "Outside 'The System,'" *Occupy Baton Rouge*, June 20, 2012, http://occupybr.com/2012/06/20/outside-the-system.

4. *Generation UNESCO: 8th Annual International Leadership Training Programme: A Global Intergenerational Forum, August 3-12, 2012* (Storrs, Ct: University of Connecticut, 2012), 65, 67–68.

5. Ibid., 108–9.

6. Ibid., 150–51.

7. For more information about new economics, see David Korten, *Agenda for a New Economy: From Phantom Wealth to Real Wealth* (San Francisco: Berrett-Koehler, 2010), and Korten's website, Living Economies Forum (www.livingeconomiesforum.org).

8. For a wonderful discussion about the emerging ideal of monasticism, see Francis Tiso, "Raimundo Panikkar on the Monk as Archetype," *Monastic Interreligious Dialogue*, DATE, www.dimmid.org.

9. See Frithjof Schuon, "The Universality of Monasticism and Its Relevance in the Modern World," in *Merton and Sufism: The Untold Story: A Complete Compendium* ed. Rob Baker and Gray Henry (Louisville, KY: Fons Vitae, 1999).

10. To learn more about Universal Sufism as articulated by Hazrat Inayat Khan and Pir Zia Inayat-Khan, see www.sufiorder.org, www.sulukacademy.org, and www.sevenpillarshouse.org.

11. Leonardo Boff, "Encouragement for Those Disappointed with the Church" *Leonard Boff*, August 13, 2011, http://leonardoboff.wordpress. com/2011/08/13/encouragment-for-those-disappointed-with-the-church.

12. For more on Creation Spirituality Communities, see their website (http://originalblessing.ning.com).

Conclusion

1. Edward F. Grier, ed., *Notebooks and Unpublished Prose Manuscripts of Walt Whitman* (New York: NYU Press, 1984), 6:2089.

2. William Everson, ed., *American Bard: The Original Preface to Leaves of Grass Arranged in Verse* (New York: Viking, 1981), 33.

3. Walt Whitman, *Complete Poetry and Collected Prose* (New York: Library of America, 1982), 1234. We are deeply indebted to Steven Herrmann's

forthcoming book, *Spiritual Democracy and the Shamanistic Mind,* for insights in this chapter.

4. For much of this discussion on Whitman we are indebted to the excellent in-depth study of Whitman by Steven B. Herrmann, *Walt Whitman: Shamanism, Spiritual Democracy, and the World Soul* (Durham, CT: Eloquent Books, 2010).

5. Walt Whitman, *Leaves of Grass* (New York: Library of America, 1992), 236.

6. Herrmann, *Walt Whitman,* 286–87.

7. Cited in Bruce Feiler, *Generation Freedom: The Middle East Uprisings and the Remaking of the Modern World* (New York: Harper Perennial, 2011), 53–54.

Index

About the Authors

Adam Bucko is an activist and spiritual director to many of New York City's homeless youth. He grew up in Poland during the totalitarian regime and spent his early years exploring the anarchist youth movement as a force for social and political change. At the age of seventeen, Bucko immigrated to America where his desire to find his path towards a meaningful life led him to monasteries in the U.S. and then to India. His life-defining experience took place in India, where on his way to a Himalayan hermitage, he met a homeless child who lived on the streets of Delhi. This brief encounter led him to the "Ashram of the Poor" where he began his work with homeless youth. After returning to the US, he worked on the streets of various American cities with young people struggling against homelessness and prostitution. He eventually co-founded The Reciprocity Foundation, an award-winning nonprofit dedicated to transforming the lives of New York City's homeless youth.

In addition to his work with homeless youth, Bucko established HAB, an ecumenical and inter-spiritual "New Monastic" fellowship for young people that offers formation in radical spirituality and sacred activism.

He collaborates with spiritual leaders across religious traditions and mentors young people, helping them discover a spiritual life in the twenty-first century and how to live deeply from the heart in service of compassion and justice.

Bucko is a recipient of several awards and his work has been featured by ABC News, CBS, NBC, *New York Daily News*, *National Catholic Reporter*, *Ode* magazine, *Yoga International* magazine and *Sojourner* magazine.

To learn more about his work see his personal website and the Reciprocity Foundation website (www.reciprocityfoundation.org and www.adambucko.com).

Photo: Bridgette O'Leary

Matthew Fox is an internationally acclaimed theologian and spiritual maverick who has spent the last forty years revolutionizing Christian theology, taking on patriarchal religion, and advocating for a creation-centered spirituality of compassion and justice and re-sacralizing of the Earth.

As a spiritual theologian, he has written over thirty books, including *Original Blessing*, *The Coming of the Cosmic Christ*, *A Spirituality Named Compassion*, *Christian Mystics*, and *The Pope's War*. His books have been translated into forty-nine languages and have been known for pioneering a unique approach to spirituality as a powerful force to transform religion, education, and culture.

The late Thomas Berry said, "he might be the most creative, the most comprehensive, surely the most challenging theologian in America." Fox was described as "the most important living theologian" by Bishop Marc Andrews.

Originally a Catholic priest, Fox was silenced for a year and then expelled from the Dominican Order, to which he had belonged for thirty-four years, by Cardinal Ratzinger for teaching liberation theology and creation spirituality. Matthew Fox currently serves as an Episcopal priest, after he received what he calls "religious asylum" from the Episcopal Church. With exciting results he has worked with young people to create the Cosmic Mass (www.thecosmicmass.org) to revitalize worship by bringing elements of rave to the western liturgical tradition.

In 2005, when Cardinal Ratzinger became Pope Benedict, Fox went to Martin Luther's church in Wittenberg, Germany, and pounded ninety-five contemporary theses at the door to call people to a New Reformation. In 2010, on a Sunday morning, he pounded the same theses, translated into Italian, at the entrance of the Basilica of St. Maria Maggiore in Rome to protest the arch-priest Cardinal Law, who presided there. Law was guilty of protecting pedophile priests in his previous position as cardinal in the diocese of Boston, Massachusetts, where, among other things, he moved a priest from parish to parish, where he abused over 150 boys. He was subpoenaed to testify but instead fled to Rome, where he was promoted to this prestigious position and where he served on a Vatican committee that appoints bishops worldwide.

His action was motivated by a belief that "At this critical time in human history, when the Earth is being ravaged by the violence of war, poverty, sexism, homophobia, and eco-destruction, we need to gather those who offer a future that is one of compassion, creativity, and justice to speak their conscience as never before. Religion and Spirituality ought to be part of the solution, not the problem."

He has worked extensively and consciously to reinvent forms of education for thirty-one years in master's degree and doctor of ministry programs with adults and currently with inner city high school students in his program called YELLAWE. Key to that reinvention, he believes, is putting Creativity first.

His work has been featured by the *New York Times, Washington Post, Los Angeles Times, Chicago Tribune, San Francisco Chronicle, Rolling Stone* magazine, *Tikkun* magazine, *National Catholic Reporter,* the *Today Show, The Young Turks,* and *Democracy Now!* He is a recipient of numerous awards, including the Courage of Conscience Award by the Peace Abbey of Sherborn, Massachusetts. Other recipients of this award include the Dalai Lama, Mother Teresa, Ernesto Cardinal, and Rosa Parks.

Fox is currently a visiting scholar at the Academy of the Love of Learning in Santa Fe, New Mexico, and lives in Oakland, California. For more information, see his website (www.matthewfox.org).

Heart in Action

Sacred Activism Series Titles

When the joy of compassionate service is combined with the pragmatic drive to transform all existing economic, social, and political institutions, a radical divine force is born: Sacred Activism. The Sacred Activism Series, published by North Atlantic Books, presents leading voices that embody the tenets of Sacred Activism—compassion, service, and sacred consciousness—while addressing the crucial issues of our time and inspiring radical action.

Collapsing Consciously
Carolyn Baker

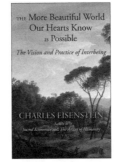

The More Beautiful World Our Hearts Know Is Possible
Charles Eisenstein

Earth Calling
Ellen Gunter and Ted Carter
APRIL, 2014

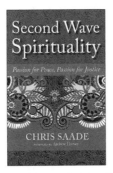

Second Wave Spirituality
Chris Saade
MAY, 2014

Animal Wisdom
Linda Bender, DVM
JUNE, 2014

For more information about the Sacred Activism series, go to:
www.nabcommunities.com/sacredactivism

North Atlantic Books
Berkeley, California

Personal, spiritual, and planetary transformation

North Atlantic Books, a nonprofit publisher established in 1974, is dedicated to fostering community, education, and constructive dialogue. NABCommunities.com is a meeting place for an ever-growing membership of readers and authors to engage in the discussion of books and topics from North Atlantic's core publishing categories.

NAB Communities offer interactive social networks in these genres:

NOURISH: Raw Foods, Healthy Eating and Nutrition, All-Natural Recipes

WELLNESS: Holistic Health, Bodywork, Healing Therapies

WISDOM: New Consciousness, Spirituality, Self-Improvement

CULTURE: Literary Arts, Social Sciences, Lifestyle

BLUE SNAKE: Martial Arts History, Fighting Philosophy, Technique

Your free membership gives you access to:

Advance notice about new titles and exclusive giveaways

Podcasts, webinars, and events

Discussion forums

Polls, quizzes, and more!

Go to www.NABCommunities.com and join today.